VANITY FAIR'S HOLLYWOOD

EDITED BY GRAYDON CARTER
AND DAVID FRIEND

WITH TEXT BY
CHRISTOPHER HITCHENS

VIKING STUDIO

PRECEDING PAGES

FAYE DUNAWAY "Golden lads and girls all must, / As chimney-sweepers, come to dust." But while we wait—and the madding crowd bats its locust wings—let the games begin! First up, Ms. Dunaway, also known as *Chinatown*'s mysterious Evelyn Mulwray and the vagabond gun moll from *Bonnie and Clyde* who left the Dust Bowl to go for the gold. PHOTOGRAPHED IN 1996 BY **DAVID LaCHAPELLE**

EDITED BY

GRAYDON CARTER
and DAVID FRIEND

TEXT CHRISTOPHER HITCHENS

DESIGN MIMI PARK
PHOTOGRAPHY EDITOR SUNHEE C. GRINNELL

PRODUCTION Martha Hurley REPORTING/RESEARCH Justin Bishop, James Buss EDITORIAL ASSISTANCE Daisy Ho, Katharine Marx RIGHTS AND PERMISSIONS Anthony Petrillose, Michael Stier PHOTOGRAPHY RESEARCH ASSISTANCE Ian Bascetta

SPECIAL THANKS TO
AIMÉE BELL, PETER DEVINE, CHRIS GARRETT, DAVID HARRIS, PUNCH HUTTON, ELLEN KIELL, BETH KSENIAK, WAYNE LAWSON, SARA MARKS, ELIZABETH SALTZMAN, JANE SARKIN, PATRICIA J. SINGER, MATT TYRNAUER, and SUSAN WHITE of *Vanity Fair*, and their staffs

Riza Cruz, Bruce Handy, Elise O'Shaughnessy, Krista Smith, Douglas Stumpf, Robert Walsh, Ned Zeman

Lisa Berman, Gregory Mastrianni, Wendy Stark Morrissey, Jeannie Rhodes, Sharon Schieffer

Anna Bakolas, John Gillies, Chris Lawrence, Sebastian Mlynarski

Archival imagery from the pages of *Vanity Fair*, 1914–36, courtesy of the CONDÉ NAST ARCHIVE.
Thanks to Charles D. Scheips, director of the archive, and to Josh Dennis.

FOR MAKING THIS BOOK POSSIBLE, VERY SPECIAL THANKS TO
Phyllis Grann
Christopher Sweet
The Viking Studio team
Andrew Wylie

S. I. Newhouse Jr.
Steven T. Florio
James Truman

IN APPRECIATION OF THE PREVIOUS EDITORS OF *VANITY FAIR*
Frank Crowninshield, 1914–36
Richard Locke, *March to June 1983*
Leo Lerman, 1983–84
Tina Brown, 1984–92

VIKING STUDIO
Published by the Penguin Group

Penguin Putnam Inc., 375 Hudson Street, New York, New York 10014 U.S.A.

Penguin Books Ltd, 27 Wrights Lane, London W8 5TZ, England

Penguin Books Australia Ltd, Ringwood, Victoria, Australia

Penguin Books Canada Ltd, 10 Alcorn Avenue, Toronto, Ontario, Canada M4V 3B2

Penguin Books (N.Z.) Ltd, 182–190 Wairau Road, Auckland 10, New Zealand

Penguin Books Ltd, Registered Offices: Harmondsworth, Middlesex, England

First published in 2000 in the United States of America by Viking Studio, a member of Penguin Putnam Inc.

This paperback edition published in 2001.

1 3 5 7 9 10 8 6 4 2

Copyright © 2000 by The Condé Nast Publications Inc.
All rights reserved.

Vanity Fair is a registered trademark of Advance Magazine Publishers Inc.

CIP DATA AVAILABLE
ISBN 0-14-200500-2

VIKING STUDIO PRODUCTION Della R. Mancuso

THE PHOTOGRAPHERS
ANNIE LEIBOVITZ
EDWARD STEICHEN
Slim Aarons, James Abbe, Jack Albin, Victor Barnaba, Peter Beard, Cecil Beaton, Jonathan Becker, Harry Benson, Alan Berliner, Peter C. Borsari, Fernand Bourges, Anton Bruehl, Eric Carpenter, Michel Comte, Ralph Crane, Andrew Eccles, Frank Edwards, Larry Fink, John Florea, David Geary, Greg Gorman, Paul Hesse, Horst P. Horst, Jean Howard, George Hoyningen-Huene, George Hurrell, Yale Joel, Dafydd Jones, Sam Jones, David LaChapelle, Mary Ellen Mark, Robert Maxwell, Patrick McMullan, Steven Meisel, Leo Mirkine, Jean-Baptiste Mondino, Nickolas Muray, Lusha Nelson, Helmut Newton, Michael O'Neill, Irving Penn, Herb Ritts, Norman Jean Roy, Martin Scorsese, David Seidner, Susan Shacter, Joe Shere, Peggy Sirota, Eric Skipsey, Snowdon, Bert Stern, Phil Stern, Art Streiber, Mario Testino, Michael Thompson, Albert Watson, Bruce Weber, Firooz Zahedi

THE ILLUSTRATORS
Ralph Barton, Miguel Covarrubias, David Cowles, Bruce McCall, Robert Risko, Andy Warhol

THE WRITERS
Peter Biskind, Patricia Bosworth, Amy Fine Collins, Dominick Dunne, Margaret Case Harriman, Christopher Hitchens, David Kamp, D. H. Lawrence, Clare Boothe Brokaw Luce, Dorothy Parker, Frank Peale, Carl Sandburg, Martha Sherrill, Walter Winchell, P. G. Wodehouse

Captions accompanying the photographs in this book were set in VF Sans, a typeface drawn exclusively for *Vanity Fair* by James Montalbano of Terminal Design, Inc. A geometric sans serif, it was inspired by early-20th-century typefaces such as Futura, Kabel, and Johnston Underground. The text pieces were set in Times Roman.

This book was printed in Japan by Toppan Printing Co.

LOUISE BROOKS There *is* a relationship between bangs and bucks, but Louise Brooks inverted it. Stepping from behind Ziegfeld's fringe, she beat Marlene Dietrich to be Lulu in Georg Wilhelm Pabst's *Pandora's Box*, which brought her instant fame on both sides of the Atlantic. A pioneer of eros on the screen and no mean player in the sheets (bedding 430, by her own count), the great gamine parted ways with Paramount in 1928, then suffered Hollywood's revenge. Yet she had her own, by becoming—what else?—a movie critic and essayist. PHOTOGRAPHED IN 1929 BY **EDWARD STEICHEN**

ARNOLD SCHWARZENEGGER Gentle giant? It's possible. Little children don't cower when they see the pumped-iron man; they giggle and shriek at the friendly *Kindergarten Cop*. Only the forces of darkness need quail. A Kennedy by marriage and a Conan by adoption, he is actually made of terminable human clay rather than cyber-flesh.

PHOTOGRAPHED IN 1997
BY **ANNIE LEIBOVITZ**

CONTENTS

By Graydon Carter

Very few things about my unbearably happy childhood I recall in such a glow of mystery and romanticism as I do the first time I ever went to see a movie. It was a decade or so after the end of the Second World War, and we were staying in a small town on the rim of the Black Forest. I was four, maybe five years old at the time. One winter night after an early dinner, my father announced that he was taking me somewhere. He bundled me up and led me by the hand over dimly lit cobblestone streets to a tiny movie house in town to see a masterpiece of early color that was his favorite film, and would later become one of mine as well.

The movie was Zoltán Korda's *The Four Feathers,* a tea-and-sand epic of cowardice and redemption (in English, with German subtitles). It was released in 1939, that Olympus of movie years. (*Gone with the Wind* and *Gunga Din* were released that year, as were *The Hunchback of Notre Dame, Mr. Smith Goes to Washington, Ninotchka, Stagecoach, The Wizard of Oz, The Women,* and *Wuthering Heights.* So were *Dark Victory, Destry Rides Again, Drums Along the Mohawk, Goodbye, Mr. Chips, The Hound of the Baskervilles, Intermezzo, Love Affair,* and *Only Angels Have Wings.*)

I also remember the first novel I ever read. I still have it, in fact: an illustrated edition of *The Adventures of Huckleberry Finn.* I also remember the first album I ever bought (*The Doors*). I haven't reread *Huckleberry Finn* in years and I haven't listened to that Doors album in decades. But I do manage a late-night twirl with *The Four Feathers* every now and again.

A novel, after a single reading, sticks to your ribs for a lifetime. The great ones do, anyway. Music's different. Music can take you up or down in a heartbeat. And it marks the mileposts of adolescence: first dance, first kiss, first love, first arrest, and so on. Movies, on the other hand, provide a different sort of emotional and intellectual service. They are, in their way, the perfect jet-age entertainment. You bolt your own world, go to a new one, and return home in two hours. Really, what better weekend is there than to stay in bed for two days with an endless supply of videos? Curling up with a book is wonderful, too. But, I confess, I'd rather have the videos.

When I was a kid, in the days before VCRs, being a movie nut was hard work. I'd plan my entire school sick-day schedule around a weekly highlighting session of the TV section of the newspaper, combing the meager listings for matinees of *His Girl Friday* or *The Wages of Fear* or *Stalag 17.* An old Ealing comedy on Wednesday at two P.M.? I'd begin planning my Wednesday-morning cough and fever the night before.

As a writer for *Time* magazine in the 70s, I found any excuse to slip off to Southern California. I'd land, get settled in at the hotel, and when I wasn't doing what I was out there to do, I'd be figuring out how to finagle my way into the studios. You know, just to look around.

I'd beg an appointment with some lower-level functionary, and when the meeting was over, I'd take off my suit jacket, roll up my shirtsleeves, and wander the lot for hours, prowling the streets between soundstages like a stray, terrified of being found out for the intruder that I was. In situations like this, never underestimate the power of a purposeful walk and a rolled-up file in one hand. I may have looked like a development hireling on a vital mission, but I was a truant and a hopeless romantic, starved for a taste of what life must have been like when the MGM and Warner Bros. and Paramount back lots were bustling with stars and extras, and writers were quartered away in stucco bungalows with typewriters and bottles of scotch.

I would have to say that movies brought me to New York from the gray, Protestant, post-Victorian city in Canada where I grew up. In front of the television and in the back rows of big movie palaces and in open-top cars at the local drive-in, I was transported by movies to this fabulous city, a city so unlike the one I knew. Movies like *The Awful Truth* and *Holiday,* through *My Man Godfrey, Nothing Sacred,* and *Sweet Smell of Success,* to *The French Connection* and *Mean Streets*—these were my surrogate New York until I managed to get my hands on the real thing. Jazz also brought me here. So did the photographs of wits and intellectuals and bohemians in Greenwich Village that ran in big-league magazines such as *Life, Look,* and *Esquire.*

But mostly it was movies that brought me to New York.

Unlike a lot of people who love films, I was not really interested in being in the movie business—just in movie theaters. Before I got to New York, I had never met anyone who actually worked in the movies, except for a friend of my father's who had been a stuntman in a couple of Michael Curtiz features before the war. So, unlike a kid growing up in Beverly Hills, I didn't know what movie people were like or how they even became movie people. My first week in Manhattan I saw Cary Grant walking up Sixth Avenue outside the Time & Life Building and Myrna Loy at the '21' Club. *This,* I thought, was living.

I love so many types of movies, but most of all I still love the ones set in New York. Beyond that, my tastes are all over the place. I revere Truffaut, Clouzot, Renoir, and Godard. I love anything by Capra, Sturges, Lubitsch, or Hawks. Same for Wilder, Wyler, Spielberg, LeRoy, and Hitchcock. Same, too, for Ford and Lean, Scorsese, Kubrick, Coppola, and Peckinpah. Give me Sonnenfeld and Soderbergh. Fellini and Fassbinder. Oh, and the Farrelly brothers too. Also anything with Irene Dunne, Jean Arthur, Robert De Niro, John Cusack, or Dennis Farina. My favorite periods are the 30s, the 70s, and right now. And also everything in between.

Not that it necessarily shows, but we've been chipping away at this book in fits and starts for five years. In 1995, along with my two deputies, Aimée Bell and Matt Tyrnauer, I began going through old issues of the magazine, beginning with copies from 1914 (the year publisher Condé Nast launched the publication, under the stewardship of its storied editor, Frank Crowninshield) and proceeding through to 1936. John Gillies and Chris Lawrence, a pair of fresh-scrubbed summer interns that year, made photocopies of stories and photographs that we liked. This took three or four months. Then, given my full-time responsibilities putting out *Vanity Fair,* raising four children, and putting on weight, things just sort of drifted.

In late 1998, David Friend, a former colleague of mine from *Life* magazine who had just joined *V.F.,* pressed me to finish the project. Together, we went back through all 470-odd issues of *Vanity Fair.* Did it twice, in fact. We pulled all the best photographs, stories, and essays involving Hollywood published during the magazine's two incarnations. (For those older readers who may have thought their subscriptions had lapsed for 47 years, *Vanity Fair* appeared monthly from 1914 to 1936; the current publication was launched in 1983.)

Over a few insanely hot days the following summer, David and I spread out the first edit of 1,805 photographs (tear sheets, color-laser copies, and digital scans of rare images from the Condé Nast Archive) on a long dining-room table in my house in the West Village. We pruned down the lot to come up with a more manageable batch of 513 so-called selects: all of them images previously published in, or shot for, the magazine. For the next several months, with the help of *Vanity Fair's* design director, David Harris, Mimi Park, the book's designer, and SunHee Grinnell, its photography editor, we pushed around these pictures—on conference-room walls, miniaturized-layout boards, and computer screens. It's not what you put in a book that's important. It's what you leave out. And with that in mind, we winnowed our selects down to the 292 essential Hollywood photographs assembled here—a good many taken, not surprisingly, by *Vanity Fair's* two signature photographers, Edward Steichen and Annie Leibovitz. A guiding hand through this whole process was Jane Sarkin, *Vanity Fair's* features editor. Over the past 15 years she has set up every Hollywood cover and portfolio.

Christopher Hitchens was conscripted to write captions for the photos; he spent a good stretch of the winter of 1999–2000 holed up in Room 1415 of New York's Mayflower Hotel, with a Sharp PC-3030 laptop, 251 research files, and a supply of Johnnie Walker Black. The 14 essays and articles that are woven throughout the book include some of the most memorable Hollywood stories we've run in recent years as well as offerings from early *Vanity Fair* contributors such as D. H. Lawrence, Clare Boothe Luce, Dorothy Parker, Walter Winchell, and P. G. Wodehouse. Together, they trace nearly a century of Hollywood power and glory, myth and mystery.

In spite of the fact that *Vanity Fair* is a New York–based magazine, it nevertheless has an outsize presence in the movie business, what with our covers, our annual Hollywood Issue, and the party we throw each year on Oscar night. And how fitting is it that the magazine and the movies came of age around the same time? When the first issue of *Vanity Fair* appeared on newsstands in January 1914, moving pictures were just evolving from novelty to necessity. Mary Pickford and Charlie Chaplin were already famous when Volume 1, Number 1 was published. But D. W. Griffith's *The Birth of a Na-*

tion wouldn't come out for another year. And *Intolerance* a year after that. Officially, there was no such thing as Beverly Hills (it wouldn't be incorporated until later that month, on January 28, 1914) or Paramount Pictures (which would be formed that May) or Technicolor (it was established at year's end). Talkies wouldn't arrive for another 13 years. And *Ishtar* for another 60 after that.

Throughout the 20s and early 30s, *Vanity Fair* was a pioneer in what came to be known as celebrity portraiture. In fact, the magazine was virtually alone in treating portraits of stars as serious photography and even as art. By having masters such as Cecil Beaton, Anton Bruehl, Baron de Meyer, and Edward Steichen cover the Hollywood beat, *Vanity Fair* was elevating screen players and their new craft. Many of the photographs here, such as those of Paul Robeson, Charles Laughton, Greta Garbo, and Louise Brooks, are the iconographic images of their subjects.

Yes, there has always been a steady, two-way flow of traffic between the New York offices of *Vanity Fair* and the bungalows of Los Angeles. Many contributors to the old *V.F.* went on to become noted screenwriters or filmmakers, or playwrights whose work made it to the big screen. Among their ranks: Robert Benchley (*Foreign Correspondent, The Reluctant Dragon, Sky Devils*), James M. Cain (*Mildred Pierce, The Postman Always Rings Twice*), Jean Cocteau (*Orpheus*), Colette (*Gigi*), John Dos Passos (*The Devil Is a Woman*), Paul Gallico (*The Pride of the Yankees*), Anita Loos (*Gentlemen Prefer Blondes*), George S. Kaufman (*You Can't Take It with You, The Man Who Came to Dinner, Animal Crackers*), Ring Lardner (*Woman of the Year*), Compton MacKenzie (*Carnival*), Dorothy Parker (*Trade Winds*), and Robert Sherwood (*Rebecca, The Best Years of Our Lives, The Bishop's Wife*).

Actors such as Douglas Fairbanks and Douglas Fairbanks Jr. were frequent essayists, and there were occasional pieces by a variety of early Hollywood bluebloods, including Mary Pickford, Leslie Howard, and Theda Bara. In 1921, while still a 21-year-old actor in Britain, Noël Coward received his first American paycheck—from *Vanity Fair*—for a wry whisper on secret love affairs in the royal courts of Europe.

And for those whose photographs appear in *Vanity Fair,* well, they just become larger than life. And strangely intimate too. How many of us have had the experience of walking down the street and spotting a familiar face, and smiling in recognition, only to realize once he or she has passed that you don't really know the person at all—that the passerby was a movie star? The good ones will smile politely back, aware of the mistake you have made.

Like Dominick Dunne, who wrote the afterword to this book, I am not at all embarrassed to admit that I am a simple, unabashed fan. Of movies, of the people who make them, and of Hollywood. This book is for them and for it, and for the little people like Dominick and you and me—all of us out there in the dark. □

THE FOUR KINGS Clark Gable, Van Heflin, Gary Cooper, James Stewart These are not just four crowned heads (though Gable, in fact, was anointed the King of Hollywood in the MGM commissary in 1938). Here you see the epitome of debonair camaraderie: Rhett Butler and Athos the Musketeer, Mr. Deeds and Mr. Smith (to say nothing of *The Man Who Shot Liberty Valance*), enthroned together in the Crown Room at Romanoff's.

PHOTOGRAPHED IN 1957
BY **SLIM AARONS**

AUDREY HEPBURN In Nazi-occupied Holland she actually did starve. And before she went, lightly, in 1993, she was a UNICEF ambassador to the world's malnourished children—their fair lady. Cecil Beaton said she resembled a Modigliani with the paint still shining; she came by her coltishness honestly. In *Roman Holiday* she was princess of a country with no name; of her Eliza Doolittle and Sabrina Fairchild and Holly Golightly you could say the same.

PHOTOGRAPHED IN 1991
BY **STEVEN MEISEL**

GRETA GARBO Tolstoy doesn't tell us about Anna Karenina's cheekbones, but Greta Garbo improved upon the master's design. Her silent Swedish melancholy carried her over the threshold of the talkies and saw her in works by Pirandello and O'Neill, and directed by Cukor and Lubitsch. Early cinema's most massive star (*A Woman of Affairs, Anna Christie, Grand Hotel*), she was also a *Vanity Fair* fixture. In *Ninotchka* she showed she could be upbeat, but the purple-blue eyes were always wistful, and the desire to be alone was not an act.

ILLUSTRATED IN 1932
BY **MIGUEL COVARRUBIAS**

JACK NICHOLSON Ever since he edged into that prison-cell scene in *Easy Rider* (1969), Jack Nicholson's lupine charm and maniacal grin have made him part of the American ("Wendy, I'm home") family, or anyway that antic, attic part of it, located just past *Chinatown*. Jack-of-all-trades, he has earned 11 Oscar nominations across three decades (winning for *One Flew over the Cuckoo's Nest, Terms of Endearment,* and *As Good as It Gets*). Witches love him, too.

PHOTOGRAPHED IN 1992
BY **ANNIE LEIBOVITZ**

DOUGLAS FAIRBANKS JR. AND **JOAN CRAWFORD**
Douglas Fairbanks Jr. was a contributing editor at *Vanity Fair*, and in every other respect a gentleman, also. (He was even knighted by King George VI.) As *Sinbad the Sailor* he maintained poise, and was the first of Joan Crawford's four husbands. What ever did happen to baby Joan? Should we ask the author of *Mommie Dearest*?
PHOTOGRAPHED IN 1929
BY **NICKOLAS MURAY**

THE KINGS OF COMEDY Robin Williams, Eddie Murphy, Jim Carrey Any director who wants to send in the serious clowns had better be able to call on these three. Robin Williams was among the first to dare wring a laugh out of the carnage in Southeast Asia (in *Good Morning, Vietnam*). Eddie Murphy (*48 Hrs.*, *Beverly Hills Cop*) has extracted a million nervous guffaws—best of all in *Trading Places*—from our race-charged society, while rubberized Jim Carrey (*The Mask*, the Ace Ventura films) has made it fashionable to be irritating (*Man on the Moon*), and in *The Truman Show* probably came closest to the clown who weeps under the made-up-ness of everything. PHOTOGRAPHED IN 1997 BY **ANNIE LEIBOVITZ**

Charlie Chaplin Playing
for His Friends After Dinner:

A Poem by Carl Sandburg

T he woman had done him wrong.
Either that . . . or the woman was clean as a white rose in the morning
gauze of dew.
It was either one or the other or it was the two things, right and wrong,
woven together like two braids of a woman's head of hair hanging
down woven together.

The room is dark. The door opens. It is Charlie playing for his friends
after dinner, "the marvelous urchin, the little genius of the screen"
(chatter it like a monkey's running laughter cry).
No . . . it is not Charlie . . . it is somebody else. It is a man, gray shirt,
bandanna, dark face. A candle in his left hand throws a slant of light
on the dark face. The door closes slow. The right hand leaves
the doorknob slow.

He looks at something. What is it? A white sheet on a table. He takes
two long soft steps. He runs the candlelight around a hump in the
sheet. He lifts the sheet slow, sad-like.
A woman's head of hair shows, a woman's white face. He takes the head
between his hands and looks long at it. His fingers trickle under the
sheet, snap loose something, bring out fingers full of a pearl necklace.
He covers the face and the head of hair with the white sheet. He takes a
step toward the door. The necklace slips into his pocket off the fingers
of his right hand. His left hand lifts the candle for a good-bye look.

Knock, knock, knock. A knocking the same as the time of the human
heartbeat.

Knock, knock, knock, first louder, then lower. Knock, knock, knock,
the same as the time of the human heartbeat.
He sets the candle on the floor . . . leaps to the white sheet . . . rips it
back . . . has his fingers at the neck, his thumbs at the throat, and
does three slow fierce motions of strangling.
The knocking stops. All is quiet. He covers the face and the head of hair
with the white sheet, steps back, picks up the candle and listens.
Knock, knock, knock, a knocking the same as the time of the human
heartbeat.

Knock, knock, knock, first louder, then lower. Knock, knock, knock,
the same as the time of the human heartbeat.
Again the candle to the floor, the leap, the slow fierce motions of
strangling, the cover-up of the face and the head of hair, the step
back, the listening.
And again the knock, knock, knock . . . louder . . . lower . . . to the time
of the human heartbeat.
Once more the motions of strangling . . . then . . . nothing at all . . .
nothing at all . . . no more knocking . . . no knocking at all . . . no
knocking at all . . . in the time of the human heartbeat.

He stands at the door . . . peace, peace, peace everywhere only in the
man's face so dark and his eyes so lighted up with many lights, no
peace at all, no peace at all.
So he stands at the door, his right hand on the doorknob, the candle
slants of light fall and flicker from his face to the straight white sheet
changing gray against shadows.
So there is peace everywhere . . . no more knocking . . . no knocking at
all to the time of the human heartbeat . . . so he stands at the door
and his right hand on the doorknob.
And there is peace everywhere . . . only the man's face is a red gray
plaster of storm in the center of peace . . . so he stands with a candle
at the door . . . so he stands with a red gray face.

After he steps out the door closes: the door, the doorknob,
the table, the white sheet; there is nothing at all; the owners
are shadows; the owners are gone; not even a knocking;
not even a knock, knock, knock . . . louder, lower, in the time
of the human heartbeat.

The lights are snapped on. Charlie, "the marvelous urchin, the little
genius of the screen" (chatter it with a running monkey's laughter
cry). Charlie is laughing a laugh the whole world knows.

The room is full of cream yellow lights. Charlie is laughing . . . louder . . .
lower . . .
And again the heartbeats laugh . . . the human heartbeats laugh . . . □

CHARLIE CHAPLIN The little guy was not a small man: he made a 20th-century point out of the distinction and became part of *Modern Times.* (George Bernard Shaw called him the only genius to be produced by the medium.) He co-founded United Artists (with Douglas Fairbanks; Mary Pickford, and D. W. Griffith), was harried by Joseph McCarthy, and cut the *Führer* down to size in *The Great Dictator:* there were giants in those days.

PHOTOGRAPHED IN 1931
BY **EDWARD STEICHEN**

MARILYN MONROE Before she broke the hearts of Joe DiMaggio, Arthur Miller, and at least one Kennedy, Norma Jean was the all-American bombshell—seen here bursting in air, before U.S. troops in Korea. (An adoring G.I. took the shot, which was first printed 44 years later, in the European edition of *Vanity Fair*.) For those who liked it hot, there was *always* Marilyn.

PHOTOGRAPHED IN 1954
BY **DAVID GEARY**

CLINT EASTWOOD A hard man is good to find. Actor (and director) Clint Eastwood's rail-tough huskiness has defined the cop, the cowboy, and the loner for almost two generations. And his laconic utterances—"Go ahead, make my day"—have penetrated the vernacular with *Magnum Force*. The frontier may have shifted from the plains (*The Good, the Bad and the Ugly*) to the inner city (*Dirty Harry*), but the frontiersman still lives on.

PHOTOGRAPHED IN 1995
BY **HERB RITTS**

JULIA ROBERTS In Robert Altman's *The Player*, the very name of Julia Roberts is synonymous with "bankability." One critic was moved to say that her dentist-defying visage was the loveliest since faces were invented. None other than Rupert Everett has called her "Miss America"; *Pretty Woman* doesn't quite cover it. She took our breath away as the dying Shelby Eatenton Latcherie (*Steel Magnolias*); won hearts, breathlessly, as the strident dynamo *Erin Brockovich*.

PHOTOGRAPHED IN 1990
BY **HERB RITTS**

DORIS DAY A muted siren for a more innocent age. Much married (and much abused by men) in real life, Doris Day personified that bubbly but untouchable girl next door, who could sing and dance like an angel. Also, as is the way with angels, she had no—uh—downside. ("I knew Doris Day," Oscar Levant remarked, "before she was a virgin.") Though she explored the bedroom-farce theme on-screen with Rock Hudson (*Pillow Talk, Lover Come Back, Send Me No Flowers*), in private her template has been *Calamity Jane.* PHOTOGRAPHED IN 1953 BY **JOHN FLOREA**

PETER LORRE Born—rather promisingly—in Transylvania, he looked as guilty as sin even when he was innocent, which wasn't all that often. (He was guilty as charged in Fritz Lang's *M* and here, as Raskolnikov, in *Crime and Punishment*.) As it had in Hitchcock's *The Man Who Knew Too Much* (1934), the creepy scent of Weimar clung to him perfectly in *Casablanca*. Clammy and obsequious, he was an Edgar Allan Poe cameo, though he did manage to play a clown, beautifully, in *The Big Circus*.

PHOTOGRAPHED IN 1936
BY **LUSHA NELSON**

SPENCER TRACY AND **KATHARINE HEPBURN**
Reel off the names of their nine movies together
(this shot is from *Adam's Rib*, number six) and
you have a hint: *Woman of the Year, Keeper of
the Flame, Without Love, The Sea of Grass,
State of the Union, Pat and Mike, Desk Set,
Guess Who's Coming to Dinner.* The fluctuating
state of their union endured a quarter-century.
PHOTOGRAPHED IN 1949

KATE WINSLET She may have let Leonardo DiCaprio succumb to the big chill in *Titanic*, but she cut a magnificent figurehead in the meantime. Her maiden voyages were all as distraught types—a mom-slayer in *Heavenly Creatures*, Ophelia in Kenneth Branagh's *Hamlet*, Sue Bridehead in *Jude*—but she demonstrated a more robust style as Marianne Dashwood in Ang Lee's *Sense and Sensibility*, which prompted an Oscar nomination.

PHOTOGRAPHED IN 1998
BY **ANNIE LEIBOVITZ**

SAM SHEPARD AND **JESSICA LANGE** Nineteen eighty-two was a banner year for Jessica Lange: nominated for *Frances* and won for *Tootsie*. She prefers *Frances*, not least because she first connected with *The Right Stuff* on the set. Sam Shepard, playwright and player, has filled out the role of lover ever since. Together, they made *Country* matter. Yet they can flourish apart, he with *Fool for Love* and she shining in *Blue Sky* and on the magazine page: few stars have assumed more guises before the *Vanity Fair* lens than Lange. "Like a delicate fawn crossed with a Buick," Jack Nicholson once mused.

PHOTOGRAPHED IN 1984
BY **BRUCE WEBER**

ANTHONY HOPKINS Raised in the same Welsh village as Richard Burton, he escaped from a similar booze problem (going on to be knighted). His gentle, melancholy, and ruminative aspects (C. S. Lewis in *Shadowlands*, Stevens the servitor in *The Remains of the Day*, John Quincy

THE WHIZ KIDS Martin Scorsese, Steven Spielberg, Francis Ford Coppola, George Lucas Someone has to make the magic happen. And reading left to right you have the conjurers of *Mean Streets*, *Raging Bull*, and *GoodFellas*; *Jaws*, *Close Encounters of the Third Kind*, *Schindler's List*, and *Saving Private Ryan*; *The Conversation*, *Apocalypse Now*, and the *Godfather* triptych; *American Graffiti* and the *Star Wars* and *Indiana Jones* sagas (the latter with Lucas producing, Spielberg directing). The gentleman on the left routinely appears in his own movies—once (in *Taxi Driver*) because an actor failed to show. Having directed more than 60 features (and securing 6 of the top 10 slots on the all-time box-office roster), they have caused acting to occur, and animation, and special effects, and commanded sets big enough for a major coup or a small war.

PHOTOGRAPHED IN 1996
BY **ANNIE LEIBOVITZ**

DENZEL WASHINGTON Taking off as the key ebony note on the board, and striking the highest liberating chords as Steve Biko, Malcolm X, and the slave-warrior in *Glory*, Denzel Washington outgrew race-casting—his first movie was actually called *Carbon Copy*—to exert authority from *Crimson Tide* to *Philadelphia* to *The Hurricane*. Seen to great effect as Don Pedro in *Much Ado About Nothing*, he owns the most slaying smile on-screen. PHOTOGRAPHED IN 1995 BY **HERB RITTS**

DAVID NIVEN Oh please, don't let's say "dapper." Mr. Niven—at ease here with Jacqueline Kennedy, then a senator's wife—was poised, assured, immaculate, even raffish when he chose. (He was considered for the role of James Bond—and once lampooned Bond in *Casino Royale*—but would have found 007 far too energetic and theatrical.) Never breaking a sweat, he took the entire planet in his smooth stride (*Around the World in 80 Days*), took *The Guns of Navarone* with equal flair (having been a real commando—at Normandy—in a real war), and composed two superb volumes of Hollywood memoir. Elegant, if you insist. Dapper? We think not.

PHOTOGRAPHED IN 1958
BY **YALE JOEL**

JOHNNY DEPP Perhaps you *should* let the Valentino look fool you: young Mr. Depp has reminded many critics of the stars of silent film. Plucked from the world of nightlife and rock 'n' roll, he did fine—and almost wordlessly—in *Platoon* and *Edward Scissorhands*, becoming more articulate in *Ed Wood*, *Donnie Brasco*, and *Sleepy Hollow*. Meanwhile, his relationship with former girlfriend Kate Moss made enough noise.

PHOTOGRAPHED IN 1996
BY **ANNIE LEIBOVITZ**

KEANU REEVES In the Hawaiian tongue, "Keanu" means "cool breeze over the mountains," and some of the lad's reserve (we used to call it inscrutability) may come from his Pacific-Chinese ancestry. Raised in other cool and windy places such as Canada, and a private Idaho embellished with his friend River Phoenix, the man who braved *The Matrix* has been evolving away from teen androgyny at warp *Speed*.

PHOTOGRAPHED IN 1995
BY **ANNIE LEIBOVITZ**

By Clare Boothe Brokaw Luce

Every age has had its Helen, and every Helen has had the people for her willing historians. The Circes of history—Helen of Troy, Cleopatra, Salome, the Queen of Sheba, Mary Queen of Scots, Madame de Pompadour, Ninon de Lenclos, Nell Gwynn, Mrs. Hamilton, Lola Montez—march (if any such martial word may be used for the thrilling rhythms of their sensuous bodies) in exquisite pageantry through the annals of art and literature. They are not forgotten, their remembered stories still have the power to touch men's hearts, and often the taste of their ghostly lips seems more real than the warm embrace of living flesh.

Alone of all the centuries, the 20th seems so far to have produced no beauty who might deserve the word historical, no charmer whose sweet legend will live in the minds of future generations of men, no feminine form which will gloriously survive in the works of poets and artists.

There is one possible exception. There is Greta Garbo—Greta Garbo, the strange and angular siren of the "movies," the legend of the studios, the sole survivor of the tawdry publicity, the spotlight madness, the vulgar exhibitionism of Hollywood. Better known to the average man than either the Queen of Sheba or Helen of Troy, her cinematic image has encircled the entire globe, and domestic as well as alien audiences, who understood no word of what she was saying, have thrilled, again and again, to the vibrant mystery of her voice and her form.

Surely the worldwide fame of this fair Scandinavian, whose every movement is instinct with beauty, whose name evokes mystery, and whose image evokes desire . . . surely she will outlast our generation and will join the deathless throng of lovely ladies—one is almost tempted to say—in . . . Hell?

She is a likely candidate. The only one, indeed, that our decade has had to offer. There are more beautiful women in Hollywood, where the most beautiful women in the world are to be found. But perfection of face or figure is often a chilling thing, and defeats the very emotion which it is ordinarily supposed to arouse in the beholder. Garbo fortuitously escapes this cold perfection. Her often sullen and too large mouth is beautiful only because it is mobile as music; her hollow cheeks beneath high, Nordic cheekbones have not the poet's smooth, rounded flow from temple to chin; her coiffure, which has been aped by the fashionable women of two continents, falls in a limp, untidy, dun-colored mop upon her thin shoulders; only her eyes, "like jewels in a shroud," heavy-lidded and slumberous beneath the gloom of her lashes (which quite literally sweep her cheeks), approach perfection, and even they are marred by shaved eyebrows, which have been replaced by inane penciled hieroglyphics, springing upward like the antennae of a butterfly.

She is broad-shouldered, flat-chested, long-legged, rawboned, and she moves with the awkward grace of an adolescent.

That is the physical image of Garbo. It shows forth, but does not explain her magnetism and her allure. These far transcend her beauty, as they also transcend her ability as an actress. (Not that she is a poor actress, but that Garbo herself is so much more real and vivid in her audience's mind than the character which she is playing. Her role is like the dress she wears—a sometimes attractive garment which permits her to expose herself decently to the public gaze.)

Perhaps the inability to define Garbo's magic in the usual physical or artistic terms is partially responsible for the inordinate interest in her "private life." It is precisely here that the average person is more than ever baffled, although

he should find in that "private life," and the Garbo legend which has grown out of its very impenetrability (or is it vacuity?), his most valuable clue to her personality, and his answer to the question: Is Garbo a woman of history?

Garbo, of all Hollywood's glittering legion, *has* a private life. She entertains, she receives, she interviews—no one. Her contacts with the studios are reduced to the minimum required by her actual cinema work; nothing more is tolerated. She forms few, if any, friendships, and does not seem to cherish them for long. Even those in Hollywood who have come to know her well— that is to say, who have shared her physical society—have left her more baffled than when they first met, for the theories which they brought to the encounter have been shattered by the almost vicious quality of her reticence. Her indifference to all the recognized Hollywood values, her long silences, her brutal independence, her famous "I tank I go home," with which she frustrates every wish counter to her own, her sphinxlike air of ageless wisdom, of always being on the verge of saying something of vast import, have never deserted her for a single second. There is no chink in her magnificent armor of aloofness. Yes, there *was* one . . . one small, vulnerable spot—Garbo's Achilles tendon (I had almost said heel): John Gilbert. For him and with him, during a brief while Greta Garbo emerged from the cocoon of personal anonymity which she had been spinning about herself ever since she came to Hollywood. A gay butterfly, she wafted about the Hollywood scene, and, according to numerous eyewitnesses, she was—under the Gilbertian influence—"just like anybody else."

Here, perhaps, is the answer to the question about Garbo's place in history.

Beautiful and gifted women always have been, and always will be, judged and evaluated by their weakness—since the strength of a woman is at best a negative quality of virtue. Are not "the beautiful" and "the damned" synonymous terms? Their weaknesses give them what historical glamour they possess. Therefore it is inevitable that Garbo should be judged in the light of her only, if brief, attachment—John Gilbert. In this light she fails not the picture fans, not her studio, not her generation, but—history. History has never reserved a place for a beautiful woman who did not love, or who was not loved by, at least one interesting, powerful, or brilliant man. Love, magnificently, a little recklessly, and certainly publicly—the loves of the great can no more be hidden than the burning of the topless towers of Ilium. When we speak of Helen, we speak in the next breath of Menelaus, of Paris. Pompadour reminds us of Louis XV, Salome would have mattered little but for John the Baptist, and although it is sacrilege, the Baptist would have mattered little but for Salome. Cleopatra had her Caesar, and Mark Antony had Cleopatra. Is the most magnetic woman of her generation, the greatest beauty of her era, to be remembered because her name was "associated with" (to use a genteel euphemism worthy of Will Hays, but hardly of Garbo) John Gilbert's? The answer is yes, or, rather, the answer is no. Neither name will be remembered.

A woman who becomes "just like anybody else" when she is in love *is* just like anybody else. A great love maddens with joy, or crushes with sorrow, it debases or exalts, deifies or brutalizes, but it does *not* standardize. The Garbo-Gilbert romance was a standard product of the Hollywood fleshpots and, as such, must be used as an index to the inner Garbo. (The fact that the attachment was not a success does not excuse its inception, although it is customary to demand forgiveness for bad taste in

love affairs on the quaint grounds that they so often turn out badly.)

The only way a woman can gloriously succeed in impressing herself upon her age—the way of love—Garbo has, until now, failed in. If she does not remedy this oversight one day, then those shadowy, gigantic six-foot close-up embraces, the microphoned passions spent in the arms of celluloid Gilberts, Novarros, Montgomerys, and Gables, will be her only epitaph—faintly humorous celluloid strips, of interest only to antiquarians or other-day humorists of, say, 50 years hence, who may conceivably show them to their friends to provide a curious or mirthful evening.

There was left to Garbo another way in which she might have, had she wished, survived the Oblivion awaiting her: the way of the intelligence—of art and literature. Here, too, she has failed. With enviable consistency, with admirable independence, but with lamentable stupidity and egotism, she has refused to pose for good artists, to interview, or even to meet socially men and women of acknowledged intelligence and ability. To be sure, the veil of mystery which has piqued the fans has not intrigued the artists, who instinctively feel the paucity of interest that it cloaks. Garbo has never inspired a single piece of fine criticism or writing (not excepting this) nor any artistic appreciation of worth. To know that this can be done by a cinema star one has only to witness the career of Charles Chaplin, who has received the serious consideration of the finest writers of his day, and whose intellectual contacts with great men of the world have been profitable and pleasant to both himself and to them. Chaplin will take his place beside Dan Leno, Grimaldi, Debureau, and Coquelin. Garbo will be forgotten as a woman in 10 years, and her legacy as an actress will be dead when Helen Hayes's, Lynn Fontanne's, and Katharine Cornell's are beginning to grow greenest.

GRETA GARBO This classic photograph metamorphosed from an inspired instant on the set of *A Woman of Affairs* to become Garbo as our readers knew her. Steichen's study still illuminates a fellow photographer's pronouncement that no woman in the world would refuse to change her face for Garbo's.

The world must take her at her own valuation: a woman with a chip (although it flew there from some Hollywooden head) on her shoulder, a woman with a grudge against life, a woman who cares nothing for literature, little for love, and for art only what she brings to that ofttimes puerile, hardly endurable, and limited medium, the silver screen.

The only first-rate artist with whom, willingly, she ever permitted herself to come in contact—Edward Steichen, the photographer—instantly discovered the truth about her while he was making those photographs which may, curiously enough, prove to be her only lasting claim to fame. He said, "She is like a lovely wild-wood animal ... or a child."

Child or animal, whichever you please. I prefer to think of her as a deer, in the body of a woman, living resentfully in the Hollywood Zoo, suffering in the bonds of a complex civilization, startled by human contacts, disinterested in human things, graceful and beautiful and mysterious with the untutored grace and native mystery of the wild thing of the forest. This would explain the famous "walks in the rain," the sunbaths, the intense need of physical exercise, the long silences (for, since nothing is ever the result of her thoughts, common sense dictates that she must be thinking about nothing), the nostalgia for her native heath, the intense discomfiture among people, and the inability or the lack of desire to make and hold friends.

You may prefer to think of her as a child who has never grown up. Sulky and spoiled, indifferent to all desires but her own, suspicious of bribes, bewildered by adult psychology, impervious to threats, since being a spoiled and talented child she knows that They will not, They dare not, hurt her. Selfish, shrewd, ignorant, self-absorbed and whimsical, perverse, and innocent—the perfect realization of the child left to itself, unhampered and uncontrolled by mature authority.

"Every man has the love affairs he deserves." This is true collectively as well as individually. Our generation's loveliest woman is but a phantom upon a silver screen—a shadow with the face of an angel of Perdition, as substantial as a mist before the moon, the inarticulate, the bad-tempered, and the "great" Garbo. □

HOLLYWOOD ISSUE COVER, 1995 Sunset Boulevard never looked as glamorous as when *Vanity Fair* put up this gatefold cover as an extended billboard—around Oscartime '95. Left to right, as the traffic piles up: Jennifer Jason Leigh, Uma Thurman, Nicole Kidman, Patricia Arquette, Linda Fiorentino, Gwyneth Paltrow, Sarah Jessica Parker, Julianne Moore, Angela Bassett, Sandra Bullock.

PHOTOGRAPHED IN 1995
BY **ANNIE LEIBOVITZ**

MARLON BRANDO A *streetcar* named desire? How about a whole *street*? Brando, *The Wild One*, conquered Broadway, then Hollywood and Vine. A young lion, a guy who was Sky Masterson to the dolls, a mercurial Zapata. In *Julius Caesar* he even persuaded Romans to lend him their ears. Then came *The Ugly American*, followed by the jowly Don Corleone and the rotund Colonel Kurtz. But those hectic first tangos will never fade away.

PHOTOGRAPHED CIRCA 1950
BY **JACK ALBIN**

JAMES DEAN Romantic (Byron actually was his middle name). And restless. And forever young. Three leading roles, four bit parts, two dozen years, and then, in 1955, wiped out in his Porsche by a Ford sedan. For no cause. Like many such, he's had a second life in our imaginations, not least for being a premature, if closeted, gay emblem. His Eden of innocence lost, he has honorary *Giant* status for all that.

PHOTOGRAPHED IN 1955
BY **PHIL STERN**

NANCY AND **RONALD REAGAN** On golden pond, the former First Couple tripped the light utterly fantastic. Their first waltz came when R.R. was the man to see at the Screen Actors Guild and the young upstart (troubled that others had mistaken her for *another* actress named Nancy Davis) needed to get her name off the blacklist. Benson's classic *Vanity Fair* cover shot of two players turned politicians turned players was entirely apt: as the 40th president, the one on the right used Hollywood punch lines; the one on the left used Hollywood astrologers.

PHOTOGRAPHED IN 1985
BY **HARRY BENSON**

SYLVESTER STALLONE AND **BRIGITTE NIELSEN**
Sylvester Stallone's first movie credit (eons before
playing *Rocky* and *Rambo*) was for a 1970 blue
movie with the title *Party at Kitty and Stud's,* later
renamed *The Italian Stallion*. Brigitte Nielsen's
first credit: *Rocky IV*. For a while, this looked like
a meeting of bodies if not of minds, but later,
with *Snowboard Academy* (hers) and *Cop Land*
(his), even bodies tended to drift apart. And yet,
as Ritts's picture reminds us: Somehow we just
had to watch.   PHOTOGRAPHED IN 1985
                                   BY **HERB RITTS**

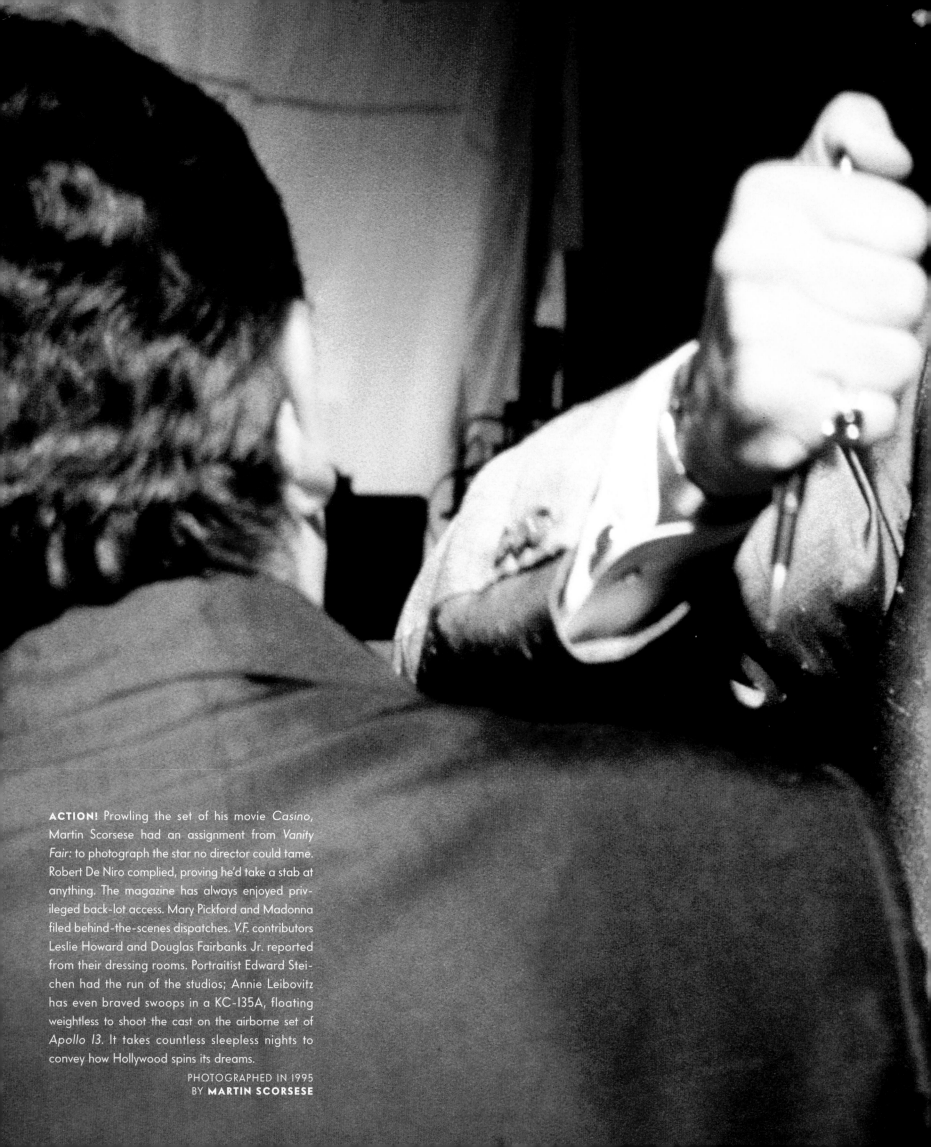

ACTION! Prowling the set of his movie *Casino*, Martin Scorsese had an assignment from *Vanity Fair*: to photograph the star no director could tame. Robert De Niro complied, proving he'd take a stab at anything. The magazine has always enjoyed privileged back-lot access. Mary Pickford and Madonna filed behind-the-scenes dispatches. *V.F.* contributors Leslie Howard and Douglas Fairbanks Jr. reported from their dressing rooms. Portraitist Edward Steichen had the run of the studios; Annie Leibovitz has even braved swoops in a KC-135A, floating weightless to shoot the cast on the airborne set of *Apollo 13*. It takes countless sleepless nights to convey how Hollywood spins its dreams.

PHOTOGRAPHED IN 1995
BY **MARTIN SCORSESE**

JULIE ANDREWS A female deer? A drop of golden sun? Victor? Or Victoria? Modern Millie? Or is that *Mary Poppins* gracing 14th Street? Julie Andrews has been the most perennial of the English roses: the secret may be a tincture of acid and mystery hidden among the dewy petals. Her director husband, Blake Edwards, matched her against Bo Derek in *10*. Good call.

PHOTOGRAPHED IN 1995
BY **ANNIE LEIBOVITZ**

SAMMY DAVIS JR. Stop the world—he wants to blast off. Spring-heeled Sammy Davis Jr. had to tap-dance and croon past a lot of barriers; an ugly racist cabal in the industry forbade his romance with Kim Novak. To become the only black face in the Rat Pack *and* the Nixon gang may not seem like much, but the self-proclaimed man with "three handicaps" (a one-eyed Jewish African-American) broke through in grand style.

PHOTOGRAPHED CIRCA 1949
BY **PHIL STERN**

PEE-WEE HERMAN As giddy as some Howdy Doody on speed, the alter ego of comedian Paul Reubens inhabits a man-child's mock-topia, zanily deconstructing his own bedpan-humor world—best translated to the screen in the Tim Burton kitsch farce, *Pee-wee's Big Adventure* (1985). Though he slinked into an eight-year exile after a trip to another strange film (*Nurse Nancy*), the indefatigable Pee-wee lurks in the dim theater of our ids: cackling, subversive, and sweetly dark. PHOTOGRAPHED IN 1984 BY **ANNIE LEIBOVITZ**

WHOOPI GOLDBERG First revered as a revved-up monologuist, now she's pitchwoman, sometime Oscar-ceremony M.C., and, yes, a Hollywood Square. In *The Long Walk Home* and *Ghosts of Mississippi*, she was a dignified reminder of suffering and survival in the bad old days; *The Color Purple* made the same point in a different way. Another spirited role as the black-magic woman Oda Mae (Oscar for *Ghost* in 1990). A nun when the mood takes her: black-and-white habit could be the key. The cognoscenti may argue over who saw her first; Leibovitz, as evidenced here, rendered her best.

PHOTOGRAPHED IN 1984
BY **ANNIE LEIBOVITZ**

KIM BASINGER O.K., keep your hat on. Kim Basinger's best practical joke was to play a body-double call girl in *L.A. Confidential;* her character's clients would have parted with good money for a few moments of *9½ Weeks*, or a *Blind Date*, or a taste of *The Real McCoy*. Batfans could also form a line, never saying never and expecting no mercy.

PHOTOGRAPHED IN 1989
BY **HERB RITTS**

By Walter Winchell

That Ina Claire can cuss like a parrot and does. A snappy retorter, too, is she. Her ace comeback being the one about the movie interviewer who, shortly after Ina became Mrs. J. Gilbert, queried, "Well, now, tell me. How does it feel to be married to a star?" and Ina snapped, "Why don't you ask Mr. Gilbert?"

That George M. Cohan pays $45 for his shoes, which are made to order. Wears high heels, but so does Lee Shubert, who wears a monocle only when in London.

Fency Thet!

That Helen Morgan drinks highballs for breakfast. The best gag about her in a long spell was the one in *Vanity Fair* that went: "It would be news if a piano would sit on Helen Morgan!"

That the funniest thing about George Jessel is an old-maid aunt who has a slight dialect. The type of woman who went to see the *Follies* recently (her first show) and she shook her head, smacked her tongue against her teeth, and said: "Oh, my, my. Look how those goils show themselves all over for a few dollehs a veek. I vouldn't show myself for a millyun dollehs even!"

That Eddie Cantor swore he was through with the stage when *Whoopee* closed.

Then he changed his mind two years later.

After he lost two million in Wall Street. Because he guaranteed friends against losses, friends he urged to buy stock.

That James J. Walker was glad, in a way, that the press went after him about his private life. He said that it was a terrific headache trying to dodge matters and now that it is over there is no longer a headache.

When he was told that his line "I'll match my private life with any man's!" was a humdinger, Walker replied: "It was a good line, at that. A decent man wouldn't dignify it with an answer and a scoundrel who had any conscience couldn't afford to!"

That Beatrice Lillie, when it is chilly, sleeps with socks on.

Anything for a laugh.

That Leslie Howard is one of the Britishers who is nice about it. I mean his adenoids never get in your hair. But he wears a beret!

That Al Jolson is said to be much older than he admits, but it doesn't appear to matter. He is rich enough to own numerous stables of racehorses and a rumor has it he is raising 800 of them.

Think of all the races they'll lose!

That Groucho Marx is the favorite of the Marx Four. He resembles F.P.A., the columnist, and was once his contributor until he discovered that publications actually pay for that sort of stuff.

Is now a successful author, too, but he wears hard collars.

That Damon Runyon's suspenders contain the likeness of his Favorite Person.

That Maurice Chevalier sends you shirts from France but doesn't pay the $25 duty on them. So you send them straight back!

That Peggy Joyce weeps if you write anything about her that doesn't please her. Let her have a good cry over this.

That Walter Winchell, one of our most notable illiterates, was actually left back four times in the same grade at Public School 184, New York City, in 1910. He was finally expelled from the school in 6B. Captain Kidd was the name of his principal, and one of his teachers, a Miss O'Donnell, a robust-looking brunette, kept him after hours on numerous occasions to kiss him full on the lips.

Among other things he has never printed is that when he was a vaudevillian his act was canceled after the opening matinee at the Grand Opera House in New York City.

His most annoying boast is that while he was expelled for illiteracy in New York, 20 years later a student at Ohio State lifted the entire contents of a column he wrote about Broadway. The student turned it in to his English professor as his own essay and it came back with an A!!!!

Once when his four-year-old daughter, Walda, was coming out of the St. Moritz Hotel, where the Winchells dwell, a strange woman stopped the child and exclaimed: "Aren't you Walter Winchell's child?"

And Walda, stamping a foot, screamed, "Dood Dod! Do I have to hear that, again?" □

WALTER WINCHELL From Ciro's to the Stork Club, Walter Winchell was the echo chamber of American showbiz gossip (and every other kind as well: Ernest Hemingway once called him the only newspaperman "who would last three rounds with the Zeitgeist"). We're indebted to the columnist for our concept of celebrity buzz. Winchell made it all the way from the Runyon era of radio to become the narrator of *The Untouchables*—on TV, no less. A little longer and we might have had the W. W. Web. PHOTOGRAPHED IN 1930

LAURENCE OLIVIER The great white knight of the theater, seen here as Archie Rice in *The Entertainer*. Director of three classic Shakespeare movies— *Henry V, Hamlet, Richard III*—he was also married to Scarlett O'Hara (Vivien Leigh) and played Lord Nelson to Leigh's Emma in *That Hamilton Woman* (1941). Could "do" upstairs or down, from Lord Marchmain in *Brideshead Revisited* to a dentist (and a Nazi dentist at that) in *Marathon Man*, acquiring 12 Oscar nominations along the way, and honorary Academy Awards in 1946 and 1978.

PHOTOGRAPHED IN 1957
BY **SNOWDON**

SIGOURNEY WEAVER Amazonian, she appears, in the swelter of this Helmut Newton tease. She poached her name, Sigourney ("gypsy" at root), from *The Great Gatsby*. Since then, we have come to know her as the talented Officer Ripley (in *Alien* pursuits), a hardworking girl, used to living dangerously. Death versus maiden; great primates versus feral humans; ghosts versus busters.

PHOTOGRAPHED IN 1994
BY **HELMUT NEWTON**

WALT DISNEY Hoover, Kleenex, Xerox—some artifacts will always be known by their original brand name. Disney, likewise, is a global synonym for animation and entertainment. The term's progenitor, Walt, formed a company that won 29 Oscars during his reign—only one aspect of his mass production of universal symbols. Needless to list the whole bestiary, though you might care to note that the little fellow on the left was originally christened Mortimer Mouse. *That's* what's in a name. It's Disney's world—we just live in it.

PHOTOGRAPHED IN 1933
BY **EDWARD STEICHEN**

SHIRLEY TEMPLE The keepers of the Temple made a mint out of her as long as she was in her prime, which was between the ages of 6 and 10. *Wee Willie Winkie, Heidi,* and *Rebecca of Sunnybrook Farm* were credited with helping pull America out of the Depression, while her own blues were just beginning. (Adolescence is a tough time to hit your sell-by date.) Readers caught the innuendo of exploitation that this shrewd caricature conveyed; they would have been relieved by her later career as a Republican matron and ambassador to Ghana and Czechoslovakia. ILLUSTRATED IN 1934 BY **MIGUEL COVARRUBIAS**

SEAN PENN Once unfairly shadowed by turbulent offscreen scenes, here's a steadily growing talent who—for all that he looks like a sheep-killing dog—has moved beyond Madonna to become mobile. Stuck with bad-boy and crazed-vet stuff until he outpaced it in *Dead Man Walking*, he found a still center in *The Thin Red Line* and looks as if he's holding it. PHOTOGRAPHED IN 1996 BY **ANNIE LEIBOVITZ**

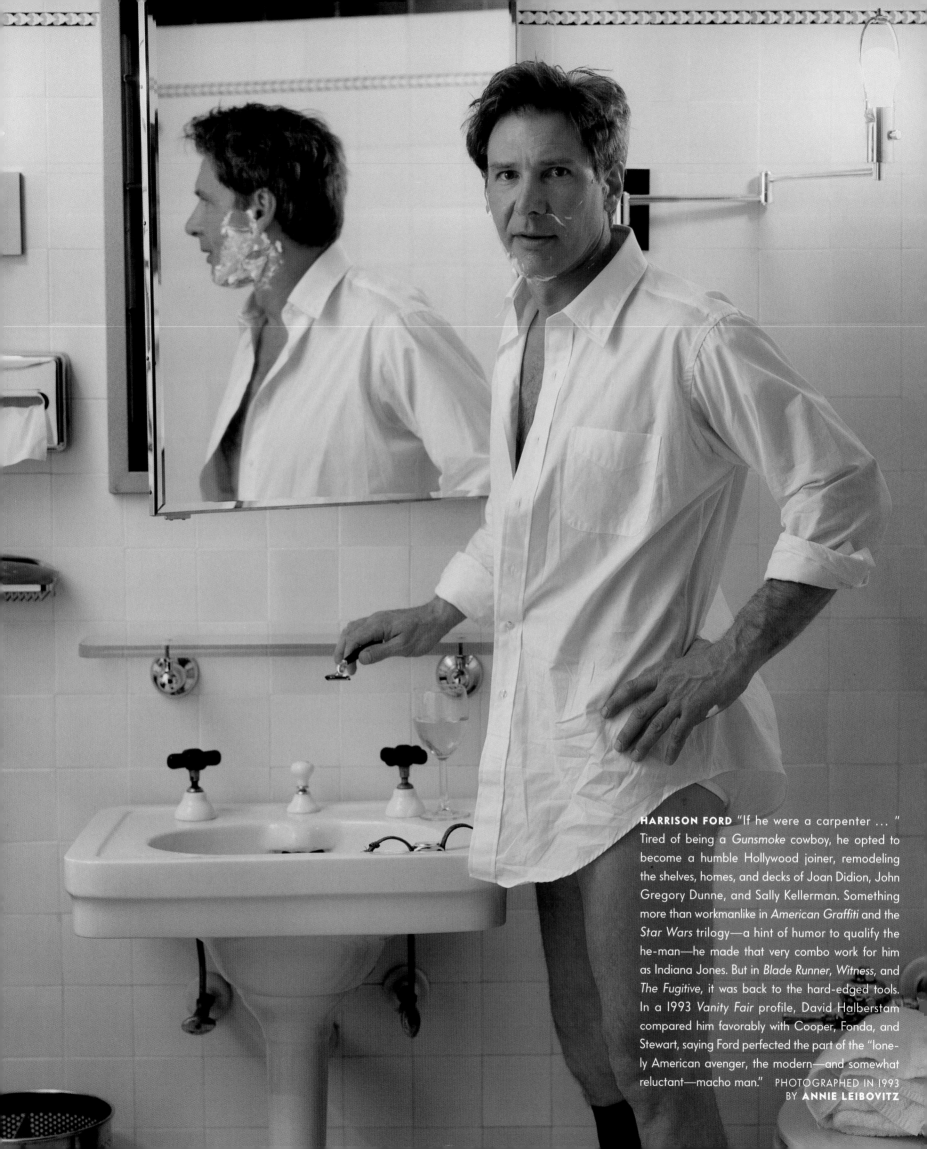

HARRISON FORD "If he were a carpenter ... " Tired of being a *Gunsmoke* cowboy, he opted to become a humble Hollywood joiner, remodeling the shelves, homes, and decks of Joan Didion, John Gregory Dunne, and Sally Kellerman. Something more than workmanlike in *American Graffiti* and the *Star Wars* trilogy—a hint of humor to qualify the he-man—he made that very combo work for him as Indiana Jones. But in *Blade Runner*, *Witness*, and *The Fugitive*, it was back to the hard-edged tools. In a 1993 *Vanity Fair* profile, David Halberstam compared him favorably with Cooper, Fonda, and Stewart, saying Ford perfected the part of the "lonely American avenger, the modern—and somewhat reluctant—macho man." PHOTOGRAPHED IN 1993 BY **ANNIE LEIBOVITZ**

GENE KELLY Ever *Singin' in the Rain*. Storm or shine, boy could he sing and dance, for Busby Berkeley in *For Me and My Gal*, for Stanley Donen in *On the Town*, for Vincente Minnelli in another town (*An American in Paris*) and in *Brigadoon*. Though he played it straight in *Inherit the Wind*, and co-directed and choreographed as well, it was for the virtuosity of heel and toe that he was tapped for a special Oscar in 1951.

PHOTOGRAPHED IN 1990
BY **ANNIE LEIBOVITZ**

BLACKLIST SURVIVORS In June 1950, the U.S. judicial system sent a group of screenwriters, known as the Hollywood 10, to jail for refusing to testify before the House Committee on Un-American Activities; of those 10, only Ring Lardner Jr. survives. The blacklist years, which stretched roughly from 1947 to 1960, damaged the careers of everyone pictured here.

PHOTOGRAPHED IN 1999
BY **SAM JONES**

Actors, *this page*, clockwise from left: Mickey Knox (*The Godfather, Part III*), Madeline Lee Gilford (*The Birdcage*), George Tyne (*Sands of Iwo Jima*), Marsha Hunt (*Johnny Got His Gun*), Jeff Corey (*Little Big Man*), Karen Morley (*M*), John Randolph (*Seconds*), Lee Grant (*Defending Your Life*), Frances Chaney (*When Harry Met Sally . . .*), Phil Brown (*Star Wars*). Writers, *opposite*, clockwise from left: Robert Lees (*Holiday in Havana*), Walter Bernstein (*The Front*), Bernard Gordon (*Escape from San Quentin*), Norma Barzman (*Never Say Good-bye*), Maurice Rapf (*Dancing on a Dime*), Joan Scott (*Cairo*), Jean Rou~~~~el Butler (*The Miracle*), Ring Lardner, Jr. (*M*A*S*H*)

CLAUDETTE COLBERT Cleopatra is for women what Hamlet is for men: the role to beat. Born a Parisienne, Claudette Colbert aced the part of Mark Antony's Isis for DeMille in 1934, and collected an Oscar the same year for Frank Capra's *It Happened One Night*. Preferring comedy to tragedy thereafter—queen of the screwballs in such efforts as Preston Sturges's *The Palm Beach Story*—she was never quite as majestic again.

PHOTOGRAPHED IN 1934
BY **GEORGE HOYNINGEN-HUENE**

ELIZABETH TAYLOR Joseph L. Mankiewicz said that *Cleopatra* with Liz Taylor was "the toughest three pictures I ever made": there is scar tissue all over the industry to prove it. She was 12 when her violet eyes shone in *National Velvet*—and younger than James Dean in *Giant*. She dazzled again in *Butterfield 8*, helping bring her the first of two Oscars. Star-crossed, she railed through *Who's Afraid of Virginia Woolf?* and whirled, offscreen, through eight marriages. Of late, she's been regal once more, as our Madonna of the AIDS crisis.

PHOTOGRAPHED IN 1961
BY **BERT STERN**

CECIL B. DeMILLE Ready for his close-up with Edward Steichen, for *Vanity Fair*, in 1931. Cecil Blount DeMille believed that moviegoers were interested only in money and sex, and he invented Gloria Swanson to prove it. But pagan and biblical afterschlock is what endures; the MegaloMillia of *The Ten Commandments* (twice!) and *Cleopatra* eclipses quieter attainments such as *The Plainsman* (1936). He was, indeed, alongside D. W. Griffith, the first director to become a celeb.

PHOTOGRAPHED IN 1931
BY **EDWARD STEICHEN**

MEL GIBSON With those eyes—hidden here, regrettably—he barely needed to expose butt and pudenda in *Braveheart*. Yet, as *Gallipoli* proved, Brits are always worth taunting, and physique is, at times, a *Lethal Weapon*. Handsome enough to play a man without a face; tried his hand at the Prince of Denmark—and, come to think of it, revenge and brooding have fueled him (*Mad Max*, *The Patriot*) over long stretches of road. PHOTOGRAPHED IN 1996 BY **ALBERT WATSON**

By D. H. Lawrence

It is a pity that "sex" is such an ugly little word. An ugly little word, and really almost incomprehensible. What *is* sex, after all? The more we think about it, the less we know.

Science says it is an instinct: but what is an instinct? Apparently an instinct is an old, old habit that has become ingrained. But a habit, however old, has to have a beginning. And there is really no beginning to sex. Where life is, there it is. So sex is no "habit" that has been formed. Again, they talk of sex as an appetite, like hunger. An appetite: but for what? An appetite for propagation? It is rather absurd. They say a peacock puts on all his fine feathers to dazzle the peahen into letting him yearn for propagation. But why should the peahen not put on fine feathers, to dazzle the peacock, and satisfy *her* desire for propagation? She has surely quite as great a desire for eggs and chickens as he has. We cannot believe that her sex urge is so weak that she needs all that blue splendor of feathers to rouse her. Not at all. As for me, I never even saw a peahen so much as look at her lord's bronze-and-blue glory. I don't believe she ever sees it. I don't believe, for a moment, that she knows the difference between bronze, blue, brown, or green. If I had ever seen a peahen gazing with rapt attention on her lord's flamboyancy, I might believe that he had put on all those feathers just to "attract" her. But she never looks at him. Only, she seems to get a little perky when he shudders all his quills at her, like a storm in the trees. Then she does seem to notice, just casually, his presence.

These theories of sex are amazing. A peacock puts on his glory for the sake of a walleyed peahen who never looks at him. Imagine a scientist being so naïve as to credit the peahen with a profound, dynamic appreciation of a peacock's color and pattern. Oh, highly aesthetic peahen!

And a nightingale sings to attract his female. Which is mighty curious, seeing he sings his best when courtship and honeymoon are over, and the female is no longer concerned with him at all, but with the young. Well then, if he doesn't sing to attract her, he must sing to distract her, and amuse her while she's sitting.

How delightful, how naïve theories are! But there is a hidden will behind them all. There is a hidden will behind all theories of sex—implacable. And that, strangely enough, is the will to deny, to wipe out the mystery of beauty. Because beauty is a mystery. You can neither eat it nor make flannel out of it. Well then, says science, it is just a trick to catch the female and induce her to propagate. How naïve! As if the female needed inducing. She will propagate in the dark, even—so where then is the beauty trick?

Science has a mysterious hatred of beauty, because it doesn't fit in the cause-and-effect chain. And society has a mysterious hatred of sex, because it perpetually interferes with the nice moneymaking schemes of social man. So the two hatreds made a combine, and sex and beauty are mere propagation appetite.

Now, sex and beauty are one thing, like flame and fire. If you hate sex, you hate beauty. If you love *living* beauty, you have a reverence for sex. Of course you can love old dead beauty and hate sex. But to love living beauty you must have a reverence for sex.

Sex and beauty are inseparable, like life and consciousness. And the intelligence which goes with sex and beauty, and arises out of sex and beauty, is intuition. The great disaster of our civilization is the morbid hatred of sex. What, for example, could show a more poisoned hatred of sex than Freudian psychoanalysis—which carries with it a morbid fear of beauty, "alive" beauty, and which causes the atrophy of our intuitive faculty and our intuitive self? The deep psychic disease of modern men and women is the diseased, atrophied condition of the intuitive faculties. There is a whole world of life that we might know and enjoy by intuition, and by intuition alone. This is denied us, because we deny sex and beauty, the source of the intuitive life and of the insouciance which is so lovely in free animals and in plants.

Sex is the root of which intuition is the foliage, and beauty the flower. Why is a woman lovely, if ever, in her 20s? It is the time when sex rises softly to her face, as a rose to the top of a rosebush.

And the appeal is the appeal of beauty. We deny it wherever we can. We try to make the beauty as shallow and trashy as possible. But, first and foremost, sex appeal is the appeal of beauty.

Now, beauty is a thing about which we are so uneducated, we can hardly speak of it. We try to pretend it is a fixed arrangement: straight nose, large eyes, etc. We think a lovely woman must look like Lillian Gish, a handsome man must look like Rudolph Valentino. So we *think*. In actual life, we behave quite differently. We say: She's quite beautiful, but I don't care for her. Which shows we are using the word *beautiful* all wrong. We should say: She has the stereotyped attributes of beauty, but she is not beautiful to *me*.

Beauty is an *experience,* nothing else. It is not a fixed pattern or an arrangement of features. It is something *felt,* a glow, or a communicated sense of fineness. What ails us is that our sense of beauty is so bruised and blunted, we miss all the best. But to stick to the films: there is a greater essential beauty in Charlie Chaplin's odd face than ever there was in Valentino's. There is a bit of true beauty in Chaplin's brows and eyes, a gleam of something pure. But our sense of beauty is so bruised and clumsy, we don't see it, and don't know it when we do see it. We can only see the blatantly obvious, like the so-called beauty of Rudolph Valentino, which only pleased because it satisfied some ready-made notion of handsomeness.

But the plainest person can look beautiful, can *be* beautiful. It only needs the fire of sex to rise delicately, to change an ugly face to a lovely one. That is really sex appeal: the communicating of a sense of beauty. And in the reverse way, no one can be quite so repellent as a really pretty woman. That is, since beauty is a question of experience, not of concrete form, no one can be as acutely ugly as a really pretty woman. When the sex glow is missing, and she moves in ugly coldness, how hideous she seems, and all the worse for her externals of prettiness.

What sex is, we don't know, but it must be some sort of fire. For it always communicates a sense of warmth, of glow. And when the glow becomes a pure shine, then we feel the sense of beauty.

We all have the fire of sex slumbering or burning inside us. If we live to be 90, it is still there. Or if it dies, we become one of those ghastly living corpses which are unfortunately becoming more numerous in the world. Nothing is more ugly than a human being in whom the fire of sex has gone out. You get a nasty clayey creature whom everybody wants to avoid.

But while we are fully alive, the fire of sex smolders or burns in us. In youth it flickers and shines, in age it glows softer and stiller, but there it is. We have some control over it, but only partial control. That is why society hates it. While ever it lives, the fire of sex, which is the source of beauty and anger, burns in us beyond our understanding. Like actual fire, while it lives it will burn our fingers if we touch it carelessly. And so social man, who only wants to be "safe," hates the fire of sex.

Luckily not many men succeed in being merely social men. The fire of the old Adam smolders. And one of the qualities of fire is that it calls to fire. Sex fire here kindles sex fire there. It may only rouse the smolder into a soft glow. It may call up a sharp flicker. Or it may rouse a flame, and then flame leans to flame, and starts a blaze.

Whenever the sex fire glows through, it will kindle an answer somewhere or other. It may only kindle a sense of warmth and optimism. Then you say: I like that girl, she's a real good sort.

flickers through her face and touches the fire in our hearts. Then she becomes a lovely woman; then she is, in the living flesh, a lovely woman, not a mere photograph of one. And how lovely a lovely woman! But alas! How rare! How bitterly rare, in a world full of handsome girls and women!

Handsome, good-looking, but not lovely, not beautiful. Handsome and good-looking women are the women with good features and the right hair. But a lovely woman is an experience. It is a question of communicated fire. It is a question of sex appeal, in our poor, dilapidated modern phraseology. Sex appeal!—applied to Diane de Poictiers!—or even, in the lovely hours, to one's wife! Why, it is a libel and a slander in itself.

There is, of course, the other side of sex appeal—it can be the destruction of the one appealed to. When a woman starts using her sex appeal to her own advantage, it is usually a bad moment for some poor devil. But this side of sex appeal has been overworked lately, so it is not nearly as dangerous as it was. The sex-appealing courtesans who ruined so many men in Balzac's novels no longer find it smooth running. Men have grown canny. In fact, they are inclined to think they smell a rat the moment they feel the a-little-too-obvious touch of feminine sex appeal.

It may kindle a glow that makes the world look kindlier, and life feel better. Then you say: She's an attractive woman; by Jove, I like her. Or she may rouse a flame that lights up her own face first, before it lights up the universe. Then you say: She's a lovely woman. She looks lovely to me.

Let's say no more.

It takes a rare woman to rouse a real sense of loveliness. It is not that a woman is born beautiful. We say that to escape our own poor, bruised, clumsy understanding of beauty. There have been thousands and thousands of women quite as good-looking as Diane de Poictiers or Mrs. Lillie Langtry or any of the famous ones. There are today thousands and thousands of superbly good-looking women. But how few lovely women!

And why? Because of the failure of their sex appeal. A good-looking woman becomes lovely when the fire of sex rouses pure and fine in her, and

Which is a pity, for sex appeal is only a dirty name for a bit of life flame. No man works so well and so successfully as when some woman has kindled a little fire in his veins. No woman does her work at home with real joy unless she is in love—and, of course, a woman may go on being quietly in love for 50 years, almost without knowing it. If only our civilization had taught us how to let sex appeal flow properly and subtly, how to keep the fire of sex clear and alive, flickering or glowing or blazing in all its varying degrees of strength and communication, we might all of us have lived all our lives in love, which means kindled and full of zest, in all kinds of ways and for all kinds of things. Whereas, what a lot of dead ash there is in our lives at present! □

GRETCHEN MOL In the sizzling summer of '98, her pert visage made the cover of *Vanity Fair.* Suddenly, she was that actress on the brink—an "It girl" in the wings.

PHOTOGRAPHED IN 1998
BY **ANNIE LEIBOVITZ**

POWERS for HEALTH

HAROLD LLOYD An American Candide in the zaniest of all possible worlds, his character was Mr. Average in skyscraper scrapes. *Safety Last* (that film with the big clock hands) was also his motto on the set, such as this Coney Island one (for *Speedy*): the silent-film comedian, who later leavened talkies, bravely refused to use a double, tempting us to conclude that there was only one of him.

PHOTOGRAPHED IN 1928
BY **EDWARD STEICHEN**

TOM HANKS He has the empathy that comes with the vulnerable, and he's milked it prettily— and made it *Big.* Fell in love with a fish in *Splash.* Splashed down safely in *Apollo 13.* The Jimmy Stewart of his generation (and a two-time Oscar winner for *Philadelphia* and *Forrest Gump*), he also won hearts and minds in *Saving Private Ryan* and *The Green Mile.*

PHOTOGRAPHED IN 1988
BY **ANNIE LEIBOVITZ**

COCOANUT GROVE, 1927 **Table 1** The Magnates—from left: William Randolph Hearst, Walter Wanger, Joseph Schenck, D. W. Griffith, William Fox, Louis B. Mayer, Cecil B. DeMille, Marcus Loew, Samuel Goldwyn, Carl Laemmle, Jesse Lasky, Adolph Zukor, and Morris Gest. **Table 2** Clockwise from top left: actors Antonio Moreno, Betty Compson with her husband, director James Cruze, Mae Murray, Lew Cody with his wife, Mabel Normand, Conrad Nagel, and Carmel Myers. **Table 3** Clockwise from bottom left: actors Noah Beery and his brother Wallace, Colonel Tim McCoy, Hoot Gibson, Victor McLaglen, Lon Chaney, and Tom Mix. **Table 4** Clockwise from bottom left: legendary gossip columnist Louella Parsons, actors Harold Lloyd, Colleen Moore, and Matt Moore with his brothers Owen and Tom, and silent-screen star May Allison with her husband, *Photoplay* publisher James R. Quirk. **Table 5** Clockwise from top left: actors Corinne Griffith, H. B. Warner, and Ramon Novarro, director Edmund Goulding, and actor Richard Dix. **Table 6** Clockwise from bottom left: actors Lya de Putti, Emil Jannings, and Vilma Banky, director Mauritz Stiller, actress Lil Dagovar, directors Ernst Lubitsch, Lothar Mendes, and F. W. Murnau, actors Joseph Schildkraut and Pola Negri, and directors Erich von Stroheim and Max Reinhardt. **Table 7** Actress Aileen Pringle, top center, surrounded by, clockwise from bottom left: writers Carl Van Vechten, Paul Morand, Anita Loos, George Jean Nathan, Konrad Bercovici, H. L. Mencken, F. Scott Fitzgerald, Jim Tully, Theodore Dreiser, Joseph Hergesheimer, and Elinor Glyn.

Table 8 From left: actors Buster Keaton, Bebe Daniels, Will Rogers, Lillian Gish and her sister, Dorothy, Constance Talmadge and her sister Norma, and screenwriter Frances Marion. Table 9 Clockwise from bottom right: actors Ronald Colman and Beatrice Lillie, director George Fitzmaurice, actresses Bessie Love and Florence Vidor, theater owner Sid Grauman, and actress Mary Philbin. Table 10 Clockwise from bottom left: actress Estelle Taylor with her husband, boxer Jack Dempsey, actors Alla Nazimova, Richard Barthelmess, and Louise Brooks, and director Mickey Neilan and his wife, actress Blanche Sweet. Table 11 Clockwise from bottom left: actors Tom Meighan and Adolphe Menjou, director Mack Sennett, and actors Lionel Barrymore, Eddie Cantor, Harry Langdon, Renée Adorée, and Syd Chaplin. Table 12 Clockwise from bottom right: actors Anna Q. Nilsson, Clara Bow, Lowell Sherman, Justine Johnston, and W. C. Fields. Table 13 Clockwise from bottom left: MGM's Irving Thalberg with actors Gloria Swanson, John Gilbert, and Greta Garbo, director King Vidor, and actors Pauline Starke, Norma Shearer, John Barrymore, Mary Pickford, Douglas Fairbanks, Eleanor Boardman, and Marion Davies. Table 14 Clockwise from bottom left: actors Dolores Costello, Douglas Fairbanks Jr., Betty Bronson, Billy Haines, Patsy Ruth Miller, Baby Peggy, Baby Fannie Ward, Joan Crawford, Mary Astor, Sally O'Neil, Jackie Coogan, and Lois Moran. The maître d'hôtel: Will Hays. And Charlie Chaplin is the late arrival.

ILLUSTRATED IN 1927
BY RALPH BARTON

MORTONS, 1996 **Table 1** Clockwise from top left: Sumner Redstone, Rupert Murdoch, producer Arnold Kopelson, and Paramount executives Sherry Lansing and Jonathan Dolgen. **Table 2** Clockwise from top: CAA's Kevin Huvane, Bryan Lourd, and Rick Nicita. **Table 3** Clockwise from top: Sid Sheinberg with Steven Spielberg and Jeffrey Katzenberg. **Table 4** Michael Eisner, top, and Michael Ovitz. **Table 5** Clockwise from top: Julia Roberts, Disney studio chief Joe Roth, Sandra Bullock, and director Joel Schumacher. **Table 6** The Men of MCA with their wives, clockwise from top: Clarissa Bronfman, Ron Meyer, Kelly Chapman Meyer, and Edgar Bronfman Jr. **Table 7** Alec Baldwin, Kim Basinger, and their baby, Ireland. **Table 8** Record exec Mo Ostin pays a visit to the table of, clockwise from top left: Barbara and Marvin Davis, Jackie Collins, Sean and Micheline Connery, Frank and Barbara Sinatra, and Joanna and Sidney Poitier. **Table 9** Clockwise from top: Dominick Dunne, Nancy Reagan, Billy Wilder, Betsy Bloomingdale, Dennis Hopper and his then fiancée, Victoria Duffy, and Jennifer Jones. **Table 10** Pierce Brosnan walks by, clockwise from bottom left: Dolly Parton, Sandy Gallin, Barry Diller, and David Geffen. **Table 11** Clockwise from top left: Anne and Kirk Douglas, Aaron and Candy Spelling, and Edie and Lew Wasserman. **Table 12** Clockwise from left: Warner Bros.'s Bob Daly, Carole Bayer Sager, Jane Semel, Terry Semel, and Joel Silver. **Table 13** Clockwise from bottom left: writer Fiona Lewis with producer Art Linson, screenwriter Mitch Glazer

with Kelly Lynch, and Sean Penn. **Table 14** Producers Mark Canton and Peter Guber. **Table 15** Clockwise from left: Frank Biondi, Michael Fuchs, and Mickey Schulhof. **Table 16** Clockwise from top left: producer Leonard Goldberg, Barbara Walters, Warnaco's Linda Wachner, and Wendy Goldberg. **Table 17** Clockwise from bottom left: managers Brad Grey and Bernie Brillstein with Eddie Murphy and Jerry Seinfeld. **Table 18** Clockwise from left: lawyer Jake Bloom with producers Larry Gordon and Jerry Bruckheimer. **Table 19** Rob Reiner and Michael Douglas. **Table 20** Proprietor Peter Morton and Steve Tisch. **Table 21** Clockwise from top left: director Renny Harlin and Geena Davis, Ted Turner and Jane Fonda, and producer Dawn Steel. **Table 22** Clockwise from left: Ray Stark, Joan Collins, James Woods, Howard Austen, Gore Vidal, and Sue Mengers. Sharon Stone sashays by. **Table 23** Clockwise from bottom left: producers Lili and Richard Zanuck, Wanda McDaniel Ruddy, Clint Eastwood, producer Al Ruddy, and Patricia Duff and Ronald Perelman. **Table 24** Clockwise from top left: Tom Hanks and Rita Wilson and Tom Cruise and Nicole Kidman. **Table 25** Tony Curtis and Jill Vanden Berg. **Table 26** Alana Stewart and George Hamilton. **Table 27** Clockwise from bottom left: Jack Nicholson, Robert Evans, and Warren Beatty. **Table 28** Clockwise from bottom left: Kevin Costner surrounded by ICM's Jeff Berg, Ed Limato, and Jim Wiatt. **Table 29** Clockwise from bottom left: sculptor Robert Graham and Anjelica Huston with architect Richard Meier and decorator Rose Tarlow.

ILLUSTRATED IN 1996
BY **DAVID COWLES**

CATHERINE DENEUVE When the people of France were asked to put a face to their national symbol, Marianne, for the bicentennial of 1789, they chose the face of Catherine Deneuve. Had the rest of humanity been polled, the result would probably have been the same. Innocence under *The Umbrellas of Cherbourg;* depravity in *Belle de Jour;* abandonment in *Repulsion;* coming back by way of scent and fashion—and *Indochine* in 1992—she is *la Révolution* in reverse.

PHOTOGRAPHED IN 1989
BY **HELMUT NEWTON**

RUDOLPH VALENTINO What did women want? Valentino. What did *he* want? Difficult to say, since he died of an unromantic perforated ulcer at the age of 31—just weeks after posing for this *Vanity Fair* portrait— probably before making up his mind. His was the biggest funeral a busboy ever had. The term "Latin lover" was his property: even as an Arabian lover in *The Sheik* (1921), he did enough work for four horsemen. Helped create the tourist trade in North Africa—for women, oddly enough.

PHOTOGRAPHED IN 1926
BY **EDWARD STEICHEN**

JULIANNE MOORE Ingres or empress? Titian or Titania? Julianne Moore has done some classic disrobing: as a porn-film veteran in *Boogie Nights*, as Marian Wyman in *Short Cuts*, as Ralph Fiennes's partner in adultery in *The End of the Affair*—and for *Vanity Fair*, naturally. But she's no less potent when fully clad, as she was as Laura Cheveley in *An Ideal Husband* and as Linda Partridge in *Magnolia*. Notice how it's the face that draws the eye.

PHOTOGRAPHED IN 2000
BY **MICHAEL THOMPSON**

HOLLYWOOD ISSUE COVER, 1996 From left: Tim Roth,
Leonardo DiCaprio, Matthew McConaughey, Benicio Del
Toro, Michael Rapaport, Stephen Dorff, Johnathon Schaech,
David Arquette, Will Smith, Skeet Ulrich.

PHOTOGRAPHED IN 1995
BY **ANNIE LEIBOVITZ**

HEDY LAMARR The quintessential femme fatale never recovered from the nude scene in *Ecstasy* (1933), and why should she have?
PHOTOGRAPHED IN 1942
BY **ERIC CARPENTER**

AVA GARDNER Married to Mickey Rooney, Artie Shaw, and Frank Sinatra, she hit her high point in *The Killers* (1946), and liked Hemingway characters and bullfights.
PHOTOGRAPHED CIRCA 1950
BY **PAUL HESSE**

VERONICA LAKE Alan Ladd's opposite in *This Gun for Hire, The Glass Key,* and *The Blue Dahlia* preferred to be depicted peekaboo-style but let Hurrell shoot her double-barreled gaze.
PHOTOGRAPHED IN 1941
BY **GEORGE HURRELL**

JEAN HARLOW At 16 she caught the eye of Hal Roach, film-comedy kingpin. By 19 she was courted by Howard Hughes, landing a starring role in his 1930 picture, *Hell's Angels*. By 26 her life would be cut short due to illness, but for one riotous spell Harlow was white-hot, advancing from bit player to bombshell to accomplished screen comedienne (*Red Dust, Dinner at Eight*). Here, Hurrell used milky shoulders, caressing sidelight, and a vanquished bear to create the consummate image of the Platinum Siren.

PHOTOGRAPHED IN 1935
BY **GEORGE HURRELL**

RUPERT MURDOCH Devilishly played by Anthony Hopkins, he was the model, in part, for press lord Lambert Le Roux in David Hare's theater piece *Pravda;* played himself in voice-over on Fox's *The Simpsons* in the episode "Sunday, Cruddy Sunday" in 1999. (It helps to own the network, and he owns a few.) Raised the *Titanic* to blockbuster status; ditto for the mammary gland in Fleet Street. Inescapable by land, sea, or air with his imperium of film, cable, satellite, sporting, newspaper, and book outlets.

PHOTOGRAPHED IN 1994
BY **ANNIE LEIBOVITZ**

ANNETTE BENING Starting slow with *Valmont* for Miloš Forman (1989) and *The Grifters* for Stephen Frears, this stage filly paced herself beautifully and was suddenly everywhere, from Vegas with *Bugsy* to the White House with *The American President*. Did the apparently impossible by closing Warren Beatty's conspicuous gender gap. Won all the remaining— or leftover—hearts with *American Beauty*.

PHOTOGRAPHED IN 1999
BY **ANDREW ECCLES**

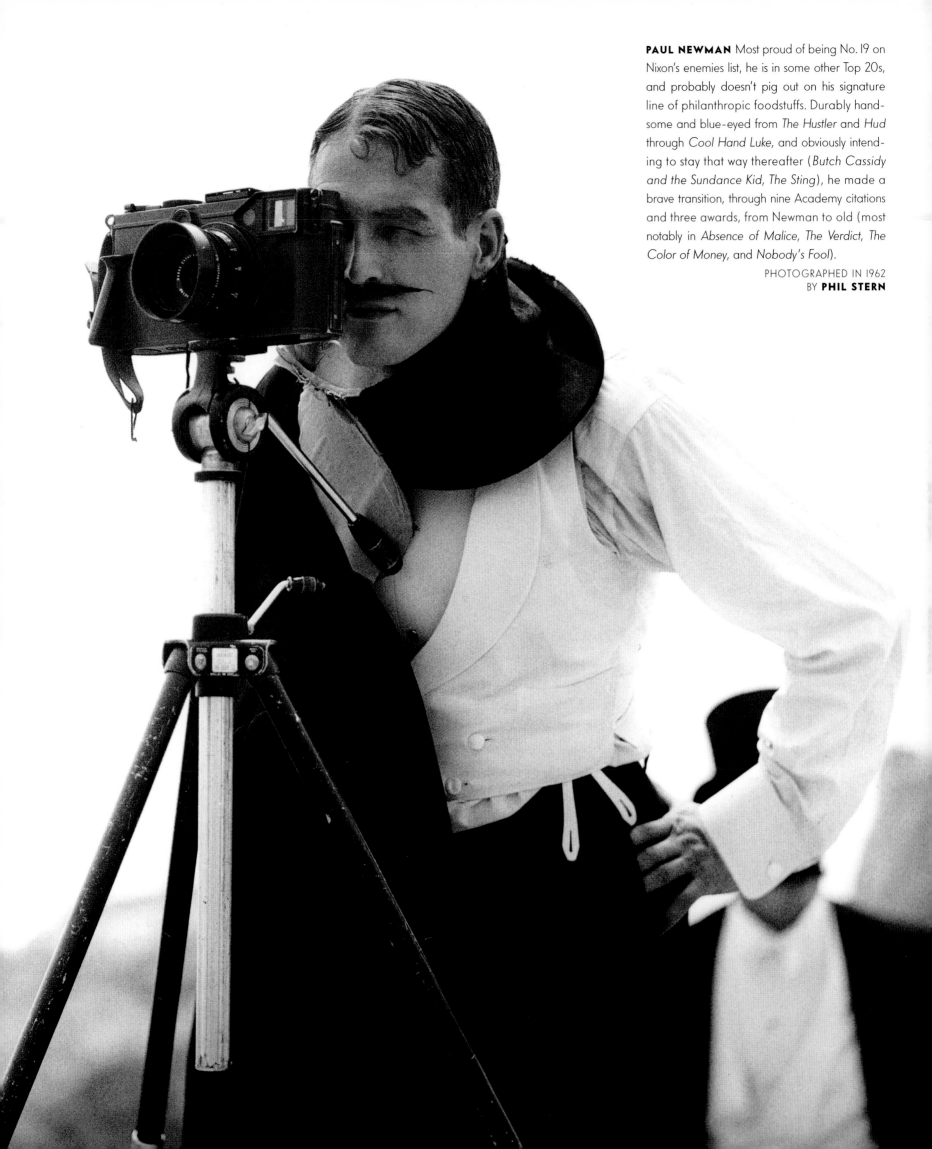

PAUL NEWMAN Most proud of being No. 19 on Nixon's enemies list, he is in some other Top 20s, and probably doesn't pig out on his signature line of philanthropic foodstuffs. Durably handsome and blue-eyed from *The Hustler* and *Hud* through *Cool Hand Luke,* and obviously intending to stay that way thereafter (*Butch Cassidy and the Sundance Kid, The Sting*), he made a brave transition, through nine Academy citations and three awards, from Newman to old (most notably in *Absence of Malice, The Verdict, The Color of Money,* and *Nobody's Fool*).

PHOTOGRAPHED IN 1962
BY **PHIL STERN**

ELAINE MAY AND **MIKE NICHOLS** Seldom seen together, seldom thought of separately: cerebral and funny by turns and in combination, they fashioned entertainment for the smart set. Jules Feiffer on celluloid, said one critic; proved half right by Nichols's *Carnal Knowledge* in 1971. His: *Who's Afraid of Virginia Woolf?*, *The Graduate*, *Catch-22*, *Silkwood*, *Working Girl*. Hers (as writer): *Heaven Can Wait*, *Reds*, *Tootsie*, and (oh dear) *Ishtar*. Together again for *The Birdcage* (1996) and as part of Hollywood's Clinton rescue team via *Primary Colors*.

PHOTOGRAPHED IN 1996
BY **ANNIE LEIBOVITZ**

By Frank Peale

Perhaps the easiest way for the layman to gain a comprehensive idea of what the producers of moving pictures have already accomplished would be for him to put himself back into that not very distant period when the cinema was still a scientific curiosity rather than a general source of amusement. It should after all—so recent is their development—not be very difficult for anyone approaching 30 or beyond it. If he then will imagine a number of theatrical producers setting out to give to every town, to every crossroad village even, theaters in which they would be shown every successful play produced on Broadway, with an identical cast and the same elaborate production seen in New York; if he will imagine these plays changed weekly, or in many cases nightly, without the least change in the manner of their showing; if he will remember that the intended audience of these plays is to be, weekly, not less than 55 million people and that the average price of admission must not exceed 25 cents—then, substituting the one word "films" for "plays," he will have some idea of what the motion-picture producers have accomplished within less than two decades.

Fifty-five million people attend moving-picture theaters weekly—in the United States alone. Paid admissions amount to $550 million annually. These figures take no account of foreign countries; and yet there is not a country today where American films are not shown. It is no jest that Charlie Chaplin is the best- and most genially known person in the world. And the crowds that waited nightly outside the Théâtre de la Madeleine in Paris for the showing of *The Covered Wagon* were, during its run, only less numerous than those that filed past the ticket booths during the first months of its showing in New York.

The Famous Players–Lasky Corporation is the greatest single producer, distributor, and exhibitor of motion pictures in the world. And for this reason it is not unfair to take it as representative. To give, even briefly, its record and to offer a fairly detailed account of its various activities will make it easier for the layman to appreciate the magnitude of the industry as a whole than for me to attempt a more comprehensive history.

Within the last 12 months, the Famous Players–Lasky Corporation produced 74 pictures of feature length, that is, pictures running from 6,000 to 7,000 feet of film. Of these, 45 were made at the company's studios in Hollywood, 28 in the studio at Astoria, Long Island. The screen version of Sardou's *Madame Sans Gêne* was made, for the sake of authentic settings, in France. Thirty-five of these pictures were comedies; 19, dramas; and 20, melodramas. The proportion was not the result of chance but of long experience in the demands of the public.

For the films made in the eastern studios, over 225 principals—actors and actresses with more or less important roles—and some 3,000 extras were employed. During the same period 500 principals and 7,000 extras were required for the Hollywood productions. For the most part these extras are "regulars," that is to say, the same people used again and again to act bits, fill up the scenes, or take their place in the crowds. It is only when pictures are being made that require hundreds of people in the background that extras are brought in for a single performance. There were, for instance, 18,000 extras used in producing *The Ten Commandments,* most of whom—a large number of them were professional soldiers, not actors—had never before been seen on-camera.

As for the stars, many have risen from obscurity with a romantic rapidity befitting the industry. Ten years ago, Gloria Swanson was an extra in the old Essanay Studio in Chicago. From there she went to California to do small bits in Mack Sennett comedies; soon Cecil B. DeMille, with admirable foresight, secured her for Famous Players. She is now indeed a "famous player," with a larger following than any other actress on their lists. And she has—to complete the romantic tale—just returned from making *Madame Sans Gêne* in Paris, the bride of the Marquis de la Falaise de la Coudraye.

Each of the most popular actors is expected to make four to six pictures each year. The material for their films will be gathered alike from the most obvious and the most remote sources. The story department has its agents in every European capital, constantly searching for available plots, and every novel that is published, every play that appears in New York, London, or Paris, has its interested observer. Of the 74 films made last year, 38 were adaptations from novels, 21 from plays, and 15 from original stories.

Once it is decided to produce an adaptation, it is turned over to the scenario department, who undertake to provide the director with a workable "script." Before the script is handed to the director, the art department will have prepared the settings, determined the costumes, and so on, while throughout both the preparation and the actual photographing of a picture, hundreds of technical assistants will be at work—wardrobe men and women, designers of scenery and costume, dressmakers, painters, carpenters, property men, scene shifters, electricians—all controlled and coordinated toward a definite, limited end: the picture which the public sees.

The "screening" may take place at one of the two studios, or in the open air. At Hollywood the studio is provided with five stages, all of which may be used simultaneously, and there is, besides, a ranch of 500 acres—for outdoor scenes. Further, there are times when the directors abandon all the settings provided for them and resort variously to that section of the United States which lies between New Mexico and Wyoming, to Cuba, Bermuda, or any attainable end of the earth.

JESSE LASKY, whose studio merged with Zukor's Famous Players, was a 20s powerhouse.

JACK WARNER, film czar incarnate, launched Warner Bros. with three siblings in 1923.

During the making of the 74 pictures of 1924, over 11 million feet of film were exposed in order to procure the necessary 400,000 feet. This indulgence on the part of the director is apt to seem an incredible extravagance, but at the present, decidedly experimental stage of the movies it is strictly necessary. Under the studios' present conditions, it is impossible to completely visualize a scene until it is "shot"; the results may be good, bad, or indifferent, and to ensure any sort of quality in the completed picture it is still requisite that there be, for any given episode in the story, a wide variety of possibilities from which the editor of the film may choose, in the interests of economy of narration, dramatic effectiveness, or good photography.

As a matter of fact, it is not among the directors of the Famous Players–Lasky Corporation that one will find the most extravagant users of film. Erich von Stroheim "shot" 350,000 feet of film to get the 12,000 he needed for *Foolish Wives,* while in making *Greed* he persisted in following Frank Norris's novel *McTeague* detail by detail until a million and a half feet of film had been used, although it was obvious from the start that not more than 12,000 could ever be shown. Robert J. Flaherty, who was at once the director and photographer of *Nanook of the North,* has recently returned from two years in the Samoan Islands, where he exposed more than 240,000 feet of film in order that some 12,000 feet may eventually record the essence of all that he has observed, and set before the camera, of that beautiful and romantic life of the South Seas, which has now all but perished under contact with a civilization that is either too ignorant or too wise.

Once the film has been cut to the desired length any number of negatives may be made from the positive that results. For instance, in the case of a spectacular success like *The Covered Wagon,* which ran for 59 weeks in New York, 10 reprints were made and sent simultaneously—in September 1923—to as many cities. Each print was transported as though it were a theatrical company; its bookings were prearranged; and each print played 40 weeks, each being seen on an average by 10,000 persons weekly.

Once the picture is completed there comes the problem of its exhibition. To assist in meeting it, the Famous Players–Lasky Corporation has acquired an interest in 166 theaters. The corporation also owns the company of Charles Frohman, Inc., and this company, in conjunction with David Belasco, controls both the Empire and Lyceum Theatres in New York and has a certain interest in other purely theatrical houses in various parts of the country.

There are some 8,000 persons on the payroll of the corporation, not including extras. There are not only those connected with the production of Paramount pictures (closely affiliated with Famous Players–Lasky); there are also thousands concerned with the administrative end of the industry or with theaters scattered throughout the world. And their salaries will range from the $7.50 a day for extras—and less for office boys—to the fabulous sums paid the stars, sums which run into thousands.

Such is the Famous Players–Lasky Corporation after a little more than nine years of existence. The company had its inception in the mind of a quiet, mannerly little man who one day walked into the office of the Motion Picture Patents Company and sought an audience. He was asked to sit down and wait. For three hours he waited. He was then shown into an office where those

MGM's **LOUIS B. MAYER,** Luise Rainer, Mrs. Spencer Tracy, Frank Capra at the Oscars in '38.

SAMUEL GOLDWYN ruled with DeMille and Lasky, roared with Mayer (MGM), then went solo.

HARRY COHN, despot of Columbia (with Rita Hayworth), was the mogul Hollywood most despised.

who were then accounted the magnates of the industry solemnly and most pompously debated the astonishing possibility of making big "feature films" in two reels! He walked, gravely and respectfully, into this sanctum of a new industry so grandly erected on a foundation of nickels. In his quiet, grave voice, he said to the men seated about the table:

"Gentlemen, I came to you with a legitimate business proposition. I meant to offer you the chance to make money—in return for an opportunity which you were to give me. But you wanted only to show me how big you were and how small I am. So, you have had me sit for three hours on a wooden bench—just to speak to you. I brought you a picture by Sarah Bernhardt, *Queen Elizabeth,* a great film by a great actress—but you made me wait three hours. I am going to make you wait three years. You might have had this picture for $15,000. Now you can't have it for 10 times that amount. I am going to play it myself, in independent theaters. If there are no independent theaters, I'll make them. But from now on, as long as I live, I intend to be independent. Good day, gentlemen!"

And Adolph Zukor walked out.

His next step was to interest Daniel Frohman. Together they persuaded Sarah Bernhardt to make her famous *Queen Elizabeth.* The idea had, doubtless, come to Mr. Zukor years before. Starting in the penny-arcade business, he had in time graduated into that of the "store show." He then acquired the old Comedy Theatre on 14th Street, New York, where he presently amazed his patrons by showing them a film of the unheard-of length of five reels—*Oliver Twist,* with Nat Goodwin as Fagan. With *Queen Elizabeth* an unprecedented success, Mr. Zukor set about organizing Famous Players. It was in 1916 that the company was finally incorporated.

One of Mr. Zukor's first moves was to engage Mary Pickford at a salary of $500 a week and, practically at once, to advance her to a salary of $2,000 a week. The course of the movies in the next 10 years was determined by this one gesture of generosity.

There was at this time in the West a young man who had been successively a musician in small-town theaters, a newspaper reporter, an unsuccessful prospector during the Alaska gold rush, and, finally, a not much more successful vaudeville actor. It was after the last venture that this gentleman of misfortune decided, along with another young man, the son of a celebrated playwright, to come east and enter the movies. His name was Jesse L. Lasky; that of his companion, Cecil B. DeMille. The immediate result of their venture was the Jesse L. Lasky Feature Play Company.

It was three years after this that the Famous Players–Lasky Corporation was formed. The 4 original stockholders were shortly increased to 10—all executives of the company. Today there are very nearly 1,900 holders of common stock, 1,800 of preferred. Preferred stock to the amount of $8,300,000 has been issued, and there are at present 235,931 shares of common stock outstanding. The most recent financial statement of the corporation showed a profit of $5,422,349 for the year, equivalent to $20.08 a share on its common stock, while the total assets of the company are officially placed at $49,018,395.

In brief, the Famous Players–Lasky Corporation is today the most significant figure in the most romantic industry in America—or, for that matter, the most romantic in the world. □

THE NEW ESTABLISHMENT Titans of the New Establishment assemble during Herbert A. Allen's annual conference in Sun Valley, Idaho. All are identified by their titles in 1997.
PHOTOGRAPHED IN 1997
BY **ANNIE LEIBOVITZ**

Back row: Berkshire Hathaway chairman Warren Buffett, Universal chairman Frank Biondi, Time Warner president Richard Parsons, TCI chairman John Malone, NBC president Bob Wright, Sony president Howard Stringer, Seagram president Edgar Bronfman Jr., Universal president Ron Meyer, Intel chairman Andrew Grove, Warner Bros. chairman Terry Semel, Comcast chairman Ralph Roberts (father of Brian), News Corp. chairman and chief executive Rupert Murdoch.

Center row: Microsoft chief technology officer Nathan Myhrvold, Time Warner chairman Gerald Levin, Orca Bay Capital Corp. chairman John McCaw Jr. (brother of Craig), ICM chairman and C.E.O. Jeff Berg, DreamWorks partner David Geffen, Washington Post Company chairwoman Katharine Graham, Microsoft chairman Bill Gates.

Front row: Allen & Co. C.E.O. Herbert A. Allen, Sony president Nobuyuki Idei, H.S.N. chairman Barry Diller, DreamWorks partner Jeffrey Katzenberg.

CAMERON DIAZ Well, at which point in *My Best Friend's Wedding* did you notice: *There's Something About* ... well ... the other girl? You've sure noticed since. She can make funny sexy. She emerged fragrant and unpolluted from the rough world of *Feeling Minnesota*. And she can switch from sultry Latin dancer—she's Cuban on her daddy's side—to natural blonde, which she is in her own right. But in either mode, we know which one she is now.

PHOTOGRAPHED IN 1999
BY **MARIO TESTINO**

AL JOLSON "You ain't heard nothin' yet!" yelled Asa Yoelson in the 1927 film *The Jazz Singer*—considered the first sound picture—and suddenly there was another dimension to the movies. Al Jolson was born to music and could have been a cantor; instead he did a holding action down on the Swanee River, and worked with D. W. Griffith, clowning until such time as black faces could appear on their own. PHOTOGRAPHED IN 1922 BY **NICKOLAS MURAY**

RICHARD HARRIS AND **PETER O'TOOLE** The luck of the Irish. Seen here in recovery (and it better be decaf in that pot) are: left, *A Man Called Horse*, who's also been zoological in *Orca*, *The Wild Geese*, *Tarzan the Ape Man*, and as "Bull" McCabe in *The Field*; on the right, the only man who'll ever play *Lawrence of Arabia*, and whose brilliant career includes *Lord Jim*, *My Favorite Year*, *The Last Emperor*, Tiberius in *Caligula*, and King Henry II (twice, in *Becket* and *The Lion in Winter*). If the titles make him sound like a member of the ruling class, it's because, like his friend, he belongs to the natural cinema aristocracy.

PHOTOGRAPHED IN 1995
BY **SNOWDON**

SIDNEY POITIER Detective Virgil Tibbs always insisted on being called "Mister": he was polite but very firm on the point, from *In the Heat of the Night* (1967) to *The Organization* (1971). Polite but firm might describe the way in which this man from the Bahamas was confined to "black" parts in a slate of pictures that drew him critics' praise (*The Defiant Ones, To Sir with Love, Guess Who's Coming to Dinner*) and a coveted Oscar (*Lilies of the Field*). It certainly describes the dignified way in which he played the hand he was dealt—as a forerunner in the struggle to be addressed as a human being.

PHOTOGRAPHED IN 2000
BY **HERB RITTS**

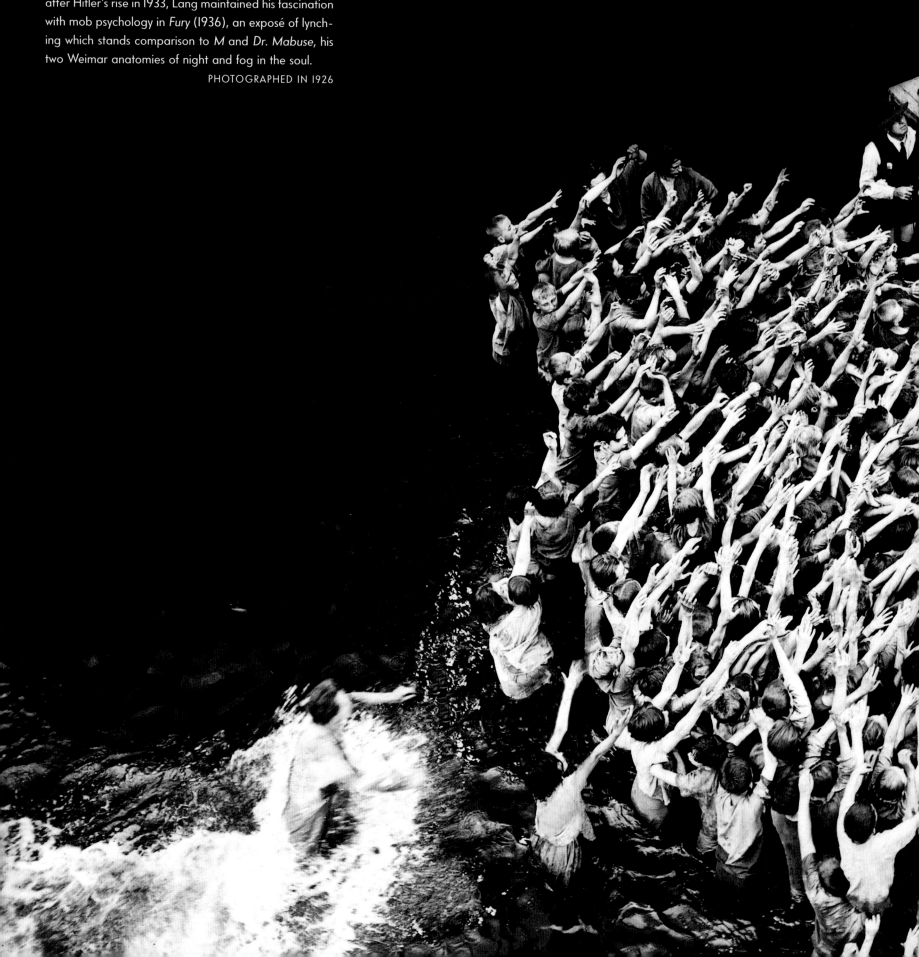

METROPOLIS An eerie prefiguration of the adoring, abject mass rally, on the set of Fritz Lang's *Metropolis*. (*Vanity Fair*, on occasion, published silent-film movie stills, offering many readers their first glimpse of *The Birth of a Nation* in 1915 and *The Cabinet of Dr. Caligari* in 1921.) Like Kafka's *Amerika*, Lang's picture took its inspiration from the Manhattan skyline and helped make New York the capital of modernity. Fleeing to the U.S. after Hitler's rise in 1933, Lang maintained his fascination with mob psychology in *Fury* (1936), an exposé of lynching which stands comparison to *M* and *Dr. Mabuse*, his two Weimar anatomies of night and fog in the soul.

PHOTOGRAPHED IN 1926

THE LOST BOYS Jean-Pierre Léaud, Pascal Lamorisse, Enzo Staiola On memory's resilient scrim, there is still a shining. A flicker of the dreams of our youth. The flame of a youngster's wide eyes. Or is it three pairs, actually? These boys endure, in body and spirit, from three pivotal works of the European cinema at mid-century: from left, the former child actors who played Antoine Doinel (in François Truffaut's 1959 film, *The 400 Blows*), the dawdling boy (in Albert Lamorisse's *The Red Balloon*, 1956), and little Bruno (in Vittorio De Sica's 1948 neo-realist *The Bicycle Thief*).

PHOTOGRAPHED IN 2000
BY **JEAN-BAPTISTE MONDINO**

DIANE KEATON Actress-director-producer-photographer, she charmed Woody *and* Warren: she's the apotheosis of the bicoastalite. As the title character in *Annie Hall* (for which she earned best-actress honors) and as Louise Bryant in *Reds*, she showed brains under various hats. Waspy when asking for pastrami on white in Allen's deli, even more so when married to the Mob: she reacted rather than acted in *The Godfather*.

PHOTOGRAPHED IN 1997
BY **ANNIE LEIBOVITZ**

BRIGITTE BARDOT She loves animals, and all the animals we know used to love her right back. Featured in many shorts until 1956, when God created Woman, with an assist from Svengali director Roger Vadim. Kittenhood gave way to feline angst; the Côte d'Azur gave her the blues; pouting replaced purring in Godard's *Contempt* in 1963. Now she's a pinup for the French National Front, often putting creature rights before human wrongs.
PHOTOGRAPHED IN 1959

DUSTIN HOFFMAN He refused to go into plastics as *The Graduate*, and has successfully resisted the synthetic ever since. The biggest little man in the biz (five Academy Award nominations; two statues, for *Kramer vs. Kramer* and *Rain Man*)—and game enough to channel Salvador Dalí here—he has been, more often, our image of the two-time loser (*Midnight Cowboy, Straw Dogs, Papillon, Death of a Salesman*). His underdogs came out ahead in *All the President's Men* and even more in *Tootsie*.

PHOTOGRAPHED IN 1996
BY **HERB RITTS**

THE STUDIO KIDS First row: Gene Autry, Ginger Rogers, Robert Young, Gloria DeHaven, Carroll Baker, Van Johnson, Lassie, Ernest Borgnine, Jane Wyatt, Jackie Cooper, Ann Blyth, Shelley Winters, Douglas Fairbanks Jr. **Second row:** Burgess Meredith, Milton Berle, Roddy McDowall, Howard Keel, Nancy Olson, Eddie Albert, Cyd Charisse, Robert Stack. **Third row:** Celeste Holm, Virginia Mayo, Sylvia Sidney, Eva Marie Saint, Anne Francis, Shirley Knight, Virginia O'Brien, Eva Gabor, Kathryn Grayson, Tony Curtis. **Fourth row:** Jane Powell, Rod Taylor, Jane Withers, Maximilian Schell, Richard Widmark, Janet Leigh, Sid Caesar.

PHOTOGRAPHED IN 1995
BY **ANNIE LEIBOVITZ**

NICOLAS CAGE Born Nicholas Coppola (Francis is his uncle), he did punkish roles in *Fast Times at Ridgemont High, Rumble Fish,* and *Raising Arizona* before Cher saw he had something and drew him into the orbit of *Moonstruck.* Hit the Strip twice, first as a newlywed on a losing streak in *Honeymoon in Vegas,* then as a boozer on a dying jag in *Leaving Las Vegas,* a performance that won him an Oscar. Good cop in *It Could Happen to You, Guarding Tess,* and *Snake Eyes;* bad guy in *Face/Off.*

PHOTOGRAPHED IN 1996
BY **ANNIE LEIBOVITZ**

MAE WEST Fair Mae, shown on the set of *Belle of the Nineties,* was depicted by the magazine in caricature, in essay, in review ("Her first starring picture, *She Done Him Wrong* [opposite Cary Grant], is a lusty and rowdy masterpiece"). Through her "affable vulgarity" and her "torrid . . . brilliantly calculated" camp, she threw a curve at staid society, making "the black lace corset of our grandmothers a sinful symbol of our times." Concluded *V.F.* writer George Davis, "I love you, Miss West, because *you* are the greatest female impersonator of all time."

PHOTOGRAPHED IN 1934
BY **GEORGE HOYNINGEN-HUENE**

EDWARD NORTON Niceness isn't everything. Introduced to us in likable roles such as the persuasive First Amendment lawyer in *The People vs. Larry Flynt*, and as a sweet gent in *Everyone Says I Love You*, Edward Norton chose that same year (1996) to appear as the schizoid slasher in *Primal Fear*. Since then, the bad Ed has been winning out on-screen, as a Nazi skinhead (*American History X*) and a sado-masochistic pugilist (*Fight Club*), but there's still a fighting chance he'll be in demand for the next remake of *Love Story*, or even *Bambi*.

PHOTOGRAPHED IN 1997
BY **HERB RITTS**

MORGAN FREEMAN The face is somehow that of a runaway slave—a good, swift runaway at that, and a long time gone. As Sergeant Major John Rawlins in *Glory,* he displayed a martial bearing that caused the driest eyes to prickle. As Miss Daisy's driver, he appealed to a gentler sensibility. In *The Shawshank Redemption* and *Amistad,* it was stoicism and fortitude that bore the heat and burden of the day, and indeed made it thinkable for him to play Nelson Mandela in *Long Way to Freedom* (1999).

PHOTOGRAPHED IN 1989
BY **SUSAN SHACTER**

LAUREN BACALL AND **HUMPHREY BOGART** Just a few friends: Laurence Olivier (far left) and Vivien Leigh (fourth from left) at actor Clifton Webb's place for a Sunday gin-rummy tournament. Yet note the natural centerpiece duo. Lauren Bacall's sassy ways and bedroom eyes, in *Key Largo* and *Dark Passage*, were only for Humphrey Bogart, to whom she was devoted until the big sleep overtook him in 1957. "Anybody got a match?" was her first-ever line, in *To Have and Have Not*, and it turned out that the answer was yes, one made in heaven. Bogart lit up the screen in *Casablanca* as well and ... you must remember these: *They Drive by Night, High Sierra, The Maltese Falcon, The African Queen*, and *The Caine Mutiny*.

PHOTOGRAPHED CIRCA 1947
BY **JEAN HOWARD**

SAN SIMEON'S CHILD

By Martha Sherrill

The huge, glowing indoor pool at San Simeon—where people swam in winter, and met at night—has the stars and planets paved in blue-and-gold mosaic on its bottom. They are magnified and illuminated, these heavenly bodies, so they seem not settled under the water but rather floating on its surface. Above, on the ceiling of the pool house, is a representation of the ocean floor: fish and seaweed and shells.

"It's an upside-down world," a tour guide says, her voice echoing gently off the far wall. "And when you stand at the end of the diving board and look down, you are diving into the night sky."

Inside San Simeon, in the Assembly Room, a wedding is progressing. It is the wedding of Patricia Van Cleve and Arthur Lake. She is very young, maybe 16 or 17. Her hair is still dark and unlightened. He is older but doesn't look it. She is a creature of money and indulgences. He is the son of circus people. They both like to drink. Right now, Lake is not all that famous, or recognizable, but next year, at 33, he will become Dagwood Bumstead, the silly, bumbling, bellowing, skyscraper-sandwich-eating physical comedian and star of the *Blondie* series.

William Randolph Hearst, the newspaper publisher and would-be movie mogul, is watching the wedding take place. This is his house. This is La Cuesta Encantada, the castle he built on a remote coastal hill halfway between San Francisco and Los Angeles. It is the greatest of the excesses that almost made him broke. He calls the place "the ranch," a lowbrow affectation as conspicuous as the ketchup bottles and paper napkins he always keeps on the dining-room table.

It is July 1937, but the weather is the weather of all Julys on the central California coast—dull and overcast in the morning, burning off by 10, then clear and warm and blue. Hearst doesn't own the sky, of course, but he's got 250,000 acres around the castle, including 50 miles of oceanfront. The hills are brown and bald for as far as you can see, shaped like knuckles on a laborer's fist, and high up, on the lushest one, with live oaks and oleander, Spanish broom and cypress, sits his house. It looks like a colossal white Spanish cathedral, like a place where you'd want to pray.

Today, the bride and groom are standing in front of an old altarpiece. It is smothered triumphantly with flowers. Empty choir stalls, carved black walnut from the 15th century, are plastered up against the sides of the 2,500-square-foot room like cheap wallpaper. Massive Flemish tapestries rise up to the ceiling, 24 feet. Near the middle of the room is a 16th-century mantelpiece, in soft beige-gray stone carved like soap, over a fireplace you can walk into.

The actress Marion Davies has planned the wedding, clearing the Assembly Room of her jigsaw puzzles and Monopoly games and gramophone, and is the maid of honor too. She is 40, and has the most delightful stutter. She is sweet, and bighearted—why, this very year she coughed up $1 million in cash to help bail out the Hearst empire, selling real estate, furs, jewelry. She is about to retire from pictures, but will keep being the maid of honor at weddings for years and years to come, over and over, and for most of her life, for the 36 years she will spend as Hearst's mistress and companion, until his death in 1951. It's only then that she'll marry for the first time herself, eloping to the El Rancho Vegas Hotel on Halloween night, 11 weeks after Hearst is gone, feeling desperate, afraid, and so drunk somebody has to hold her up to say "I do."

Patricia's wedding dress is silk and as preposterous as any wedding dress, but at least it goes with the décor. She's comfortable at the castle. She's used to it. Patricia Van Cleve Lake wasn't born at San Simeon, exactly. Nobody really knows anymore where she was born—maybe France, maybe Santa Barbara or New York—but Marion Davies pretty much raised her, shuttling her around from the big beach house in Santa Monica to the castle up the coast to the Ritz Tower or the Warwick in Manhattan.

Patricia is Davies's niece, you see—if that explains anything. Summers, she'd go with Hearst and Davies on tours of Europe, becoming part of a familiar entourage, a grab bag of folks: some of Hearst's five sons and their wives, Davies's sisters and their children, a small number of business associates, corporate types, and then, of course, the nurses, governesses, maids, all creating a line of cars and cargo and people that went on and on, single file.

Arthur Lake had been on one summer tour. He was a friend of Jack Hearst, one of W.R.'s sons, and was thrown together with Patricia. Davies and Hearst had a way of doing that, throwing people at each other, making a match in their minds. Patricia and Arthur were both funny, kooky, childish. They were also sweet, and a little oblivious. And it didn't take long for the magic to happen, for the match to manifest itself physically. It was a good one, too: they would stay together for 50 years, for thinner and fatter, richer, poorer. They sang together ("She's Funny That Way"), partied, and stayed up all night until Arthur's heart stopped in an ambulance on his way to the hospital eight years ago. But it's too soon to talk about that.

Let's go first to Patricia's death, a year and a half ago: at the bitter end, she sat in her hospital bed in the desert, at the Eisenhower Medical Center in Rancho Mirage, wheezing into the microphone of a tape recorder, down to one lung and counting, slowly making tapes in which she tried to remember her life. She wanted us to know who she was, or thought she was: the child of Marion Davies and William Randolph Hearst.

The day of her wedding, she says, Hearst telephoned her in one of the bungalows and asked to see her in his private rooms below the towers of the castle. She was in awe of him. She called him "the Chief."

"So I went up there," she says on a tape. "He said to me, 'You know I'm your father.' I said, 'Yes.' He said, 'This is a secret between the three of us.' I said, 'Yes.' . . . I gave him a kiss on the cheek, and he said, 'I have to go wake up Marion. See you later.' That's it, O.K.?"

And that was it. That was the secret between Patricia and Marion and W.R., which Patricia kept until the day she died and her son, Arthur Patrick Lake, made it public. The response was mixed. The Palm Springs *Desert Sun* ran a huge spread with pictures (THEIR GREATEST SECRET, October 13, 1993). The *Los Angeles Times* followed up with a somewhat more skeptical article (OBITUARY REVIVES RUMOR OF HEARST DAUGHTER, October 31, 1993), but then things died down. First of all, there was no actual proof, unless permission was given to start exhuming bodies and doing DNA tests. There was no record of birth, birth certificate, or mention of the birth in Hearst's or Davies's papers. The Hearst family refused to comment.

Patricia Lake started making the tapes around 1990, after Arthur died and couldn't stop her anymore. So much to tell. So much to blab about, finally. She has a husky voice, a certain graceful facility with profanity, and a rich baby-talk accent. Sentences are tossed off in a babble.

Patricia meanders. She seems quickly bored by herself. Her lack of introspection and insight is stunning. She reveals things, but dispassionately, as though everything behind her were one long, flattened, dead road. What was,

was. "These things happen, baby," she says, and her shrug is almost audible. Maybe she'd been numbed by pain, but, also, maybe memories weren't as much fun as dancing, breathing easily, getting to live forever.

Patricia says she was 11 when Marion Davies found her one day, alone, bored, sitting by the side of the big Neptune Pool at the castle. Davies sat down next to her, put her feet in the water, and told her the whole story, told her that she wasn't the daughter of George Van Cleve, an Arrow shirt model, and Marion's promiscuous glamour-girl sister, Rose, but that she had been born secretly in France, to Marion, in "a château or some sort of a little private hospital." And that when Marion brought her baby back home to New York, Hearst had the birth certificate faked.

Patricia celebrated June 18, 1923, as her birthday, but thinks she could have been born as early as 1920. "It sounds a little complicated," she says in the tapes, "but for someone in the position of W. R. Hearst that could easily be arranged.... It sounds kind of strange, but much stranger things have happened, I'm sure, throughout history."

But on her wedding day, who cared about all that? *Oh, baby, who cares?* There is a big dinner for everybody in the endless, dark dining room of the castle—tapestries and choir stalls, rows of silk flags from Siena hanging from the ceiling. Patricia and Arthur change in their rooms, then walk outside, out the west entrance, where a pair of stone saints flank the doorway, and into the blinding sunlight. The church bells ring, high above them, inside the twin spires. Out front, a pickup truck waits for them. This is their idea of a joke, just the beginning of a lifetime of jokes together—pretending to be on fire, putting ice cubes down people's backs ...

Because everything is funny, isn't it? The tall, great sky was looking out for Patricia in those days. Baby, the whole world was looking out for her. Things beyond La Cuesta Encantada might have been depressed and confused in 1937, but here, in the Santa Lucia hills, the fun was continuing. The 20s were preserved inside this enormous villa—as romantic and holy and sexual a place as you've ever seen. It wasn't like *Citizen Kane* at all, that monstrous Xanadu, cold and forbidding. It was happier than that. Sunnier.

There were fruit trees—tangerines and lemons and oranges. There were colored tiles, tall Mexican fan palms, purple bougainvillea. There were zoo animals, milky statues, a stable. A breeze brought the smell of jasmine inside the house. And Hearst and Davies were looking out for Patricia then, and, despite everything you may have come to believe from seeing Orson Welles's gloomy movie, they were upbeat, unconventional, creative. And, yes, some would say a little careless.

On their honeymoon, Patricia and Arthur drive north up the coast to Carmel, Monterey, San Francisco, then eventually almost to Oregon, to another huge Hearst compound that tried too hard—this one with a Bavarian-village theme—called "Wyntoon," near Mount Shasta. They are a little bored there. A little stir-crazy. Soon enough, they get sick of the servants,

The Neptune Pool at Hearst's San Simeon estate: on this site, Patricia Lake claimed, actress Marion Davies revealed that she and Hearst were Lake's true parents.

sick of the nearby quiet town of McCloud, and sick of each other. The Lakes start calling up their pals. *Come up, join us, baby. Have some fun.*

And this tells you how they lived—for years and years. After their two children, Arthur Patrick and Marion Rose, were born, they became part of the group, too, just another subset of the entourage, the traveling show of "pals" and family members who wandered from place to place, from the beach to the desert, from Scandia to the Del Mar racetrack. For several years after they were married, the Lakes simply lived with "Aunt Marion" in Santa Monica, at her white plantation plopped down on the sand—110 rooms, 55 bathrooms, 37 fireplaces—but soon enough they were given a house of their own, and a staff.

Arthur Lake found a job. The *Blondie* movies began in 1938, and Arthur would play Dagwood pretty much for the remainder of his career. These were light films, very successful, and he was in demand for appearances across the country. Rehearsals for various traveling shows were held at the Lakes' house, a 30-room Spanish-style place off San Vicente Boulevard in Santa Monica, and the cast and crew would come and stay for days and days. Oh, as long as they wanted. The house "was as big as a hotel," Patricia says. Nobody was ever turned away—Arthur's sister, Florence, and her family were already living in a huge apartment over the garage—a policy that became problematic later on.

The San Vicente place is gone now, torn down to make way for a development of modern homes. But the entrance remains. Cement-and-plaster pillars are standing, and two wrought-iron swinging gates—held back permanently by overgrown ivy—vestigial reminders of the old days, when endless Hearst money flowed endlessly to Davies and then from Davies to her family.

Marion's family. How do you begin to describe the Douras clan? They were outrageous, shocking. They were hilarious and, at times, disgusting. They were Irish, maybe some Dutch, maybe some French—and Catholic. There were so many Douras girls back then that it was hard to keep them straight. Ethel and Reine and Rose and Marion were all dancers under the stage name Davies, aspiring to the *Follies,* and living in a small house near Gramercy Park in New York City. Their father drank and gambled and kept a separate residence.

The spoiling started right off. When Marion was 15, she told her mother, Rose, that she wanted to go on the stage, that she hated convent school. Well, the matter was turned over to "Papa Ben," to Bernard Douras, but what did Papa know? Let the girls do what they want! And when Marion was 18 and started seeing a married man, a 52-year-old guy named William Randolph Hearst, and when he'd come by the house to have dinner and stare at her, well, who was to criticize? The man seemed honorable enough. He'd declared his intentions: he was in love with Marion, and would marry her if he could, if only his wife would give him a divorce ... That was good enough, wasn't it?

Hearst began pursuing Marion, following her, buying her watches and rings, sending her love letters. She kept them all. She started liking him back. And after a while he decided to make her a star, finance her silent pictures, then promote her way, way beyond overkill. He had all those newspapers, you see. But she wasn't talentless or charmless, like Susan Alexander, the ear-piercing soprano in *Citizen Kane,* and even Orson Welles had to say so, finally. The backing Hearst gave Marion was "less of a favor than might appear," Welles wrote in the foreword to *The Times We Had,* Davies's memoirs. "That vast publicity machine was all too visible; and finally, instead of helping, it cast a shadow—a shadow of doubt.... This question darkened an otherwise brilliant career."

Second to San Simeon, Davies would continue to be Hearst's main obsession. There was something wild about her, reckless and unpossessable. He spent his life trying to control her. Hearst wasn't just Marion Davies's lover—he was her agent, her producer, her father, her brother, and when her mother died in 1928, he said to her, "I'm awfully sorry.... May I be a mother to you?"

Welles also wrote, "Theirs is truly a love story. Love is not the subject of *Citizen Kane.*"

Hearst never did get a divorce—Millicent remained his wife until he died—but he spent a lifetime trying to make it up to Davies and her family. Bernard Douras eventually became a New York City magistrate, thanks to Hearst, and the rest of the Dourases would follow Marion to California after Hearst's Cosmopolitan Pictures signed a deal with MGM in 1924 giving her $10,000 a week. One by one, they arrived and stayed, living either with Marion in a big house on Lexington Road in Beverly Hills or later in separate houses she bought for them.

The Dourases were passionately close, but there was a certain amount of sponging. Marion's sister Reine, who was divorced from theatrical producer George Lederer, came to California with her children, Charles (who would write the screenplay for *His Girl Friday*) and Pepi (who hurled herself out a window of Good Samaritan hospital in 1935), and stayed for years. There was Marion's sister Rose, who was married six times and enjoyed countless men along the way, including a 10-year affair with Washington newspaper publisher Edward Beale McLean and a notable fling with Japanese actor Sessue Hayakawa.

It seems Rose was the wildest, the most drunken. She was also the official mother of Patricia Van Cleve. "It was a touch-and-go relationship," Patricia says. "Rose could be sweet as sugar, had a good heart, but too many gin martinis and look out—Jekyll and Hyde."

Biographer Fred Lawrence Guiles, who began researching his well-received book *Marion Davies* in 1969, wondered then about the possibility of Patricia's being Marion's daughter instead of Rose's. Since the 20s, there had been wild stories about Marion's love children—the cook's daughter at San Simeon was supposedly hers, the French actress Simone Simon was supposedly hers. One outrageous rumor even had it that Hearst's twin boys, Randolph and David, who were being raised by Millicent in New York, were really Marion's.

Guiles tends to believe Patricia's story. And he is working on a new edition of his biography of Davies that will consider her claim. Why? "Rose was totally out of the picture as a mother," Guiles says during a telephone call to his home in Florida. "Nobody could have been more unmotherly to Patricia than Rose was."

While Patricia says on her tapes that she loved "Mama Rose," she also claims there was always the danger of Rose's getting drunk and revealing the truth. At a time when Marion's career in pictures would probably not have survived further scandal, Hearst and Davies were careful to take good care of Rose—she wound up with her own house in Bel-Air. George Van Cleve, who was one of Rose's husbands and ostensibly Patricia's father, found cushy jobs within the Hearst empire. He ran off with Patricia several times between the years 1925 and 1930, and fought for legal custody of his daughter on the grounds of Rose's promiscuity and drinking, but Patricia came to believe it wasn't to protect her. He wanted ransom.

It was this mess Patricia was trying to escape by marrying Arthur Lake, she says, this confusing childhood of floating between a mother who wasn't motherly and an aunt who was—but who was also a wildly successful movie star—and floating between a father who kidnapped her and a father figure who was 74 years old and could never decide if he wanted to be a rich bohemian or the president of the United States.

"As a little girl I wanted to call them Mama and Papa," she says of W.R. and Marion on her tapes, "but I just couldn't do that. Then time marches on—I was so used to the position I was in, and as you grow up, it's easier to cope. You know what I mean?"

But, for many years beyond her wedding day, Patricia's life continued to be centered on both sets of parents. She was essentially a cheerleader, a beautiful, kept companion. Everybody wanted her around. She had grown up tall and lean and attractive, with Marion Davies's sense of the absurd. She had Hearst's long face and high-bridged nose, his horsey teeth and huge smile. "It was seeing her in a home movie," says archivist and historian Nancy E. Loe, the author of several books about Hearst and San Simeon, "that made me even consider her story."

Rose called Patricia frequently in the middle of the night, drunk and crying about something. When George Van Cleve suffered a series of strokes, Patricia took him in and gave him a bedroom suite in the back of the San Vicente house until he died in 1949. And when Hearst began having serious heart problems and moved into a house on North Beverly Drive with Davies, Patricia dutifully kept Marion company while Marion held a four-year vigil for the failing tycoon.

Hearst was wheelchair-bound toward the end of his life. The house was kept at a suffocating 80 degrees. And Davies was by then a hopeless alcoholic. "There were always a lot of nurses around," remembers Marion Rose Canessa, Patricia's daughter—nurses for both Hearst and Davies. Patricia spent nearly every day with them, but it wasn't until after W.R.'s death, in 1951, that she realized her actual status within the Hearst empire: she was nobody.

Upon hearing the news their father was gone, William R. Hearst Jr. and David Hearst went to Davies's house and had their father's body removed—presumably to save their mother any further embarrassment. As Davies sobbed over the corpse, according to Patricia, she was injected with a sedative to get her out of the way. By the time she woke up, Patricia and Arthur and their kids were there, but Hearst was gone, his stuff was gone. And no invitations came, for any of the Dourases, to attend his funeral.

In his 1991 book, *The Hearsts: Father and Son,* William junior denies that Davies was injected with a sedative at the Hearsts' request. When his father died, she was asleep, he says, already passed out in her bedroom—and never aware that the sons had arrived or that the mortician had been called to come for the body. There was no conspiracy to exclude Davies from the funeral, he says, but he writes that he "didn't want to see her drunk in a face-to-face confrontation with our mother. Nor did Mother."

Finally, he says, it's not true that he refused to give Davies information about the funeral in San Francisco—as Davies claimed. But William junior doesn't seem to realize that his version of events is only slightly less cruel: "I never had a phone conversation with Marion during that time. Therefore I could not have refused, as she asserted, to give her the time and place of the funeral. The truth is, it was published in many California papers."

Patricia becomes animated on her tapes when talking about Hearst's death. She speaks more quickly, and turns sarcastic. "Not only did they come over, knock her out, take her lover's body away, my father's body away, but later.... Christ!" Patricia says. "Years before, she had saved the goddamned Hearst empire, saved it by coming up with tremendous cash, selling jewels, furs, property, stocks, saved all the bastards, you know. And I thought, I just don't believe this. I cannot believe that people can be like this, when there is so much there, there is so much for everybody.... My mother was a very good friend to all the Hearst boys.... And I can't believe they could do that to a good, loyal woman, with a good heart."

And she adds, "Thanks a lot, gang."

Marion Davies wouldn't die for another 10 years, but it was a bad 10 years—made worse by her increased drinking and by her new husband, Horace Brown.

The minute Davies sobered up from her Vegas wedding, she called Patricia on the phone.

"I think I'm married," Davies said.

"What?" Patricia said.

Brown, a merchant marine whom Rose had dumped a year or so before, looked just like Hearst, Patricia says. She came to call him "Hor-*ass*"

Brown, but he would stay until Marion died, despite the scenes and fights and threats to divorce him. "I don't know how many times she filed," Patricia says. "Hundreds."

In 1960, Patricia and Arthur Lake moved to the beach, to Santa Monica—down the way from Marion Davies's old seaside monstrosity, which she'd sold in 1945 for $600,000, about what it had cost to put in the 37 fireplaces. The Lakes' house was big and white too, but not so grand. Times were changing. It had three floors and blue shutters, and it was located right between the sand and Highway 1: a little shabby and noisy—beachy—but with room enough for all the partying freeloaders, stray dogs, and family members in crisis. There were 10 bedrooms, 7 bathrooms.

"You should have seen the linen closet. Like Bullock's," says one of Patricia's granddaughters. "And the kitchen had restaurant refrigerators—one whole wall of them."

Davies died the following year, leaving a fortune estimated at as high as $20 million. When Patricia received roughly a third of the estate (the rest went to Charlie Lederer and Rose), the Lakes acquired not just a new monthly income and the deed to their Santa Monica beach house, but all kinds of Davies stuff as well. Cherubs carved in marble. Old ball gowns and costumes, fur coats. Patricia put up paintings of Davies everywhere, and one big portrait of Hearst. "It was totally human-looking," says another granddaughter, "with piercing eyes that would watch you wherever you went."

Patricia got the assemblage of important photographs in silver frames, too, and placed them on top of Rose's old Steinway: Davies with George Bernard Shaw, Davies with Douglas MacArthur, Davies with Lord Mountbatten, Davies with Charles Lindbergh. There was J.F.K., and Richard Nixon, and Martha Raye, and a tiny, tiny little oval gold frame containing a blurry snapshot: Hearst and Davies, heads close, smiling.

Arthur and Patricia never fought about anything, except when to start drinking. Arthur didn't approve of it until after six in the evening—unless, of course, you'd been up all night and it was suddenly morning. That was O.K. The Lakes had parties like that all the time. Patricia wouldn't stay up for just one night or two. When she was going strong, really out there, even in her last year, her 73rd, a party could last three days, three nights sometimes, without sleep, without morning newspapers and television, without the humdrum day slipping in and ruining everything. People remember her swinging her gigantic diamonds around, holding a vodka, and laughing. She was always laughing. Patricia Lake knew what fun was, and laughs.

"Pat led a tremendous life," says Peter Linder, an old friend. "She'd lie on the beach with diamond rings as big as your knuckle, getting sand in them."

She never did the dishes, or cleaned up, or made the food. She didn't know how. At the beach house, there was a housekeeper and a maid and a butler to do that. And when Patricia got older—and the money began to run out—her friends did it: just stopped reveling long enough to put on a pair of rubber gloves and squirt liquid soap into the sink, run the water. They didn't care, either.

"There was no week, or weekend, no waiting to celebrate," says Lillian Morley, who knew the Lakes for 25 years. "Every day was Christmas for

them, and every night was New Year's Eve. And I never saw either of them get mad at anybody."

Their son, Arthur Patrick—who owned eight cars by the time he was 18 years old—dropped out of school. (His dad had never gone at all, teaching himself to read and write as a teenager.) He grew tall and blond, with deep-set blue eyes—Patricia thought he looked like W.R.—and became an actor. He appeared in several episodes of *Wonder Woman* and *Baa Baa Black Sheep*. He worked as a stuntman. Between gigs, he was a drinker, a troublemaker. He laughed and called himself "a trust-fund junkie." When things got desperate, he would pawn a piece of his mother's jewelry—an American-flag pin with rubies, diamonds, and sapphires that had belonged to Davies.

Patricia didn't mind. Unconditional love: that's how she had been raised, and that's how she raised her own. "Dad did horrible things," says Arthur Patrick's daughter Patricia Lake Hashi, "but my grandparents were always there. Helping out."

"He was a bastard," says Peter Linder, "a horrible monster boy."

Marion Rose turned out quite differently from her brother. She liked school. She didn't like drinking. She was serious; as a girl, she wanted to be a nun. Later she got interested in singing: church music, gospel, then Leonard Bernstein songs. In the summer of 1963, when she was 18, she was taken to France by Rose, given the tour—although it wasn't the usual European trip with one's grandmother.

"She'd been on the wagon since Aunt Marion died," says Marion Rose. But when they got to Paris, to the Hôtel de Crillon, all Rose's old memories of her youth and her love affairs in France came back to her. She went wild, started drinking, and had to go home sick. "It killed her in a month. She went back and died of cirrhosis."

By the time Patricia's grandchildren started being born, she was 40, and she took more of an interest, had the mothering thing down better. She raised some of them in her house. Sometimes she'd tell them stories—about her childhood, how Van Cleve used to kidnap her. "When I'm dead, you're going to have to remember all this," she'd say, but even so, when she talked about Rose and George, Patricia seemed vague on the details, as though her relationship to them was a rumor she'd heard thirdhand.

She threw the kids christening parties, and birthday parties, and parties when they graduated from kindergarten—and movie stars would come, not other children. The kids called her "Mama Pat." Arthur was "Daddy Artie." And later on, Patricia would introduce her granddaughters as her "daughters" or "sisters," familial identities all jumbled up, just the way she was used to.

"They enjoyed us. They took us out," says Patricia Lake Hashi, the oldest grandchild. "They'd go out to dinner clubs—Scandia and all those places—and we'd always be there. We'd be asleep in the big round booths at three in the morning, the waiters covering us with the tablecloths."

Arthur Patrick's kids grew up beach rats and surfers. The girls would come in from the ocean and dress up in Marion's old ball gowns. His son drained all the water out of the swimming pool and started skateboarding inside, leaving wheel burns everywhere, and Patricia and Arthur loved it. Family stories include things like totaling Daddy Artie's new Cutlass ("That's O.K., baby") and how he sent the kids to the store with signed blank checks, or left money for them in their shoes if he thought they were low on cash. There were always strangers in the house, men they called "uncle" and women who were "aunts." And dogs everywhere—a family of Chihuahua-Pekingese mix that kept breeding and inbreeding.

"It was just a chaotic place," says Lillian Morley, "you know, dog turds all over the place.... But in spite of the mess it was probably one of the only Edens I'll ever find on this earth. Really and truly."

It's five or six miles up a winding, narrow road to the top, to the crest of La Cuesta Encantada—the enchanted hill—where William Randolph Hearst's big dreams lie in state forever. You make this journey sitting in a groaning tour bus, after paying $14 a ticket. As the ride begins, a little speaker up by the bus driver's head offers some crackling flapper music. A 1920s feeling breezes over you. A voice comes on, describing the history of California in brief (Mexican land grants), and then telling the story of how William Randolph Hearst came to own these gorgeous brown hills (his father, George Hearst, started buying them in 1865 for 60 cents an acre).

"Hearst Castle," as it's called on the mugs and key chains in the gift shop, receives about 800,000 visitors a year now. When Hearst died, there were attempts to sell the property (they say that Bing Crosby briefly showed interest), but it was given, finally, to the California Department of Parks and Recreation after U.C. Berkeley turned it down. The Hearst Corporation still owns 88,000 acres around the site, but the state owns the house and 160 acres of grounds and access routes. In 1958, it was opened for tours. It pays for itself, and for plenty of other sites in the state besides.

Today's tour guide, a tall young woman with a stagy voice and long, dark hair, describes Hearst three times as "a regular guy." She mentions the ketchup on the table, his love of trees and gardens, how devastated he was by his dachshund's death. How he liked to tap-dance. The tours include amusing factoids and figures, some of which are hard to verify. Hearst's father was the 15th-richest man in America "in his heyday," the guide says. His son, an only child, "surely didn't have to work for a living" and yet he came to run "92 businesses, 26 daily newspapers at his pinnacle in 1931." He was a congressman, tried to be governor of New York, and tried to be president of the United States too. And he spent money, spent, spent, spent. Never cared about making it.

Inside the dark, red damask movie theater, a projector plays some old black-and-white footage of Hearst, clowning and laughing, pulling his sweater over his head to hide from a camera. "Hollywood," the tour guide says, "doesn't have the kind of fun anymore that it used to."

There are tales and more tales, whispers of things—of parties, of romances, of nighttime swims and laughs. The castle still seems like a place that's waiting for things to happen, for people to come back, for Amelia Earhart and Jean Harlow, Clark Gable and Cary Grant. In this room, Hoagy Carmichael played the piano. Over there, on the roof of the indoor pool, Charlie Chaplin played tennis. Here is the upstairs library where Harpo Marx pushed all the furniture aside and Marion Davies did somersaults from one end to the other, losing pieces of her jewelry along the way.

The gossip about illegitimate children began as early as 1924, when a famous but disreputable New York lawyer named William J. Fallon claimed to be in possession of birth certificates of Hearst's children "born of a certain prominent motion picture actress." Newspapers across the country printed the story, except those owned by Hearst, but Fallon never produced the birth certificates. The rumors faded and resurfaced, the way unsettled things do.

Fred Guiles, the biographer who wrote *Marion Davies,* remembers visiting Patricia Lake in Rancho Mirage in 1970, when he was researching his book. She was "tight-lipped," he says, so much so that he didn't dare ask about the rumors of her parentage, but he studied her appearance carefully, because "she did look so much like Hearst."

He now proposes a possible year of birth for Patricia, 1920, when there's a brief lull in Marion Davies's moviemaking schedule. She made her first extended trip to California to see Hearst that year, and apparently had a very romantic tryst with him at an inn in Santa Maria. For months, she lived in relative isolation on a ranch outside Santa Barbara. She didn't work for a while. Then, even though Hearst hoped she'd stay with him in the West, she went back to New York. At this point, she could have gone to France with

Rose and had the child, although Guiles thinks it is more likely that the baby was born while she was still in California. "The story is probably true," Guiles says.

Patricia had nothing to gain. Hearst's will is sealed—all 125 pages of it—but according to biographer W. A. Swanberg, who reportedly had access to the will when researching his book *Citizen Hearst,* provisions were made for claims such as Patricia's. In the document, Hearst expressly denies the existence of any illegitimate offspring. He also provides for the discovery of some unknown illegitimate offspring: "then I give and bequeath to each such person the sum of one dollar."

Nancy Loe, the historian and archivist, respects Guiles's research but thinks the Patricia Lake story is bunk. When I ask why Patricia would tell the biggest lie of her life on the eve of her death, Loe suggests that perhaps Patricia believed it was true—either wanted Marion Davies to be her mother so badly that she came to believe it or was lied to by Davies.

"Marion's alcoholism was so advanced," says Loe, "and her desire to have children so strong, some wishful thinking might have become reality to her."

Loe also wonders why Hearst would have needed to hide a daughter. He lived openly with Davies after 1925, and later in his life appeared to have abandoned his political ambitions. He was known to have wanted a daughter—badly—and so, if he finally had one, why would he not have claimed her publicly? "He relished his role as an iconoclast," says Loe. "That makes me inclined to think that he wouldn't have had trouble acknowledging a child."

In the Hearst Castle gift shop, it's hard not to notice the absence of photographs of Marion Davies. No postcards of her. No gold-plated charms. On the tours, depending on the guide, her name is barely mentioned, as though she continues to be an embarrassment to the Hearsts, to the state of California, and to us. There's an old-fashioned dismissal of her, despite the fact that she had a huge career of her own, and that she ran the house, invited her friends, influenced Hearst and his newspapers, helped manage his life and his finances. (He began listening to her in the early 30s, when she made a killing in New York real estate while he was losing his shirt.) Maybe the guides don't know what to say because Davies wound up a drunk, because she was on morphine too, when her mouth cancer took over, because she somehow lost her respectability, whatever respectability she had had.

If a guide were to start talking about Marion Davies, well, suddenly he or she would be forced to discuss something as volatile and absorbing as passion and craziness, articulate to a busload of average Americans—who really just want to pay $14 to gape at splendor and big dreams and the Neptune Pool—that sometimes life doesn't follow a predictable pattern, that powerful people do as they please, live on their own terms, drive where they want, build what they want, spend and waste and use.

The desert house was nice when Patricia and Arthur bought it, as were all the houses when they first moved in, then it slowly deteriorated. The dry wind beat it up, baby. The family beat it up too, and the friends. Pat and Artie's place was still like a hotel, a refuge for countless friends whose marriages had fallen apart, for cousins on their way down or up, for people who came to drink and just stayed.

And it was still like a gallery, cluttered with pictures of dead people the Lake granddaughters could barely identify, dead people their boyfriends had never heard of.

George Bernard Shaw? Who was Marion Davies?

The sun was so strong in the summer that the air smelled like toast. Dust storms blew across Bob Hope Drive in Rancho Mirage. The Lakes came to live permanently in the desert after 1977. The Betty Ford Center wasn't far away, although it's unclear whether any of the local population was choosing to take advantage of the facilities. Certainly not Pat and Artie. They were having too much fun.

They kept the beach house in Santa Monica for a bit longer, letting Arthur Patrick live there, then sold it—had to sell it, really—in 1979. Money was starting to be a problem. They were downscaling discreetly. They moved from a house at Eldorado to one at Thunderbird—both private golf-course communities—and then finally, in their twilight years, settled at the Indian Wells Country Club, in a one-story, three-bedroom modern house in front of the 18th hole.

The dogs had taken over by then. The Chihuahua-Pekingese mix was in its fourth and fifth generations, maybe more, and inbred to the point where some of them had eyes missing, legs missing. At the beach house, there had been one dog so infirm it was kept in a drawer in the kitchen with holes drilled in it and simply called "the Dog in the Drawer." Diane Weissmuller, another friend, says they "all looked like E.T.," and pretty much everybody remarks that Patricia never focused on housebreaking them. Billie Dove, the silent-film star who was Patricia and Arthur's next-door neighbor for years, says there were 13 of those dogs. Lillian Morley says it was more like 18 or 20.

"I don't know," says Dove, "but the house got pretty rank."

"It was," says Morley, "like walking into a can of ammonia."

Mind you, this is not criticism. Everybody loved Patricia and Arthur. Everybody. They were a crackup. They were clowns, the kind of people who dove into the pool with their clothes on, and pretended to lose control of their golf cart. They were lovable, sang at benefits, played Blondie and Dagwood. Billie Dove, sitting in her living room at Thunderbird, her flecked blue eyes still as young as when she made *Blondie of the Follies* with Marion

them, which, pretty soon, was only the promissory note on the beach house.

It's obvious they were drinking too much, isn't it? You drink, and you tend to neglect things. So many of their friends drink, too: during an interview with one couple, old pals of the Lakes', I found myself downing two straight vodkas in one hour just to keep up, but those friends aren't broke. They still have two houses, clean, flat, modern California places with tidy yards and healthy-looking pets.

Other people drink like that and don't lose everything. It's more. It's something more.

Patricia went a little wild when Arthur died in 1987. She slashed a painting of Marion Davies. She talked, for the first time, about a fling she'd had with Errol Flynn. At the Hollywood Memorial Park Cemetery, standing at the Douras-family crypt—where she'd buried Marion and Rose and Ethel and Reine, George Van Cleve, and God knows what other freeloaders—Patricia leaned over to one of her granddaughters, motioned to a marble bench marking a grave nearby, and said, "Hey, can you dig up Tyrone Power for me?"

Marion Davies's Santa Monica "beach house," above, photographed here in 1930, had 110 rooms, 55 baths, and 37 fireplaces. Davies sold it in 1945 for $600,000.

Davies in 1932, says that Patricia "was the happiest person I've ever known."

Arthur Patrick and his girlfriend called the house "Horror Manor" because it looked as if nobody had taken care of it for years. The doors were off their hinges, the roses were dying, only parts of the lawn got watered. By the 1980s, Arthur spent most days in his robe or pajamas, and Patricia was down to polyester muumuus. They rarely left the house, and sometimes went months without paying their bills—Arthur could go the longest time without opening the mail or even picking it up off the floor. Daily realities often eluded them. At Thunderbird, when the electricity was turned off, or the water, their old friends Earl and Lillian Morley would run over and show them how to get it turned back on.

"Oh, honey, you know what they were?" Lillian says, smiling. "They were children, absolutely."

Patricia and Arthur sold off their assets, pawned jewelry, spent their monthly income before it came in. They were offered financial advice. They were offered temporary loans. But over time the Lakes just kept invading principal, kept getting Marion Rose and Arthur Patrick to sign off on permission to spend the Davies money that had been left in trust for

Memories of Arthur's wake: Friends and family laugh, then become protective. It was at the Linders' house. "It's just too horrendous to go into now," says Tisha Sterling, who lived with the Lakes for about a year when she was Arthur Patrick's girlfriend. So many things happened. A door got broken at the Indian Wells house when Arthur Patrick, his son, Arthur David, and Johnny Weissmuller Jr., the son of the actor who played Tarzan, got into a fight. Then one of the Lake cousins was caught trying to steal jewelry from fellow guests. And Patricia turned up at the Linders' blotto. She walked into the room, kicked off her shoes, lifted up her skirt, and said quite loudly, "Pussy says 'Hello!'"

She spent the next couple of weeks in her dark bedroom, sober. She was keeping quiet, not really eating, either, just mourning Arthur. They had been only seven months shy of their 50th anniversary.

It seemed as if there was always something terrible happening to Patricia after that—things disappearing, money missing. Her drinking got worse. She was lonely, and took in some Lake cousins who wouldn't leave—then shot out the windows of the house with a gun. Johnny Weissmuller Jr. remembers having to come down from San Francisco at least three times, at Patricia's request, to help her kick people out. "She couldn't say no to anybody," Weissmuller says.

"It was like something out of *Deliverance*," adds his wife, Diane.

Going broke, Patricia even hocked her wedding ring, hocked lots of things. She replaced them with huge fakes, big sparkling chunks that had the same effect, made her feel the same way.

And soon a guy named Paul Wallace turned up, a former Broadway dancer and onetime choreographer who was living in the desert. He was considerably younger than Patricia, lightened his hair, didn't say much. They'd go out dancing together, and Patricia loved that. They got married. But there were scenes—screaming fights, with Pat running out to the guard's kiosk at the country club—and then there was the time Wallace disappeared and was found, months later, in a nearby hospital. People liked him about as much as they had liked Horace Brown.

Patricia's granddaughters were still around—Arthur Patrick's three girls, all of whom now have kids of their own. They idolized her. They took turns living with her. And they did for her what she'd done for Marion and Rose: poured drinks, talked, laughed. Meanwhile, somebody came up with the idea of taping Patricia while she talked about her life—Marion had done the same thing after Hearst died—and talked about her real parents. Maybe something would come of it.

The last years were rough. Patricia's hair was still long and bright—but white, not blond. She still had a certain regal bearing. But Billie Dove remembers seeing Patricia being helped by two men into her golf cart outside the Hotel Indian Wells, and thinking, "I've got to call her and beg her to stop drinking." Peggy Linder remembers seeing Patricia in the bank a couple years ago, after not having seen her for a long time, and is ashamed to admit it now, but, well, "I thought as long as she didn't see me I could duck right out. And the next thing we knew, she was dead. We didn't even know she had cancer, didn't even know she was sick—anything."

She never wanted anybody to know.

'Truth is always stranger than fiction," Patricia says with a groggy laugh, her mouth a little too close to the microphone. "I think you know that."

Her death certificate listed her parents very plainly, in Courier typeface: "Marion Davies" and "William Randolph Hearst." It's an exciting sight, so final-looking, but in truth it means nothing. The next of kin provides the information about the deceased to a county official, and it's not up to the official to check. You can't help but wonder, though—as she came into this world, as she went out—who was lying about Patricia.

Arthur Patrick Lake was the next of kin who, in this case, provided the vital or not so vital information. Maybe he was doing something daring, honorable, for his dead mother, listing her parents that way. There was another reason too, of course, another motive for making this declaration so officially. Arthur Patrick wanted money. He wanted money so badly it was practically all he talked about, all he thought about.

"I'm going to make a million on this," he'd say. "We're selling this to TV and I'm making a million."

Patricia and Arthur Patrick got together with Ed Simmel, a film and TV producer who lives in Palm Desert and who, along with his wife, Honey, had been a good friend to Patricia during the final years, when some of her tonier friends were less in evidence. They even had dinner with Paul Wallace. They liked Patricia, accepted her, and believed her. And the plan, before Patricia learned she had lung cancer in the spring of 1993, was that she'd tell her story, maybe put a book deal together, do the rounds of shows—Oprah and Phil and Sally Jessy—and that Ed Simmel and Arthur Patrick would get a treatment written for a TV mini-series. They would call it *The Hidden Hearst*—a title thought up by Tisha Sterling's mother, actress Ann Sothern.

"I don't know what Arthur Patrick cared about except money," Sterling says now. "He just wanted to be loved and to have money."

But he also liked to drink—did he have much choice? Arthur Patrick was a day-long beer drinker. And a year ago, just six months after burying his mother, he ran off with a woman he had been seeing, and got married at the Universal Life Church in Bullhead City, Arizona. Both newlyweds had been drinking, and were driving back to Indian Wells when their car swerved off the road. Arthur Patrick was thrown, killed instantly.

The task of seeing through the book and TV mini-series deal, the packaging and selling of Mama Pat to the networks, fell to Arthur Patrick's four children, even as they made arrangements for his funeral and tried to deal

with his widow, who had been living at Horror Manor and was refusing to leave. Marion Rose Canessa wanted nothing to do with the mini-series, which has yet to find a buyer. She read the treatment and found it "gruesome" and "melodramatic" and "like an episode of *Dynasty*," she says, so she pretty much signed away her control over her mother's story.

And what was the story, exactly?

"Forget Jackie O," says Honey Simmel, "Pat Lake was the first American princess and nobody knew about her and that makes me very sad. Pat was the real thing."

Of course, it's hard to define "the real thing." Perhaps a hopeless alcoholic who was loved by everybody she knew, who always laughed, who took people into her house, who never got mad, who burned through millions of dollars, who was already drinking champagne at 14 and dancing close to Errol Flynn, and who used to shrug and say, "These things happen, baby," is more of an American princess than Jackie O, but I get a distinct feeling, talking to the Simmels, that some glossing is going on.

During the two days I spend in the desert with Ed and Honey Simmel and the four children of Arthur Patrick and a producer named William P. D'Angelo from Grosso-Jacobson, the firm which is packaging the Patricia Lake story, there is no mention made of Paul Wallace, or the condition of the Lakes' desert house. The dogs don't come up, either.

And when I ask, point-blank, "Did Patricia have a drinking problem?" there is a rise of objection all around. "Party drinking," says Honey Simmel. Of the grandchildren, Kimberly Lake Santori seems the most offended.

Kimberly Santori, 25, is the youngest of Arthur Patrick's children. Her voice is exactly like Dagwood's—with sudden elevations of tone, shifts in octave, and sometimes the loud, braying quality. She is pretty too, farm-girl pretty, with a few buttons on the front of her black summer dress undone. She is a secretary in Clovis, California. She has three children. Her husband is a "maintenance technician." She wears a ring that belonged to Davies, which Patricia never took off: two ruby hearts next to each other.

"It was their two hearts together," Santori says.

At the end of two long days, she looks up at me.

"So? Do you buy our story?" she asks.

I say that I do.

"Will other people?"

I look over at her brother, Arthur David Lake. It's because of him that I "buy" the story. He is tall and lean, 32, surfs a lot, works as a mason, has a 6-year-old daughter. He lives in Hawaii and Malibu. He is quiet, lets the three sisters take over. His face is haunting. Arthur David has deep-set blue eyes, a long nose, and a certain shape of brow that I've seen one other place: in a portrait of the young William Randolph Hearst that hangs at San Simeon. Of course, it proves nothing, but it's unmistakable—the resemblance—and later, after all the research and reporting, the talking to experts, it is because of Arthur David's face that I have come to believe this ridiculous story—and maybe, too, because I am the sort of person who, given a toss-up, likes to believe things.

"Growing up, we were always taught not to air certain things. We all knew basically who we were, but we didn't put on airs or tell other people," says Patricia Lake Hashi. "Maybe some paranoia was instilled in me."

Patricia Lake Hashi is 34, a manicurist on the island of Kauai. She is wearing a sash around her forehead, like a flapper. She is also wearing jeans with high-heeled bone-white pumps. She is seriously beautiful; she has Marion Davies's eyes, nose, mouth—pretty much everything. Like the other women in the family, she married young, and she has three children, aged 4, 8, and 13.

The curse of Millicent Hearst comes up several times. "When things would be going bad for Mama Pat, she'd say, 'Oh, the curse of Millicent Hearst,'" recalls Victoria Lake, another granddaughter. "Hey, I'm not afraid to say it—Millicent Hearst cursed our family." Each time I hear something like this, I think to myself that the curse of alcohol probably has more to do with the family's problems than W.R.'s wife does, but I don't feel like having to describe William Randolph Hearst using a word like "codependent." I'm not sure that Patricia's drinking has anything to do with her credibility, either. Sober people lie, too. But I do ask again, more boldly,

"Is anybody going to tell me that Patricia had a horrible drinking problem?"

"Oh no. Not at all," says Kimberly Lake Santori.

"Pat did not. Everybody else in the family had a drinking problem. Even Marion," says Victoria Lake. "Pat could drink for 24 hours," she adds, "then snap out of it, and be doing needlepoint, and say, 'I'm on the wagon.' I saw her go six weeks without drinking."

"It never stopped her from going to a meeting or a party," says Kimberly Santori.

"She did smoke," says Honey Simmel.

"It was a completely different era," says Victoria. "You drank. You smoked."

They do impressions of Mama Pat smoking—index finger and thumb pinched together, the way gangsters and German officers smoke in movies. They demonstrate how she checked out her lipstick at the dinner table—by looking at her reflection in the blade of a knife. They do her smoky, sultry voice too: *Just close the curtains on the stage of your mind, baby.*

Patricia Lake Hashi calls Orson Welles a "big pig." It's explained that "Rosebud" was the name Hearst had for Marion Davies's genitalia—and the family was outraged that Welles had been cruel enough to make a joke of it.

They have hundreds of snapshots: Arthur Lake at San Simeon with the Three Stooges. Patricia on a sailboat, gorgeous and slim. Patricia at the castle, in front of the Neptune Pool, where her kids learned to swim. And then a picture of Marion Davies at the end of her life, when she had mouth cancer, sitting in a dining room full of people, with a scarf tied around her head, "to keep her jaw from falling off," says Victoria.

Victoria Lake has a Douras face, too—but with a different configuration—and a kind of unsettling street smarts and honesty. She is 27. She has gained weight, she says, because it's been a lousy year. She lived with Mama Pat the last year of her life, and is planning to move to Kauai to be with her older sister. She has porcelain nails that extend two inches beyond the ends of her fingers. She drums them on the coffee table in the suite at the Hyatt in Indian Wells, where we have all gathered.

Looking at a picture of William Randolph Hearst, she says, "He was hideous-looking. I don't care how much money he had, I wouldn't have gone with him."

"We never talk about all this, you know," says Kimberly Lake Santori. "This is the most we've ever talked about Marion and W.R. and Pat."

Occasionally there's a ruined feeling, a corrupted Tess of the d'Urbervilles quality, to the grandchildren, a sense that before all this, before the mini-series and the claims, they were happy just to be kids, beach rats, surfers, young moms. They had nothing to worry about—never cared about proving their ancestry. Never cared much about money. That was their dad's obsession. And now they've got Ed and Honey Simmel sitting across the room from them, helping them push Patricia's story, telling them what they should say and not say, like chaperons—keeping the Lake grandchildren under control—lest the blood of their grandmother and great-grandmother should rise inside them and demand some excitement, some life, some living.

And the blood does rise, at night. The Lakes have a wonderful way of hydroplaning beyond decorum and respectability. It starts with Kimberly Lake Santori, when she brings her baby daughter to the Hotel Indian Wells bar and lets her walk around on top of it. And then Arthur David Lake sits

down next to me. "My grandmother would have liked you," he says. Why? "Because you drink vodka straight."

A huge maroon Cadillac pulls up in front of the hotel. It's rented. It has a car phone and all the extras. Patricia Lake Hashi is at the wheel. *Come on, get in, baby.* The windows are all down. We drive off too fast, into the night, with the dry desert air on our faces. The radio is blasting. The music is up so loud you couldn't know suffering. You couldn't know anything. Everybody is swinging his head, singing. We are speeding in the dark, singing along, and laughing.

It is midnight, after dinner, and we have to go dancing, they say. The Cadillac takes us to a place called the Yacht Club, in a strip shopping center in Indian Wells. It's all blue inside, and nautical and watery. The bar and dance floor are pretty much empty, except for a table of five men—where the granddaughters will eventually wind up. But, for now, we are ordering more drinks, more beer, and pretty soon Victoria Lake is out there moving around by herself on the floor and smiling. She's wearing black jeans, a black T-shirt, and a black cowboy hat. And she's really moving.

What's particularly stunning is how confident she is, how sensual she is, how unabashed, and how powerful. She says she is 20 pounds over her usual weight, but still, at a time when other women might be hiding themselves, their bodies, she is wearing skintight black jeans. And at a point when other women would be sitting down all night, not wanting to dance until they were thinner, she is out there, going it alone, and beautifully. Soon enough, Kimberly Santori joins her.

"This is where Mama Pat used to come," she says. "She never got old, you know. She was more of a kid than us."

And Patricia Lake Hashi gets out there too, in her jeans and high heels and white sash around her forehead. She is laughing, huskily, from her guts. The three girls line up together with their arms around one another, and the next song comes on—a reggae beat, Bob Marley. They whoop. They love it.

"Don't worry . . . 'bout a thing . . . 'cause every little thing gonna be all right." They start singing into their beer bottles, moving around. And suddenly it's impossible to feel sorry for them, for the beautiful granddaughters of Patricia Lake, and perhaps, if you give them the benefit of the doubt, the beautiful great-granddaughters of Marion Davies. Maybe nobody educated them, disciplined them, or nagged them. Maybe they've been cursed by Millicent, left with pieces of jewelry still in hock, left with unfinished business—a funny lie or truth in the air that nobody is going to get around to clearing up anytime soon—but here they are, gorgeous and laughing and dancing together.

And I think, It doesn't matter who the parents of Patricia Lake were, or who her grandparents and great-grandparents were. We inherit all kinds of things from our parents, biological and spiritual, and it's clear that these women didn't get sensible things that others may have—money, schooling, a last name or middle name like Hearst—but, my God, they can dance like that. And they can laugh. They can stay out late, and dive headfirst into the Hotel Indian Wells swimming pool at three in the morning.

And it isn't until some hours, some days, some weeks later, when responsibility and respectability begin creeping back into my body, that I realize this isn't a small thing at all, their inheritance. Out on the dance floor, I can see Patricia, Marion, Rose, Marion Rose too, swinging, jiving, oblivious, beautiful and unrestrained and free and completely remarkable. Oh, these Dourases. They do know this: life is about fun, about right now, right here, take a break, take a breath, exhale, that's it.

So what if the money's gone? □

AL PACINO With Pacino, the play's the thing. So ingrained is the stage in his acting marrow (he counts Lee Strasberg and Charles Laughton among his tutors) that many of his cinematic personae have seemed to come alive, walk off the screen, and become permanent characters in our culture: Michael Corleone (the *Godfather* trilogy), Frank Serpico (*Serpico*), Tony Montana (*Scarface*). He's most convincing when most intense: as trip-wired Sonny Wortzik in *Dog Day Afternoon*, as the blind (and Oscar-worthy) Frank Slade in *Scent of a Woman*, as crusading newsman Lowell Bergman in *The Insider* (spun from Marie Brenner's 1996 *Vanity Fair* article on tobacco-industry whistle-blower Jeffrey Wigand).

PHOTOGRAPHED IN 2000
BY **ANNIE LEIBOVITZ**

ROBERT DE NIRO "You talkin' to *me?*" He's our most eloquent exponent of the inarticulate (*Taxi Driver, Awakenings*) and of the man of few words (young Vito Corleone in *The Godfather Part II,* Michael in *The Deer Hunter*). Yet he was madly fluent in *The King of Comedy* and *Cape Fear,* and has been a shape-shifter *extraordinaire,* from lean Johnny Boy (in *Mean Streets*) to bruising middleweight Jake La Motta (in *Raging Bull*).

PHOTOGRAPHED IN 2000
BY **ANNIE LEIBOVITZ**

EDITH HEAD She may not have known how to dress, but she knew how to dress Hollywood. Did you admire George Peppard's *tenue* in *Breakfast at Tiffany's?* Perhaps you thought Elizabeth Taylor was well turned out in *A Place in the Sun?* Was Bette Davis attired to kill in *All About Eve?* Credit the greatest wardrobe mistress of all time—"The Dress Doctor," as she called herself—for putting eight Oscars on the rack and keeping 35 nominations in a cupboard for everyday wear.

PHOTOGRAPHED IN 1976
BY **ERIC SKIPSEY**

EDITH HEAD

ROBERT EVANS When we hicks from Hicksville picture the life of a Hollywood producer, it's Robert Evans's life we are thinking of. Discovered poolside in Beverly Hills by Norma Shearer; fast-tracked at Paramount; tapping Coppola to do *The Godfather;* producing *Chinatown* and *Rosemary's Baby;* marrying Ali MacGraw; inhabiting Garbo's old estate (where he is shown, *below*); keeping his looks. Then the downside: the cocaine bust, turkey-shoot movies like *The Cotton Club,* friendship with madam Heidi Fleiss—all of which sound quite fun, too.

PHOTOGRAPHED IN 1994
BY **MICHEL COMTE**

HOLLYWOOD ISSUE COVER, 1997 From left: Cameron Diaz, Kate Winslet, Claire Danes, Renée Zellweger, Minnie Driver (reclining), Alison Elliott, Jada Pinkett, Jennifer Lopez, Charlize Theron, Fairuza Balk.

PHOTOGRAPHED IN 1996
BY **ANNIE LEIBOVITZ**

JUDY GARLAND Her piercing, tremulous voice, still without equal, sent us over the rainbow. Though some now dwell on the pills and the pathos—and how MGM banished her from the lot in 1950—instead, let's remember Judy the child star (*The Wizard of Oz*), the soul of screen musicals (such as director husband Vincente Minnelli's *Meet Me in St. Louis*), the queen of Hollywood evensong, here joining a few friends (from left, Lenore Cotten, Moss Hart, and Richard Burton) in a raucous tribute to Cole Porter (not shown). The next year, '54, she would make one of the town's great comebacks, in producer husband Sidney Luft's *A Star Is Born;* by '69, Seconal would end it all.

PHOTOGRAPHED IN 1953
BY **JEAN HOWARD**

JEAN HARLOW AND **HOWARD HUGHES** Harlow died too soon (at 26) and Hughes lived too long (to 71): in their brief collaboration on his flier picture *Hell's Angels*, the future aeronautics magnate and famous recluse virtually invented the star of *Platinum Blonde, Goldie, Bombshell,* and *Reckless.* ("The *t* is silent," murmured Margot Asquith of her own first name, "as in Harlow.") H.H. soldiered on through Jane Russell, Kate Hepburn, and Ida Lupino, once combining his passions with his commitment to technology by designing, for Russell, a cantilevered bra. When able to concentrate, he produced *The Front Page* and—with the other H.H., Howard Hawks—*Scarface* (1932)

JERRY BRUCKHEIMER AND **DON SIMPSON**
These gentlemen ignited our engines. *Flash-dance. Beverly Hills Cop. Top Gun.* Careers were in constant overdrive. Then came *Days of Thunder.* Simpson succumbed to drugs and other vices shortly after critiquing modern life—and Hollywood—for *Vanity Fair:* "People live their childhood until they're too old to do anything else." Powerhouse Bruckheimer has rallied since (*Con Air, Armageddon, Gone in Sixty Seconds*), but the pair's derring-do ethos was best decoded in a line in James Toback's *The Big Bang* (1990), delivered by Simpson himself: "I've always, always been able to kind of teeter on the precipice." The teeter principle—credo for their town and their trade.

PHOTOGRAPHED IN 1990
BY **ANNIE LEIBOVITZ**

PAUL ROBESON The first African-American to play *Othello* on Broadway (or any other role, come to that), Paul Robeson was a colossus—seen here in character as Eugene O'Neill's *The Emperor Jones*, a part he would re-create on-screen. Often forced to find work in Europe, and for eight years deprived of his U.S. passport for his leftist politics, he twice made a fool of himself: once by acting in *Sanders of the River* and once by accepting the Stalin Peace Prize. His rendition of "Ol' Man River" in *Show Boat* outlasts the racism of his time and the tragedies of his life.

PHOTOGRAPHED IN 1933
BY **EDWARD STEICHEN**

KRISTIN SCOTT THOMAS English, yes. Patient? No. Left the convent to pursue the camera; now the camera pursues her. As Brenda Last, the scheming minx in *A Handful of Dust* (1988), she fulfilled all of Evelyn Waugh's designs for women. As Fiona in *Four Weddings and a Funeral*, she reverted to a brittleness which was the more striking for being shed in the Sahara. Notice how Parisian the luscious adulteress of *The English Patient* can look: some of her finest work is in the French cinema.

PHOTOGRAPHED IN 1997
BY **ANNIE LEIBOVITZ**

HOLLYWOOD, 1937 This loopy, twilight paean to pre-war L.A. comes courtesy of Bruce McCall, maestro of the warped vista, the outsize interior, and all manner of fanciful transport. Remember those sumptuous prop-drops from Howard Hughes's "Aeroboy" service: haute French meals, delivered piping hot, air-to-door? Alas, only McCall does. But using *Vanity Fair* as a canvas, he is forever building visual bridges to a wondrous time that never was.

ILLUSTRATED IN 1996
BY **BRUCE McCALL**

RITA HAYWORTH The atom bomb at Bikini Atoll was embellished with her likeness. While you sort out *that* image—the favorite of soldiers and prisoners everywhere—consider that she was cousin to Ginger Rogers, tempestuous companion to Victor Mature, Orson Welles, and Aly Khan, and dance partner to Fred Astaire in *You Were Never Lovelier* and *You'll Never Get Rich*. In *Gilda, left,* she pretended to strip: the reverberations extended far beyond Bikini. PHOTOGRAPHED IN 1946

JACK NICHOLSON AND **WARREN BEATTY** Women are some-times heard to complain about the unfairness of men getting older and better. And so they should (left), so they should (right). Men can be envious, too: when profiling Beatty (he of *Splendor in the Grass, Bonnie and Clyde, Shampoo, Reds, Bugsy, Bulworth,* and so much more) for *Vanity Fair,* Norman Mailer said ruefully that "a lover on such a scale cannot survive without philosophy." (He wished.) As for Happy Jack, well, *his* philosophy, as told to Hollywood's magazine of record, was that "you only lie to two people in your life—your girlfriend and the police," and the law hasn't caught up with him yet, either

DENNIS HOPPER AND **CHRISTOPHER WALKEN** "You know, Billy, we blew it," Peter Fonda told Hopper at the close of *Easy Rider.* A poor prediction. Young Hopper, who had already survived two movies with James Dean, went on to survive *The Texas Chainsaw Massacre 2, Blue Velvet,* and nearly 100 other features. He even surfaced from *Waterworld,* though his off-screen recoveries were all the more creditable. Hopper keeps coming: look at the mileage on the guy. Same for Walken; the man who put the fear of Christ into Woody Allen in *Annie Hall* has specialized in giving people the creeps ever since. Pale and abstract, ideally cast as Hopper's interrogator in *True Romance,* Walken could have landed from somewhere else. Michael Cimino wasted him in *Heaven's Gate,* and he wasted Vietnam in *The Deer Hunter,* earning an Oscar but still prone to smile in the wrong places.

PHOTOGRAPHED IN 1995
BY **ANNIE LEIBOVITZ**

By Amy Fine Collins

O n a rainy Tuesday afternoon during the spring of 1948 a roomful of Hollywood power lunchers were treated to a spectacle that equaled in sheer outrageousness the fantasies they confected in their studio dream factories. The movie industry's two gorgons of gossip, buxom columnist Louella O. Parsons and her behatted counterpart, Hedda Hopper—the town's most feared women and most notorious rivals—were sitting down together to a civilized meal of cracked crab at the No. 1 booth of the posh Rodeo Drive restaurant Romanoff's. The establishment's customers, who probably wouldn't have blinked if Harry Truman himself had walked in on the elbow of Stalin, stampeded for the telephones to broadcast the news to the outside world. These calls, Hedda said, "brought in a mob of patrons who stood six deep at the bar to witness our version of the signing of the Versailles Peace Treaty." Press agents, *Collier's* magazine later reported, scurried "from washroom to washroom tearing hair, gnashing teeth, and awaiting the end of the world." For this entente cordiale between these two Weird Sisters—who together commanded a loyal audience of around 75 million newspaper readers and radio listeners (roughly half the country)—signaled more than just a bit of stagy fence-mending. It also ominously harbingered the collapse of the crisscrossing, double-dealing structure that for years had supported the entire Hollywood publicity machine. In their quest for column mentions, a commodity worth its space in gold, studio heads, publicists, and stars had long been playing the dangerous game of pitting one woman tooth and nail against the other.

Nobody left Romanoff's until nearly two hours later, when, their standing-room-only performance complete, the two ladies sauntered out arm in arm. "Peace," Hedda reflected in her 1952 memoir, *From Under My Hat,* "it's wonderful! But it didn't last." Besides, Louella surmised, "so many people say we do not" like one another. "Who are we to argue against such an enthusiastic majority opinion?"

Neither, of course, had actually expected or even wanted a permanent reconciliation—Louella and Hedda were wise enough to the ways of Hollywood to know feuds were good business. Louella had been covering the film industry since 1915 (she was, in her boastful words, "the first movie columnist in the world"). And Hedda, originally a stage and film personality, had known Samuel Goldwyn when he was still called Samuel Goldfish, and had acted in the first movie Louis B. Mayer ever produced. Like so many sworn enemies, they were distorted fun-house-mirror doubles of each other—the one fat, the other thin—with more in common than either probably cared to acknowledge. Born four years apart and much earlier than either ever admitted (Hedda joked she was "one year younger than the age Louella claims to be"), the two women both escaped from dreary hick towns into seemingly advantageous marriages, merely to wind up single mothers struggling to support only children. Prodigiously energetic and ambitious, both eventually found themselves capable of pulling in huge incomes (around $250,000 a year, close to $2 million by today's standards), yet had such extravagant tastes that they were constantly in debt. And politically both Louella and Hedda were, in the words of one contemporary, "to the right of Genghis Khan."

Crisply summing up the difference between herself and her nemesis, Hedda observed that "Louella Parsons is a reporter trying to be a ham; Hedda Hopper is a ham trying to be a reporter!" Though Hopper was more sophisticated—"worldly, lovely, beautifully groomed, with a New York actressy polish," says Kitty Carlisle Hart—Parsons, whom John Barrymore called "that

old udder" and who Roddy McDowall says "resembled a sofa," may actually have been the more complicated of the two characters.

A s George Eells intimated in his 1971 dual biography, *Hedda and Louella,* Louella certainly was the more mendacious. In addition to fudging her birth date—she gave it as 1893 rather than 1881—Louella concealed the fact that she was born in Freeport, Illinois, to Jewish parents, the Oettingers. After graduating from high school in Dixon, Illinois (Ronald Reagan's hometown), Louella worked as a reporter on a local paper. Always as gooily romantic as a candy valentine ("I believe that love is the answer to almost all the problems the world faces"), she captivated one of the area's more eligible and affluent men, John Parsons. "Louella was very popular with men," says Dorothy Manners, the columnist's assistant for 30 years. With "lustrous brown hair and skin that a baby might envy," Louella was "much more at-

tractive than she was ever given credit for." Apparently Mr. Parsons agreed with Manners's assessment; he wed Louella in 1905, and a year later she gave birth to their daughter, Harriet. Louella's official bio neatly disposes of Parsons by having him die on board a transport ship on the way home from World War I. Though he did die young, Parsons made his exit in a more commonplace fashion—he was screwing his secretary and Louella divorced him. She expunged this, and other significant bits of her history, in order to align her life more strictly with the Catholicism she began to practice fervently in middle age.

Rid of John Parsons in all but name, Louella relocated to the nearest big city, Chicago. By around 1910 she was working for nine dollars a week in the syndication department of the *Chicago Tribune* and writing movie scenarios at night. Through a cousin's connections, she advanced to a much more lucrative job as story editor at Chicago's Essanay Studios, where she came into daily contact with such freshly coined silent stars as Mary Pickford and Gloria Swanson.

When Louella priced herself out of her Essanay job, she went to the Chicago *Record-Herald* and boldly approached the editor with an unusual proposition. "All the movie stars of the day had to pass through Chicago on their way from New York to Los Angeles," explains Dorothy Manners. "There was a two-hour wait in Chicago. Louella's idea was to go down to the train station and interview the stars while they waited. She figured they would be glad to have something to do, and that from these meetings she could put together a column about their personal lives. Her editor told her, 'Who would be interested in reading about that?' Well, you can guess what happened."

Louella's behind-the-scenes reports for the *Record-Herald* thrived, but the paper folded. In 1918 the invincible reporter transferred her talents to the New York *Morning Telegraph*. She, daughter Harriet, and a new husband she had acquired during her Chicago years, a riverboat captain named Jack Mc-

Caffrey, settled into a $90-a-month apartment on West 116th Street. Louella's grinding work schedule and ceaseless social maneuverings soon alienated McCaffrey, but their crumbling marriage was really finished off by Louella's obsessive affair with a married man, Peter Brady, a prominent New York labor leader—"the real love of her life," says Dorothy Manners. (The records of this second marriage also seem to have been obliterated in an effort to sanitize her past.)

Though Louella, by her own admission, lost her head over the married Brady, professionally she navigated a steady, upward course. Shrewdly, she began a campaign to capture the attention of the most powerful figure in newspaper publishing, William Randolph Hearst—and she aimed directly at his heart. Her column turned into a one-note instrument, tirelessly piping honeyed praise for the talent and beauty of the sprightly blonde starlet Marion Davies, whom Hearst had plucked from a chorus line at the age of 14 to become his mistress, and around whom he had built his Cosmopolitan motion-picture studio. Parsons's sugar-flecked shower of accolades (a generous counterpoint to another critic's assessment that "Miss Davies has two dramatic expressions—joy and indigestion") inevitably led to a friendship between the two ladies, and finally an offer from Hearst in 1923 to become the $250-a-week motion-picture editor of his *New York American*. The perpetual Parsons refrain "Marion Davies never looked lovelier" echoed down the decades, eventually winding up as a standard on the drag-queen circuit.

But Louella, whose gushing enthusiasm for the movie business knew no limits, did not reserve her effusions for Davies alone. She also made a minor pet of an actress named Hedda Hopper, whom she lauded for her "capable" performance in the Davies vehicle *Zander the Great*. And she took her plaudits even further, describing Hedda in 1926 as the type of woman who could lead any man astray.

Hedda, formerly Elda Furry, Quaker butcher's daughter from Hollidaysburg, Pennsylvania, was born in 1885 and became smitten with the theater as a teenager when she attended Ethel Barrymore's performance in *Captain Jinks of the Horse Marines* at the Mishler Theatre in nearby Altoona. Stagestruck, she ran away to join a Pittsburgh theatrical troupe. From there, in 1908, she escaped to New York, where, accepted into the chorus of the Aborn Light Opera Company, she became known for the best pair of legs on Broadway.

These lovely appendages, and Elda's youth, caught the rakish eye of one of the leading lights of the theater, DeWolf Hopper, a Harvard-educated actor 27 years her senior and married so many times his friends called him "the Husband of Our Country." Hopper weakened women's wills "with his voice," Hedda recalled. "It was like some great church organ"—an apparatus sonorous enough to persuade her to become his fifth wife, in 1913. When they weren't on tour, the couple lived in Manhattan's Algonquin Hotel, where Mrs. Hopper found herself in the thick of such elite theatrical personages as John Barrymore, Douglas Fairbanks, and a very young Tallulah Bankhead. "As Wolfie's wife I didn't hover around the fringes of a world of celebrated people," Hedda recalled with her farm-girl briskness. "I was pitchforked right in amongst 'em." DeWolf's greatest gifts to his young wife—whom he habitually taunted, cheated on, or simply ignored—were their son, Bill, his distinctly more euphonious surname ("Elda" was traded in for "Hedda" on the advice of a numerologist), and his impeccable instruction in diction. "In fact, I got an overdose," she wrote. "I clipped my letters so short that I sounded like an inbred British dowager mated to a Boston bull terrier.... It was that very affectation ... that got me into all the phony society-female roles that I played on the screen."

Hedda, husband, and son landed in Hollywood in 1915, where DeWolf had been lured by a lucrative contract from the Triangle Film Company. In spite of DeWolf's demands that Mrs. Hopper relinquish her acting career, Hedda persuaded him to let her take the female lead in *Battle of Hearts* (1916)—her first film—at $100 a week. This was no "society-female" role, however. Playing a rough-and-ready fisherman's daughter, she won the part

They were the dueling grandes dames of the budding gossip trade—and Hollywood's most notorious rivals. Hedda Hopper, *opposite*, in a late-50s portrait, fancied flamboyant hats; Louella Parsons, shown in '53, was the brainier of the pair.

149

simply because of her sinewy build and her height. At five feet seven and 128 pounds, she was a beanstalk in a hothouse where diminutive orchids such as Mary Pickford and Lillian Gish flourished. The movie opened to respectable notices, with one critic pointing out that Hedda looked "exceedingly well in trousers."

After Triangle foundered and the Hoppers returned to New York, Hedda began working in earnest at the studios there and in Fort Lee, New Jersey. The role that set the pattern for all her future casting was that of the faithless spouse of a millionaire in L. B. Mayer's *Virtuous Wives* (1918). Determined to upstage the star, Hedda sank her entire $5,000 salary into gowns and hats from the salon Lucile—and it paid off. *Variety* observed that Mrs. DeWolf Hopper stood out "prominently," at the expense of Anita Stewart, whose self-effacement was "a remarkable exception to the general run of stars."

By 1920, Hedda's stature as a film actress had soared so high that she demanded $1,000 a week—double her previous salary. Jealous that his protégée's earnings now matched his own, DeWolf hurled himself into the dalliances that eventually brought about the 1922 collapse of their marriage, a fact Louella duly noted in her *Telegraph* column. Independent and in need of funds, in 1923 Hedda accepted L. B. Mayer's offer of a Metro (soon to become MGM) contract in Hollywood.

Frantically trying to balance a heavy social schedule, daily deadlines, a clandestine love affair, and her checkbook, Louella—who habitually slept only two or three hours a night—found herself in failing health. Though diagnosed with tuberculosis, she ignored doctor's orders and dragged herself in the fall of 1925 to a dinner party at Hearst's home. The next morning Louella's host discharged her on full salary and sent her to the California desert to recuperate.

During her desert confinement, several of Louella's Hollywood friends made the eastward pilgrimage to visit her in Palm Springs. Darryl Zanuck came bearing books, and Hedda Hopper showed up, hoping to supplement her movie income with real-estate dealings. In fact, ever since Hedda had arrived in Hollywood two years before, she and Louella had been engaged in a sort of mutually beneficial swap meet. A continent away from the main action, Louella had grown to depend on the gossipy actress's sharp ears. "When they first knew each other," says Dorothy Manners, "Hedda was an actress, a good one. They liked each other a lot. If anything happened on a set—if a star and leading man were having an affair—Hedda would give Louella a call." In return, Hedda was guaranteed a few lines of copy under Louella's increasingly powerful byline.

Hedda sorely needed these breaks, small and sporadic though they may have been. Having refused to lie down on L.B.'s well-worn casting couch, she was making the bulk of her pictures on loan-out arrangements with other studios. As she worked infrequently, Hedda, distinguished by her mannequin-like ability to wear clothes and her social aplomb, was regularly called upon to model for MGM's head costume designer, Adrian, or to serve as studio cicerone for visiting V.I.P.'s.

Eventually, MGM canceled her contract, and Hedda found herself living with her son in a three-room basement apartment—a humiliatingly far remove from the gold-brocaded tower bedroom she occupied on her visits to her colleague and close friend Marion Davies at San Simeon, Hearst's palatial complex north of L.A. And her love life was in no less disarray. Just before Hedda lost all her savings in the Crash, she accompanied scenarist Frances Marion to Europe in 1928, and during the crossing fell madly in love with a handsome American painter. "But she refused to sleep with him," Marion told biographer George Eells. "I used to say to her, 'Hedda, for heaven's sake, throw your panties over the windmill.'" But Hedda prudishly held her ground, even when the painter followed her back to Hollywood. Despondent, her ardent suitor ended up committing suicide.

Fully recovered by March 1926, Louella, 45, called Hearst to announce she was ready to return to the *New York American*. The newspaper magnate replied, "Louella . . . the movies are in Hollywood—and right now I think that is where you belong." He surprised her further with the happy tidings that he wished to syndicate her column—a huge boon to her finances and her influence (eventually 372 newspapers, as far afield as Beirut and China, would carry her)—and appoint her motion-picture editor of his multi-tentacled International News Service. "At last," rejoiced Louella, "the Hollywood writer is going to Hollywood!"

For connoisseurs of Hollywood lore, the timing of Hearst's offer—and of Louella's all-expenses-paid retreat to Palm Springs before that—is an eyebrow raiser. Even Louella allowed that the tales explaining the origin of her lifelong position with Hearst were macabre enough to have sprung from the febrile imagination of Edgar Allan Poe. But, publicly at least, that was all she said.

There are two great unsolved mysteries in Hollywood: the first, the murder of director William Desmond Taylor, and the second, more pertinent to Louella's story, the sudden demise of Thomas Ince, a universally respected director-producer whom Hearst had hoped to lure to Cosmopolitan Pictures to bring cachet to his lackluster studio. "Louella knew exactly what happened in both cases," says Richard Gully, formerly Jack Warner's special assistant for publicity, and now, at 90, a writer for the paper *Beverly Hills 213*. So unsatisfying are all the explanations for Ince's 1924 death—officially reported as acute indigestion leading to heart failure—that last year Patricia Hearst, W.R.'s granddaughter, reopened the whole can of worms by publishing a fictional account of the affair, *Murder at San Simeon*.

The "murder," if that indeed is what it was, did not, however, take place at Hearst's mountaintop castle, but aboard the Hearst yacht *Oneida*—later known as "William Randolph's Hearse"—in November 1924. To woo Ince, Hearst organized a shipboard party for the filmmaker, attended by Marion Davies, writer Elinor Glyn, actresses Seena Owen and Aileen Pringle, some Ince and Hearst business associates, and, according to many accounts, Charlie Chaplin and Louella Parsons. George Eells was convinced that Ince simply took sick and died after swilling too much of Hearst's bad Prohibition-era liquor. A more operatic version of what happened aboard the *Oneida* was that Chaplin had been having, as Roddy McDowall puts it, "a wingding with Marion Davies." Crazed with jealousy, Hearst hired a killer, who, mistaking Ince for Chaplin, shot Ince instead. Dismissing this rumor, Dorothy Manners states, "There's not a shred of truth to any of that. Every day after lunch at Louella's house, where she had her offices, the two of us took a long walk. During one walk I asked her about this story. She said, 'I was in New York at the time. And I've got columns datelined from New York to prove it.'"

"So many alibis," sighs one of Hollywood's most senior and best-informed insiders. "How hard would it have been for a Hearst journalist to fake a dateline? Anyway, Chaplin wasn't even on that boat. But Louella was." The real story, he insists, is that Hearst, coming up from his cabin after a postlunch nap, discovered Ince playfully embracing Davies. In the same jesting spirit, Hearst pulled a long hatpin out of Davies's hat—"a very large affair, as it was windy on the ship"—and aimed for Ince's arm. Ince suddenly turned to face Hearst, and instead of pricking the producer's arm, the hatpin "entered directly into his heart, causing an instant fatal heart attack. The key to the whole story is that Hearst then put his yacht into harbor on a Sunday and had the body cremated that day so there would be no autopsy. Listen, there's no smoke without fire. There's certain things you just can't fake. And Louella was on the boat, for God's sake."

Louella, inaugurating the first column to be syndicated from Hollywood, took to her adopted town like a thirsty dromedary to a lush oasis. Immediately, she laid down the law: "You had to tell it to Louella first," says director George Sidney. Ubiquitous on the Hollywood scene, she became notorious for assuming an air of goofy vagueness in order to snap up material on the sly, and for leaving behind a puddle of urine wherever she sat (incontinence had plagued her at least since the seventh grade). In 1934 she significantly expanded her power base and income by breaking into radio, and on her popular *Hollywood Hotel* program, sponsored by Campbell's Soup, she introduced the first "sneak previews" show. Actors appeared for free to read parts from upcoming films in exchange for cases of soup (Carole Lombard's favorite: mulligatawny). Her influence was such that in a poll of moviegoers lined up at New York's Rivoli theater to see a B-grade production called *Nancy Steele Is Missing* in 1937, 78 percent said they were there as a result of Louella's broadcast.

But Louella's reputation for grasping Hollywood firmly by its scrotum arose less from her ability to lasso audiences into movies than from her skill at performing the vulturine rites of "Love's Undertaker" (one of her less scurrilous nicknames). Her informants could be found in studio corridors, hairdressers' salons, and lawyers' and doctors' offices (she sometimes learned of starlets' pregnancies before they did). When she received a tip that Clark Gable and his second wife, Ria, were about to divorce, Louella "kidnapped" Mrs. Gable, whom she held hostage at her North Maple Drive home until she was sure the story was "speeding across the wire" ahead of any other service. Her most earth-shattering scoop during her early years in California, however, was "the biggest divorce story in the history of Hollywood": the split between the town's undisputed king and queen, Douglas Fairbanks Sr. and Mary Pickford. Pickford, who made the crucial mistake—repeated reflexively by generations of stars to come—of pouring her heart out to Louella, bitterly recalled that she had "counted . . . upon the columnist's discretion" to safeguard her "against sensation." When the bombshell erupted across international headlines, Hollywood was treated to one of its first full-throttle media maelstroms.

In total command of Hollywood, Louella also succeeded in getting her hooks permanently into a man, urologist Harry "Docky" Martin, whose devilish Irish charm had at long last induced her to give up the married Peter Brady. Even before their 1930 marriage (Hearst gave the bride a $25,000 bauble as a wedding gift), Martin had earned a certain local reputation of his own as one of the town's most florid drunks. Leonora Hornblow, widow of producer Arthur Hornblow Jr., recalls that late one night at a party at L. B. Mayer's, "Docky—everyone, even the parking attendant at Romanoff's, called him that—passed out cold under the piano. Somebody shook him, trying to wake him up. But Louella shouted, 'Let Docky sleep! He has surgery at seven tomorrow morning!'" (An elaborated version of this story has Martin's famously large penis popping out of his pants as he slumped over, inviting the comment "There's Louella Parsons's column!") Under Louella's aegis, Docky, who had made an early specialty of cleaning up V.D.-infected whores, advanced to the post of Twentieth Century Fox's chief medical officer. "Basically, a studio doctor's job was to shoot stars with anything to make them perform," explains Gavin Lambert, author of Norma Shearer and On Cukor.

Hedda, meanwhile, was still desperately laboring to support herself and Bill, whom she ill-advisedly was nudging into the family profession. (Ambivalent about acting, Bill made a few movies, sold used cars for a while, and finally found his showbiz niche playing Paul Drake on the Perry Mason TV series.) Probably the most money Hedda ever saw during this bleak phase was from the life-insurance policy she collected on DeWolf when he died in the mid-30s. Her fee for acting plummeted—and she was lucky to scrape together two or three movie parts a year. In 1932, at the urging of L. B. Mayer's powerful assistant, Ida Koverman, Hedda ran unsuccessfully on the Republican ticket for a county political seat. She failed miserably as an actor's agent and, with nothing to lose, went with Bill back East, where she briefly returned to Broadway in Bea Kaufman's Divided by Three. This theatrical engagement did nothing to resuscitate her career, but it did make a monumental differ-

ence to a fledgling actor she befriended in her show—Jimmy Stewart—whom Hedda dispatched to MGM to be put on contract.

Hedda's prospects had sunk so abysmally low that, back in California in 1935, she nearly signed on as manager of a male-escort service. Around 1936, Paramount hired Hedda to work in a more appropriate capacity, teaching English to its newest import, the Polish tenor Jan Kiepura. "I believe that was the last thing she did before she became a columnist," says George Sidney.

Hedda, by nature more cynical about Hollywood than Louella—who, says Roddy McDowall, "wallowed in phony sentiment"—reflected that in their town "if you have guts enough to stick it out, and even a modicum of ability, you'll wear down Hollywood's resistance." Ironically, it was while Hedda was nestled deep in the magnanimous bosom of Hearst and Davies that the obdurate "resistance" of Hollywood to Hedda Hopper began to melt away. During a visit to Wyntoon, the pseudo-Bavarian Hearst compound in Northern California, Hedda was entertaining her fellow guests—including Eleanor "Cissy" Patterson of Hearst's Washington Herald and Louella Parsons—with a scintillating stream of chatter about Hollywood stars. "Why don't you write that?" Patterson suggested. "Write?" Hedda protested. "I can't even spell!" Patterson proposed that she simply dictate a weekly letter over the phone, for which she would receive $50 per week. Louella, secure on her lofty throne, thought so little of this new development that she reported colorlessly in her October 5, 1935, column, "Hedda Hopper engaged to do a weekly Hollywood fashion article for Eleanor Patterson . . ."

Louella was right, at least for the moment, not to feel menaced. Hedda's Washington column stopped after only four months, when the novice newspaperwoman refused to have her pay cut by $15 a week. The stint on Patterson's paper, however, turned out to be a valuable warm-up for her real break, which came early in 1937. The Esquire Feature Syndicate, which had been searching for a Hollywood columnist, called upon Andy Hervey of MGM's publicity department for a recommendation. He suggested Hedda Hopper, aged 52, with the caveat that she might not be able to write, "but when we want the lowdown on our stars, we get it from her." Luckily for Hedda, one of the first papers to pick up "Hedda Hopper's Hollywood" was the Los Angeles Times, a morning paper like Louella's Examiner. "No matter how well syndicated a writer was, if he didn't have a local outlet, no one in the industry considered him very important," explains producer A. C. Lyles.

In order to place Hedda emphatically on the map, her old MGM ally Ida Koverman threw a hen party in her honor, to which all the town's most accomplished journalists, publicists, and actresses (Joan Crawford, Claudette Colbert, Norma Shearer) were invited. One guest, Louella O. Parsons, swept in, turned on her heel, and exited in a huff. "Louella never really dreamed at first that Hedda could ever become serious competition," says Dorothy Manners. "But then, neither did Hedda."

Manners feels that MGM's reasons for handing Hedda her poison pen were perfectly honorable. "She was past the age of a leading lady, and they wanted to give her a job. It made sense—she had a great entrée into the world of the studios." But others (including Louella) took a dimmer view, saying that L. B. Mayer, with the blessing of other studio chiefs, cagily set Hedda up as a columnist to offset Louella's monopolistic power. Observes gossip columnist Liz Smith, "The studios created both of them. And they thought they could control both of them. But they became Frankenstein monsters escaped from the labs."

If Louella at first felt that by ignoring it, her new competition would go away, she soon came in for a rude awakening. In 1939, Hedda buried "Love's Undertaker" with a world-class scoop, the divorce of the president's son Jimmy Roosevelt (a Goldwyn employee), who was involved with a Mayo Clinic nurse, from his wife, Betsey. This was no mere column item, but a coveted "cityside" story splashed across the country on front pages. Hedda had ferreted out the story by employing what would become a time-honored method—dropping in on her victim unannounced in the middle of the night.

The feud between the two women was composed in equal parts of charade, sport, and vitriol. "Hedda was more inclined to see the battle as funny—as a great publicity builder. She understood that it was good for business," Manners says. "But Louella really hated the whole thing. And she saw Hedda as a rival in every possible way, even down to the clothes she wore." But, according to Richard Gully, Louella might have tolerated the flamboyantly hatted interloper if her animosity had been fueled solely by professional jealousy. "The true story of the famous feud is that it started for personal reasons," he says. "Hedda always referred to Doc Martin as 'that goddamn clap doctor,' and that's what really infuriated Louella."

Hedda's and Louella's power derived as much from the stories they withheld as from those they ran in their papers and broadcast on their radio shows. "They never ratted on Katharine Hepburn and Spencer Tracy," says Gavin Lambert. "And they never mentioned a word about Norma Shearer's affair with Mickey Rooney. Mayer put a stop to that—and then forced her to take the 'nice' part of Mrs. Stephen Haines in *The Women*." Perhaps not coincidentally, MGM gave Hedda the small but juicy part of society reporter Dolly de Peyster in the same movie.

Because of the "moral turpitude" clause in all the stars' contracts, which called for automatic cancellation if an actor misbehaved, "the studio bosses used Louella and Hedda as a weapon of intimidation to keep their employees in line," Lambert continues. "But if there was a real problem with a star, they could almost always buy these women off"—either through an exchange of information, or indirectly with cash, as when Twentieth Century Fox purchased the rights to Louella's 1943 memoir, *The Gay Illiterate*, for $75,000. (The picture, needless to say, was never produced.)

What remain deeply seared in the collective Hollywood memory, however, are those vindictive, destructive stories that the two women elected, for whatever reasons, to publish. In 1943, a high-strung redhead named Joan Barry burst into Hedda's offices in the Guaranty Bank building on Hollywood Boulevard, sobbing that she had been impregnated and then discarded by Charlie Chaplin. The columnist, who fancied herself a guardian of female virtue, went gunning for the priapic comedian, who consequently found himself on trial in a hugely publicized paternity suit. (Though the court ruled that Chaplin was not the father, he was nevertheless forced to pay child support.) In retaliation, Chaplin presented Louella with the scoop of his marriage to 18-year-old Oona O'Neill later that year. Hedda, defending her role in the Barry-Chaplin debacle, insisted that her intention had been to issue "a warning to others involved in dubious relationships." This admonition was so effective, Hedda maintained, that at a cocktail party she had only to wag her finger at one producer for him to terminate an extramarital fling.

Simply disapproving of a romance, even if there was nothing murky about it, was sufficient grounds for Hedda to attempt to torpedo it. When erstwhile costumer Oleg Cassini was dating Grace Kelly, Hedda ran an item which, Cassini recalls, "basically said, 'Of all the handsome men in Hollywood, why is she seeing Cassini? It must be his mustache.' Hedda hated Europeans. She was a real America Firster. Well, I responded with a letter which said, 'I give up. I'll shave my mustache if you shave yours.'"

Louella also ran interference with Grace Kelly when the actress began an affair with the married Ray Milland while they were shooting *Dial M for Murder* in 1953. Since her marriage to Docky, Louella had grown more Catholic than the Pope. Every Sunday she showed up for 9:45 Mass at the Church of the Good Shepherd, often still drunk from the night before, and she was god-

mother to a whole brood of Hollywood offspring, including Mia Farrow and John Clark Gable. Outraged that Kelly, a well-brought-up Catholic, could be so flagrantly compromising her honor, "Louella broke the story," Richard Gully says. "And Grace backed away from Milland, but it nearly ruined her career."

In an even more potentially dangerous move, Hedda tattled on Joseph Cotten for trysting with juvenile star Deanna Durbin while they were working together on *Hers to Hold* (1943). "Cotten was never going to leave his wife," says Leonora Hornblow. "They were just having a little fun." Hedda's exposé was "extremely painful to Lenore Cotten, Joe's long-suffering wife," but her husband got revenge for both of them. "There was some huge event going on in the Beverly Wilshire ballroom. Joe saw Hedda across the room and came toward her, saying, 'I've got something for you.' He kicked right through the gold party chair she was sitting on, and its legs buckled. The next day Joe's house was full of flowers and telegrams from all the people who would have liked to kick Hedda in the backside but didn't have the courage. Joe pasted the telegrams on his bathroom wall."

Probably the most devastating character assault ever to blaze over the newswires was Louella's immolation of Ingrid Bergman after she left her husband, neurologist Peter Lindstrom, in 1949 to live in Italy with director Roberto Rossellini. This information alone, innocuous as it may seem today, caused a worldwide uproar. In 1945, Bergman—thanks to Hedda's crusade on her behalf—had been cast as the angelic Sister Benedict in *The Bells of St. Mary's*. Her holiness thus established before the public, Bergman in 1948 stepped into the title role of Victor Fleming's *Joan of Arc*. Shocked to find that their saint had turned sinner, the press denounced Bergman in editorials, and audiences boycotted theaters showing her pictures. But the *coup de grâce* came when Louella detonated the most explosive ammunition of all. Early in 1950, the *Los Angeles Examiner* ran on its front page, above Louella O. Parsons's byline: INGRID BERGMAN BABY DUE IN THREE MONTHS AT ROME. This story of the gestating Bergman-Rossellini love child created, Louella estimated, "the greatest [sensation] ever, I believe, in relation to a story about a movie personality." So unexpected was this electrifying *Examiner* headline that other reporters, including Hedda, castigated Louella and Hearst for printing what they presumed to be an already disproved canard. That evening, Louella found her husband in his bedroom, bent piously over his rosary beads. The doctor explained, "I'm . . . praying your story is right."

Louella was right, of course—as Roberto junior's birth incontrovertibly proved—because she had been informed of Bergman's pregnancy by an unimpeachable source, whose identity she never revealed. She referred to him in her 1961 memoir, *Tell It to Louella*, as "a man of great importance not only in Hollywood, but throughout the United States." Dorothy Manners sighs deeply and then releases the long-held secret. "Howard Hughes tipped her off. And here's why. Hughes was producing films at RKO, and he had bought some play or book for Ingrid that he desperately wanted to make into a movie for her. At that moment she was the hottest thing in pictures. Ingrid was so crazy about Rossellini that she agreed to a contract with Hughes—but only if he would produce Rossellini's movie *Stromboli*. Hughes accepted these terms, and *Stromboli* was a huge bomb. Hughes then asked her to come back to America immediately to work on his movie. She told him, 'Honestly I can't—I'm pregnant.' And he was incensed. It meant it would take at least a year to recoup his losses from *Stromboli*. He then called Marion Davies and told her to tell Louella, who at first didn't print the news. When Hughes asked Marion why not, she said, 'My God, Ingrid's married to another man. This could bring about the biggest lawsuit against Hearst.' So Hughes himself verified the story of the pregnancy with Louella. He was so furious during that telephone call, I could overhear him shouting into Louella's phone. After that call, the story ran."

Most of the time, Tony Curtis maintains, Louella and Hedda "couldn't touch the major players. It was the young people coming up who suffered the most. I'll never forget a call I received one day from Hedda, on the studio phone." Like an inquisitor before an auto-da-fé, she grilled Curtis: "God help you if you lie to me, but are you going out with a

Hat-mad Hopper and Hearst's society editor Princess Conchita Pignatelli greeted Sophia Loren, seated, left, and Louella Parsons at a 1957 affair.

PHOTOGRAPHED IN 1957
BY **RALPH CRANE**

teenager?" Curtis says, "The way she invoked God—it was as if she were speaking morally for Him. It was frightening. I didn't know what the consequences would be. With Hedda you knew pretty much where you stood. But there was something uncomfortable about Louella—as if deep down something was grinding away, some secrets, maybe, from her past. And I was sure everybody was a spy. We all felt that Hedda's son, Bill, was a spy. No one wanted to be his friend."

It was not just individuals who provoked the wrath of these two harpies—they preyed on pictures and whole studios too. When MGM gave the lead in its 1934 costume drama *The Barretts of Wimpole Street* to Norma Shearer instead of Marion Davies, "on Hearst's instructions, there was no mention of the movie or of Norma Shearer for a year in Louella's column," says Gavin Lambert.

Louella inflicted more serious and lasting damage on Orson Welles and *Citizen Kane*—and in the process nearly derailed one of the greatest masterpieces ever to emerge from Hollywood. Upon hearing the rumor that Welles's first production with RKO was to be a *film à clef* about her boss, Louella lunched with the "boy genius" and listened to his litany of evasions and denials—all of which she believed. Soon after, Hedda, who had been offered a small part in the picture, managed to talk her way into its first screening. Instantly recognizing that the film was inspired by her friend Marion Davies's millionaire lover, Hedda passed on the information to Hearst, twisting the knife by adding that she couldn't comprehend why Louella hadn't already alerted him. Enraged, Hearst ordered Louella to attend a screening with two lawyers. Horrified by what she saw, Louella rushed out of the studio screening room to cable Hearst, who telegraphed back the terse message STOP CITIZEN KANE. Springing into action, Louella warned RKO that she would expose long-suppressed tales of "rape by executives, drunkenness, miscegenation and allied sports." Further, it was hinted, the American public would be informed that "the proportion of Jews in the industry was a bit high." Refusing to capitulate to Hearst's pressure, RKO chief George Schaefer—who had also been threatened by Hearst with legal action—announced that *Citizen Kane* would open in February 1941 at Radio City Music Hall. Louella hastened to call Radio City's manager, Van Shmus, advising him that exhibiting the film would result in a total press blackout. The premiere was then canceled. Louis B. Mayer, siding with Hearst (whose Cosmopolitan Pictures had been affiliated with MGM), next made Schaefer an unusual offer: he would pay the rival studio $805,000 in exchange for burning the master print and all copies of the film. Schaefer stood firm and refused to cooperate. Finally, after the Hearst press launched a savage attack on Welles, falsely accusing him of Communism, the tide turned and Welles and the movie began attracting sympathy, especially from such Hearst adversaries as Henry Luce, founder of *Time* and *Life*. Taking advantage of the general turmoil, which had turned into a publicity bonanza, RKO at last released the picture in May 1941. And though the movie was a critical triumph, Welles, branded a troublemaker, never quite recovered his position at RKO or in Hollywood again.

If RKO failed to make it up to Orson Welles, the studio did its best to appease Louella. In 1943, her daughter, Harriet, who had been toiling as a producer at Republic Studios since 1940, was awarded a long-term contract with RKO. Curiously, Louella and Hedda had an unspoken truce regarding their children. When the mannish Harriet married effeminate publicist King Kennedy at Marsons Farm, Louella's San Fernando Valley estate, in 1940 ("Truly a marriage of Louella's convenience," one wag says), Hedda was among the guests. Bill Hopper received glowing commendations in Louella's column. And it was Hedda's raves for Harriet's *I Remember Mama* (1948) that brought about the celebrated reconciliation at Romanoff's that year. Baffled observers theorized that Louella and Hedda had reached an understanding that, with mothers like themselves, these kids needed all the help they could get.

The two women, of course, extended help to many people outside their family circles; flaunting their power meant interspersing malevolent behavior with flashy displays of benevolence. In the early 40s, when Joan Crawford had been labeled box-office poison by the Theatre Distributors of America, "MGM dropped her," recalls publicist Warren Cowan, co-founder of Rogers & Cowan and now chairman of Warren Cowan Associates. Undaunted, producer Jerry Wald tapped her to appear in *Mildred Pierce* (1945)—and hired Rogers & Cow-

an to promote the tarnished star. In a press release, Cowan says, he wrote the following item: "The front office of Warner Brothers is jumping with glee over the first two weeks' rushes of Joan Crawford in *Mildred Pierce*. They're predicting she'll be a strong contender for the Oscar." To Cowan's extreme surprise, Hedda ran the item verbatim, turning the story into an "exclusive." (Explaining her indulgence toward Crawford, Hedda said, "I knew what being out of a job meant.") Then, Cowan says, "various versions of it spread around. Just before the Academy Awards, we took out an ad in the trades, reproducing that item from Hedda's column. It was the first time an ad was run directed to the Academy. That one item became the foundation for the Academy Awards campaigns which now companies spend hundreds of thousands of dollars on each year." Cowan speculates that as a result Joan Crawford won the Oscar. "And that was the power of one columnist and how it mushroomed," Cowan concludes.

For a Hollywood unknown, a summons from Louella or Hedda was tantamount to a wave of Glenda the Good Witch's wand. When Warner's child actor Jack Larson was 17, "Hedda decided to do a piece just about me," Larson recalls. "Bob Reilly, head of publicity at Warner's, told me, 'Your career is made!' I was strictly rehearsed until it made me crazy. I was told not to mention anything about how I was studying drama with Michael Chekhov, a Russian, because Hedda was so anti-Communist she'd turn on me. But she ended up being very nice to me. If Louella or Hedda liked you and plugged you, it really could help."

Their column mentions "became a sort of currency of the time," Roddy McDowall explains. "Agents would use them as contract-negotiating tools. To prove your value you could show the studio books of clippings." Adds Tony Curtis, "You only knew how good you were doing by your appearances in their columns. There was no other measure."

So closely scrutinized were the two women's daily write-ups that lyricist Alan Jay Lerner tracked down, met, and married starlet Nancy Olson after Hedda ran a "little item with a picture of me at the end of her column," she recalls. At the time, Olson was working on Billy Wilder's *Sunset Boulevard* (1950), in which Hedda played a cameo role. "The original plan," Wilder says, "was to have Hedda and Louella, after Joe Gillis's murder, try to telephone their papers at the same time from Norma Desmond's house. One would be on the phone upstairs, trying to file her report, while the other cut in downstairs on the same line. There'd be a wild, crazy fight between the two of them, with lots of foul language. It would have been a very dramatic moment, a lot of fun. But it turned out to be one of my very few defeats in the movie. Louella declined to appear, because Hedda was a very good actress and Louella knew she would steal the scene."

As the studio system began to break down, and actors, abetted by a new breed of agent demanding huge fees and greater independence for clients, began wresting control of their lives away from studio bosses, the Parsons-Hopper hegemony over Hollywood might have toppled. But in fact both women adjusted and adapted as necessary, branching out to the new medium of television. Hedda even dared to go up against Ed Sullivan on Sunday night with an NBC program, *Hedda Hopper's Hollywood*. They published more books of memoirs, all commercial successes. No up-and-coming younger columnist even brushed the hem of their garments—in Louella's case often an Orry-Kelly, Adrian, or Jean-Louis design, and in Hedda's a Mainbocher, perhaps, with a hat from John Frederick's or one made by a fan.

They lived as well as or better than the stars they wrote about. Hedda spent a tax-deductible $5,000 a year on her signature headgear alone. In addition to clothes, Hedda had a weakness for Bristol glass, which she displayed abundantly, along with her millinery, in the eight-room house she had bought in 1941 on Beverly Hills' Tropical Avenue. "This is the house that fear built," she would announce to visitors.

Financially somewhat better off than Hedda, Louella kept two houses, the one at 619 North Maple Drive, where she worked, and her Valley residence (with a peach-and-blue bathroom paid for and decorated by neighbor Carole Lombard, and a patchy lawn sometimes filled in with fake grass from a studio prop department). And even after Docky's death Louella had another comfort unavailable to Hedda—a man in her life, in the person of songwriter Jimmy McHugh. A fellow Catholic, he gave his constant companion a gift that she literally idolized: an illuminated 10-foot Virgin Mary which Louella enshrined in her backyard. The couple was a fixture at parties, premieres, and such nightspots as Dino's Lodge on Sunset Strip, where Louella could be seen "drunk and peeing on the floor" while the house picked up the check, says impresario Allan Carr.

The most conspicuous proof of Louella's and Hedda's ongoing sovereignty occurred every year at Christmastime. "Your car had to get in line at their houses to deliver presents," recalls producer A. C. Lyles. Inside, their homes were so glutted with gifts, they "looked like giant cornucopias, with presents tumbling out of closets, walls, and floors," remembers Tony Curtis.

Dorothy Manners reflects, "I can't imagine why people were so scared of Louella. But they certainly kowtowed to her. Louella, you see, was not just a columnist. She was a corporation. There were seven columns a week—Sunday was a whole section with a rotogravure. She had the radio show *Hollywood Hotel.* And then she had the Sunday-night East and West Coast gossip show with Walter Winchell—people didn't move when they were on the air. There were her articles for *Modern Screen* magazine, which I ghosted—she split the $1,000 she received monthly with me. And every year and a half we'd do a five- or six-week tour of *Louella Parsons's Stars of Tomorrow,* playing all the country's most glamorous movie houses. Just to give an idea, one year we had on tour with us Susan Hayward, Robert Stack—and Ronald Reagan and Jane Wyman, when they were beginning their romance." (According to George Sidney, Stack recently said that he joined the journalist's vaudeville troupe because Louella cautioned, "If you don't do it you'll never work again.")

In an effort to stay up-to-date, both women raced to cultivate new protégés. Jimmy McHugh made a point of introducing Louella to all the newly minted teen musical heartthrobs—Fabian, Bobby Darin, and her personal favorite, Elvis Presley. To tap into the same rock 'n' roll youth culture, Hedda enlisted the help of George Christy, then hosting his ABC radio show *Teen Town.* She developed a particular affection for Steve McQueen, who won her over by "treating her like a chorus girl." Hedda also fussed over Ann-Margret, says Allan Carr, who managed the actress in the early 60s. "She gave her motherly advice, but Hedda probably got more out of it than Ann-Margret did. Times were changing, the country was changing, and so were the movies. Hedda and Louella just didn't have the influence over the new young audiences that they had had 10 or 20 years before."

Louella, who had already begun to show signs of severe physical deterioration, suffered a cruel blow when the *Los Angeles Examiner* folded in 1962. Though her column was switched to the Hearst afternoon paper, the *Herald-Express,* she thereby lost her edge to Hedda's morning *Los Angeles Times.* Still, Louella carried on, going out every night bejeweled and bewildered, like a dowager empress whose country had overthrown her rule, tottering unsteadily on the arm of Jimmy McHugh. And despite rumors of her imminent retirement, by day she put together her column with more than a little help from Dorothy Manners and other assistants.

Drop-in gossips and would-be stars were always welcome at Hopper's office, located at the town's epicenter: Hollywood and Vine.

Finally, in 1965, blighted by further medical problems, Louella retired. Dorothy Manners took over the column and gradually substituted her byline for that of the great Louella. At 84, this living fossil of Hollywood's golden age was installed in a Santa Monica rest home. There she was attended by a private nurse, paid for by the Hearst corporation.

Hedda—once described by *Time* magazine as "blessed with eternal middle age"—carried on in perfect health straight into the mid-60s. But—estranged from Bill and Joan, her granddaughter—Hedda, warding off loneliness, insinuated herself into the cozy family life of her neighbors, filmmaker Bob Enders and his wife, Estelle. At Christmas the four Enders children helped her dig into her mountain of presents. One year a gift came from Kirk Douglas, whom she had refused to speak to for a long time. Hedda called to thank the actor, but before she did she turned to Bob and Estelle and admitted, "I've been a bitch."

Hedda had one last crack at the movies—a minor part in the sudsy melodrama *The Oscar.* Regally elegant at 80 in a jeweled gown and the kind of towering Dairy Queen hairdo that she used to preserve overnight with rolls of toilet paper, Hedda made a brief but memorable appearance. The last word she uttered on-screen was "Bye." On a Friday night early in 1966, producer Bill Frye and Rosalind Russell stopped by Hedda's house on Tropical Avenue for a cocktail. "[Photographer] Jerome Zerbe had invited us all to dinner at Chasen's," Frye says. "Hedda had on a hat and suit and she looked marvelous. Then I looked down and saw she was wearing bedroom slippers. Hedda explained, 'I don't feel up to it. If you go out, you should give. If you can't give, you shouldn't go out.' It was a kind of motto."

Hedda, who never overstayed her welcome at parties, had another motto: "Go before the glow fades"—and so she did. The following Monday, before the release of *The Oscar* and two months after Louella's official retirement, she died of complications from double pneumonia. Harriet, feeling it her duty to inform Louella of Hedda's death, visited her ailing mother at the Santa Monica rest home. "Mother, I have something to tell you," Harriet said. "Hedda died today." This announcement was followed by a long silence, then a look of confusion, and then another long silence—finally broken by the exclamation "GOOD!" And that, says Roddy McDowall, "was her last cogent word."

Louella lingered on for six more years, a decrepit, mute relic who most of the world assumed was dead. During her incarceration, "she went into a complete silence," says Dorothy Manners. "She just lay there, with no reaction, utterly expressionless." Another person close to Louella's circle says that "in her room she watched TV a great deal—sort of. Her mind was so gone, she'd sit transfixed, watching *snow* on television. It was the Twilight of the Gods."

"At the end," says Gavin Lambert, "Louella and Hedda looked more and more like bizarre dinosaurs." As with these extinct behemoths, no other creatures ever rose up from the swamp to replace them. Dorothy Manners retired in 1977, Aileen Mehle turned down offers to continue both columns, and Joyce Haber had a run at the *Los Angeles Times,* but was dropped. Liz Smith reflects, "L.A. is now a town with no gossip column. No one wants to let these demons loose again." And to all those fearful of demon columnists, past or future, Hedda had this to say: "They should know what I *haven't* written!" □

THE PRODUCERS **First row:** Lawrence Bender (*Reservoir Dogs, Pulp Fiction*), Bonnie Bruckheimer (*Beaches, For the Boys*), Art Linson (*Melvin and Howard, The Untouchables, Casualties of War, Dick Tracy, This Boy's Life*), David Brown (*Jaws, The Verdict, The Player, A Few Good Men*), Dino De Laurentiis (*King Kong, Ragtime, Blue Velvet*), Lili Zanuck (*Cocoon, Driving Miss Daisy*), Richard Zanuck (*Jaws, Cocoon, Driving Miss Daisy*), Ray Stark (*Funny Girl, The Way We Were, The Sunshine Boys, Peggy Sue Got Married, Steel Magnolias*), Danny DeVito (*Reality Bites, Pulp Fiction*), Stacey Sher (*Reality Bites, Pulp Fiction*), Lynda Obst (*The Fisher King, Sleepless in Seattle*), Wendy Finerman (*Forrest Gump, I Like It Like That*), Lawrence Gordon (*48 Hrs., Die Hard, Field of Dreams*), Edward R. Pressman (*Badlands, Wall Street, Reversal of Fortune*). **Second row:** Stanley Jaffe (*Goodbye Columbus, Kramer vs. Kramer, Fatal Attraction, The Accused*), Denise DiNovi (*Heathers, Edward Scissorhands, Batman Returns, Little Women*), John Davis (*The Firm, Grumpy Old Men*), Brian Grazer (*Splash; Parenthood; Liar, Liar; Apollo 13*), Michael Shamberg (*The Big Chill, A Fish Called Wanda, Reality Bites, Pulp Fiction*), Joel Silver (*Lethal Weapon, Die Hard, Demolition Man*), Don Simpson (*Flashdance, Beverly Hills Cop, Top Gun*), Jerry Bruckheimer (*Flashdance, Beverly Hills Cop, Top Gun*), Gale Ann Hurd (*Aliens, The Abyss, Terminator 2: Judgment Day*), Lee Rich (*The Sporting Club, The Choirboys, Passenger 57*), Robert Evans (*Chinatown, Marathon Man, Urban Cowboy, Sliver*), Lauren Shuler-Donner (*Mr. Mom, St. Elmo's Fire, Dave, Free Willy*), Arnon Milchan (*Brazil, The War of the Roses, Pretty Woman, JFK, Under Siege, The Client*). **Third row:** Arnold Kopelson (*Platoon, Falling Down, The Fugitive*), Mario Kassar (*Total Recall, Terminator 2: Judgment Day, Basic Instinct, Cliffhanger*), Steve Tisch (*Risky Business; Corrina, Corrina; Forrest Gump*), David Foster (*McCabe & Mrs. Miller, The Getaway [1972 and 1994], Tribute, The Mean Season*), Robert Rehme (*Necessary Roughness, Patriot Games, Beverly Hills Cop III*), Mace Neufeld (*The Omen, No Way Out, The Hunt for Red October, Patriot Games*), Steven Reuther (*Dirty Dancing, Pretty Woman, The Mambo Kings, The Client*), Lawrence Turman (*The Graduate, Pretty Poison, The Getaway [1994]*), Roger Corman (*Boxcar Bertha, Big Bad Mama, Grand Theft Auto, Rock 'n' Roll High School*). PHOTOGRAPHED IN 1995 BY **FIROOZ ZAHEDI**

SOPHIA LOREN AND **JAYNE MANSFIELD**
A neckline plungeth and out pops envy. Never has a still from a Hollywood party (this one snapped at the fabled Romanoff's) better captured the almost gravitational tug of interstellar curiosity and awe. Here actress Jayne Mansfield, having placed strategic dabs of makeup on her nipples, gets the twice-over from Sophia Loren, who in her day elicited her own share of astonished responses.

PHOTOGRAPHED CIRCA 1957
BY **JOE SHERE**

JEREMY IRONS Mr. Ironic, in Oscar-winning form (*Reversal of Fortune*), is shown here doing his impression of Claus von Bülow doing *his* imitation of Queen Victoria. And we *are* amused. There's been no letting up since Jeremy took the role of Charles Ryder in *Brideshead Revisited*, parlaying gaunt melancholy into roles as diverse as Polish guest worker (*Moonlighting*) and quasi-incestuous Tory M.P. (*Damage*). Off-track briefly as blond terrorist in one of the *Die Hards;* sighs of sophisticated relief when he reappeared as Humbert Humbert in *Lolita*.

PHOTOGRAPHED IN 1990
BY **HELMUT NEWTON**

TIM BURTON The caped crusader must also know the uses of enchantment; not since cartoonist Charles Addams has anyone been able to make the child-ghoul seem cute—or Christmas seem as ghoulish as it sometimes can be. Here, the creator of frightful delicacies such as *Pee-wee's Big Adventure, Beetlejuice, Batman, Edward Scissorhands,* and *The Nightmare Before Christmas* explores another of his gothic-comic head trips, on the set of *Sleepy Hollow.*

PHOTOGRAPHED IN 1999
BY **MARY ELLEN MARK**

ORSON WELLES Sent the nation into a panic on Halloween eve 1938 with his radio broadcast of H. G. Wells's *The War of the Worlds;* consistently breached the boundary between reality and art thereafter—by depicting his own marriage to Rita Hayworth in *The Lady from Shanghai* and, most notably, by making William Randolph Hearst think that he was actually the model for *Citizen Kane,* the great publishing beast depicted in Welles's masterpiece, the film many purists consider the finest ever made. (Welles, *left,* took on the role himself.) Darting and later lumbering from one side of the camera (*The Magnificent Ambersons*) to the other, he brought Shakespeare to the screen by playing and directing *Macbeth, Othello,* and the Falstaff saga *Chimes at Midnight;* as Harry Lime in *The Third Man,* he was just as successful conveying a touch of evil. PHOTOGRAPHED IN 1941

GEORGE CUKOR AND *THE WOMEN* The man who directed *The Philadelphia Story, Gaslight, Winged Victory, Pat and Mike, A Star Is Born, Let's Make Love,* and *My Fair Lady* is seen here with his fair ladies from *The Women* (written by *Vanity Fair* alumna Clare Boothe Luce): Florence Nash, Phyllis Povah, Rosalind Russell, Joan Crawford, Norma Shearer, Paulette Goddard, Mary Boland, and Joan Fontaine. (Cukor's great discovery Katharine Hepburn was not in the picture.) Probably the most sweeping shot ever taken of a Hollywood "walker," reigning with his queens. PHOTOGRAPHED IN 1939

NICOLE KIDMAN She can play an intellectual or an heiress, and has done so in *Days of Thunder* (1990) and *The Portrait of a Lady* (1996). She has combined the elements of policy wonk and action babe in *The Peacemaker* (1997), which inaugurated the DreamWorks logo. And she has been known to disrobe to startling effect, as in *To Die For* and *Eyes Wide Shut*, where she featured with her husband, Mr. Cruise.

PHOTOGRAPHED IN 1997
BY **ANNIE LEIBOVITZ**

CARY GRANT "Warm, dark, and handsome," purred Mae West, having invited him to come up and see her sometime in *She Done Him Wrong*. She got him right. He was the essence of the leading man and the definition of Hollywood Anglophilia. Hitchcock noticed that this graceful ex-acrobat could also be sinister and passionate (*Suspicion, Notorious, North by Northwest*) after the rest of the world saw he could be charming and witty (*His Girl Friday, Holiday, My Favorite Wife, Bringing Up Baby*). Not awarded an Oscar until the rightly embarrassed Academy gave him one—for everything—in 1970.

PHOTOGRAPHED IN 1934
BY **GEORGE HOYNINGEN-HUENE**

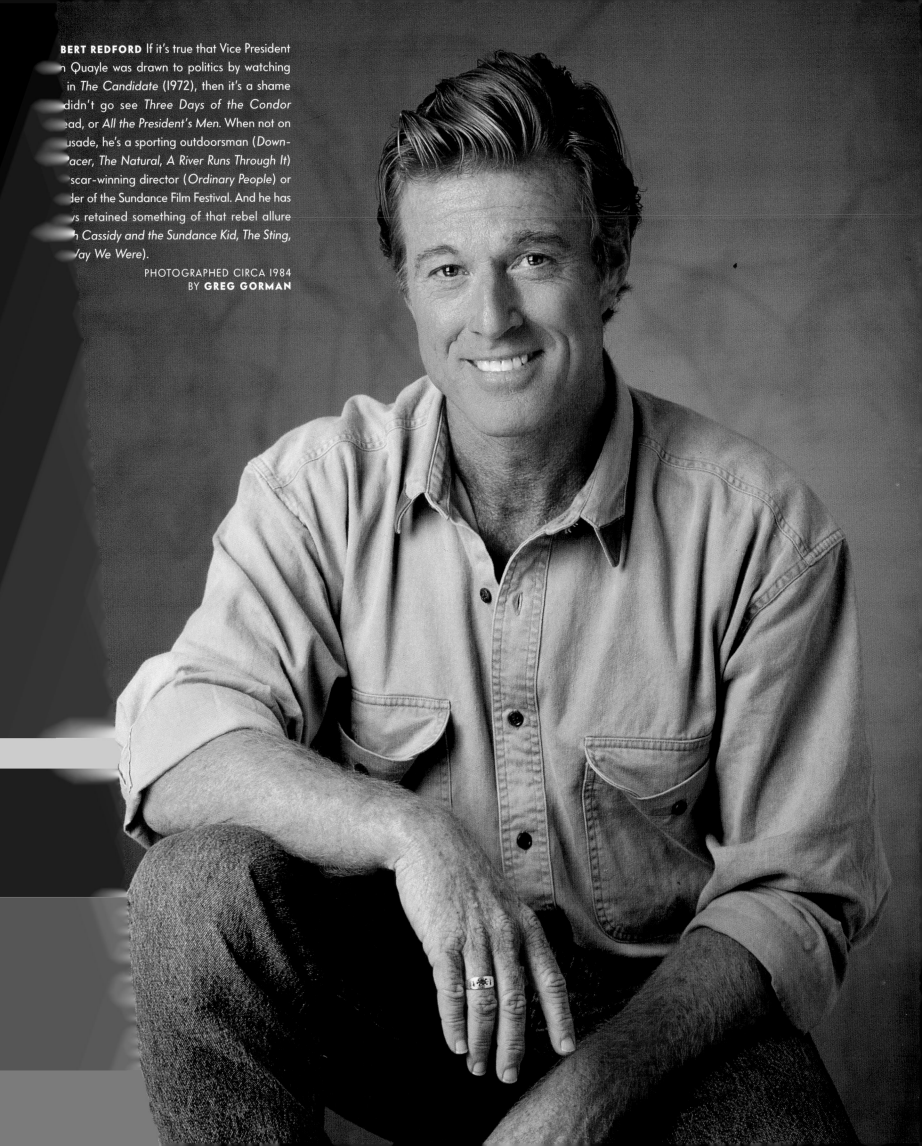

ROBERT REDFORD If it's true that Vice President Dan Quayle was drawn to politics by watching him in *The Candidate* (1972), then it's a shame he didn't go see *Three Days of the Condor* instead, or *All the President's Men*. When not on a crusade, he's a sporting outdoorsman (*Downhill Racer, The Natural, A River Runs Through It*) or Oscar-winning director (*Ordinary People*) or founder of the Sundance Film Festival. And he has always retained something of that rebel allure (*Butch Cassidy and the Sundance Kid, The Sting, The Way We Were*).

PHOTOGRAPHED CIRCA 1984
BY **GREG GORMAN**

JENNIFER LOPEZ When Gregory Nava decided that there were Latina stars overdue to be born in East L.A., and therefore cast Bronx native Señorita Lopez as Maria Sanchez in *Mi Familia* (1995), he keyed the ignition for *Money Train*, *Blood and Wine*, and *Selena*. Her culminating role was as the cop from heaven in Steven Soderbergh's 1998 adaptation of Elmore Leonard's *Out of Sight*: Miami naughty, but still Miami nice.

PHOTOGRAPHED IN 1998
BY **FIROOZ ZAHEDI**

WOODY ALLEN There is a cinematic link that connects us to the edgy world of Mort Sahl and Lenny Bruce, and he is seen at right impersonating Groucho Marx. Fatalistic, ironic, hyperbolic Allenesque humor (at its apex in *Annie Hall*) has become, like bagels, part of the national intake: the name *Manhattan* a synonym for civilization and its discontents. Barring Chaplin and Keaton, no American comedian-filmmaker has been free to play *auteur* for longer (30 films in 30 years).

PHOTOGRAPHED IN 1972
BY **IRVING PENN**

THE DIRECTORS **First row:** Wolfgang Petersen (*Das Boot*), Quentin Tarantino (*Pulp Fiction*), Lawrence Kasdan (*Body Heat, The Big Chill*), Penny Marshall (*Big, A League of Their Own*). **Second row:** Alan J. Pakula (*All the President's Men, Presumed Innocent*), Oliver Stone (*Platoon, JFK, Nixon*), Herbert Ross (*The Turning Point, Steel Magnolias, Boys on the Side*), Billy Wilder (*Double Indemnity, Sunset Boulevard, The Apartment*), Richard Donner (*Lethal Weapon, Maverick*), Barry Levinson (*Diner, Rain Man, Disclosure*), Warren Beatty (*Heaven Can Wait, Reds*), John Singleton (*Boyz N the Hood*), Norman Jewison (*In the Heat of the Night, The Hurricane*), Ron Howard (*Cocoon, Parenthood, Apollo 13*), James L. Brooks (*Terms of Endearment, Broadcast News*). **Third row:** Tim Burton (*Batman, Edward Scissorhands*), Tony Scott (*Top Gun, Days of Thunder*), Sydney Pollack (*The Way We Were, Tootsie, Out of Africa*), Ivan Reitman (*Ghostbusters*), Barbra Streisand (*Yentl, The Prince of Tides*), Robert Zemeckis (*Forrest Gump*), Andrew Davis (*The Fugitive*), Mel Gibson (*Braveheart*). **Fourth row:** Adrian Lyne (*Fatal Attraction, Indecent Proposal*).

PHOTOGRAPHED IN 1995
BY **ANNIE LEIBOVITZ**

By Margaret Case Harriman

Not long ago a writer whose work appears in the more skeptical magazines called to interview Joan Crawford. Joan arranged herself against a charming background and unleashed the movie star's customary monologue. "I hate dishonesty and insincerity," she told the writer, "but I love animals and little children." When she went on to say a great deal about life and love, and what was the matter with this sad world, he became acutely restless. "You don't seem very interested," Joan said, looking at him carefully. "Are you suggesting that my opinions about life are not important to the world in general?" The writer shrugged politely. "Well," said Joan, relaxing, "why the hell didn't you say so in the first place?"

To people who know her, there is nothing phony, no brittle assortment of fine mannerisms, about Joan. She never falls into any depressing attitudes of refinement; she puts her elbows on the table, scatters cigarette ashes around, and, on occasion, swears like a lady. She is a rather grave girl on the whole, curiously compelling to be with, perhaps because of her spectacular gift for listening. She has a knack for giving her entire attention to the people who talk to her, so that, transfixed by those astonishing eyes and by the air of expectancy which surrounds her, they begin to glow and to feel that they are being pretty interesting, after all. Entirely self-taught, she is never stilted, because everything she does is the result of a study so eager and so minute that it has come to be natural to her. She was born into an obscurely threadbare family in San Antonio, Texas, and went to work first as a telephone operator in the Oklahoma town to which her family moved when she was about 14 and, later, as a salesgirl in a Kansas City department store. The family name was Cassin, and she was known as Billie Cassin. The Cassins were always desperately on the move, and when Billie decided that she wanted to be a dancer, she got a job in the floor show at the Friars' Inn in Chicago, and went from there to the Oriole Terrace in Detroit. Finally reaching New York, she danced in the chorus of a Shubert show at the Winter Garden, and at Harry Richman's Club. She was about 18 then, and had thought up a stage name flossy enough to suit her own taste at the time. It was Lucille Le Sueur. Le Sueur had been her mother's maiden name, but the Lucille was her own idea. When a Metro-Goldwyn scout saw her and engaged her to come to Hollywood to work in pictures, the studio decided that her adopted name was too fancy and too hard to pronounce and, in collaboration with a movie magazine, conducted a contest to find a new name for her. A Mrs. Louis M. Artisdale of Rochester, New York, won the first prize of $500 by inventing the name Joan Crawford.

In Hollywood, Joan set out to bring herself to public attention less by her work in pictures than by a continuous nightlife that would have put most girls under the sod. In less than two years she had won 84 cups in nightclub contests for dancing the Charleston, or for imitating Bee Jackson, the shimmy expert. She was, then, undistinguished in appearance from any other good-looking girl, except by her curiously arresting eyes. She hid the fine structure of her face by pulling her brown hair onto her cheeks and over her forehead, and by a careless mask of makeup. Later, she dyed her hair a flaming red and rolled her stockings not quite far enough above her knee-length skirts. A good many Californians go around in sport clothes during the day, and when Joan made her first visit to New York as a Hollywood star, she appeared on Fifth Avenue and at lunch in fashionable restaurants in backless dresses with shoulder straps. When she became engaged to Douglas Fairbanks Jr., nobody was surprised at the definite raising of eyebrows that greeted the news at Pickfair, the home of Douglas's father and Mary Pickford. In those days Pickfair was referred to by other Hollywood residents, not without respect, as Buckingham Palace, and Mary and Douglas were acknowledged king and queen of the film colony. Other women stars rose and stood politely when Mary entered a room, and no premiere of a picture in a Hollywood theater was allowed to start until Mary and Douglas were in their seats. The marriage of the red-haired bombshell into Hollywood's reigning family startled columnists everywhere into reviving the old story of the prince and the beggar's daughter. In the excitement, nobody noticed that Joan's improvement upon herself, which was to become calculating and relentless, had started some time before.

Because it had seemed a good idea at the time to be a hot-cha girl, Joan had concentrated on being the hottest hot-cha girl in town. She had, however, a stark streak of discernment in her. When she perceived that there were higher goals for a Hollywood star, she set out, with the same tireless concentration, to learn everything that seemed necessary. She took lessons in voice, diction, and French every day, and still does. She gave away her collection of long-legged dolls, souvenirs of nightclub parties, and began gravely to collect old silver and china. When she found out that it was pretty silly to collect antiques without knowing about them, she read a lot of books about silver and china. She progressed, by stages, from a houseful of fairly pally servants to a Scandinavian couple, laconically correct. She modified her hair to a deep shade of auburn, and learned to buy clothes from good dressmakers in Paris and New York. The dresses in her own wardrobe, now, are a good deal less extreme than those she wears in pictures. Off the screen she wears no makeup except lip rouge. When she stopped using powder, a year or so ago, her defiantly shiny face turned out to be a success. It seemed to be the cleanest face in Hollywood. She scrubs it every night with soap and water and looks more attractive, ready for bed, than many women more expensively anointed. Her speech, trained by continual study, is carefully modulated, but never seems affected, because her manner is entirely direct. She has a shrewd eye and ear for nuances. In the course of her merciless observations she fell upon a great truth one time when she said, over a bowl of crackers and milk, "It's funny, you can always say that your foot hurts, and it sounds all right, but if you say that your feet hurt, it sounds perfectly lousy."

Joan is as house-proud as any suburban matron who ever got into a pretty flush over a new icebox. She puts away her linen herself when it comes home from the laundry. (If that sounds like a press agent's notion, it is only the fate to which a good many curious facts are doomed.) Her reasons for putting away her own laundry are simple: she worked hard to acquire fine linen, and she likes to handle it and to know, each time, that she has got it all back. If a towel or a sheet is missing, she knows which one it is. She changes the whole aspect of her house in Brentwood Heights, outside of Hollywood, about once a year, adding wings, transplanting trees and gardens in a fine frenzy. A month or so ago, a woman from New York who had frequently dined at Joan's house last year returned to Hollywood and was asked to dinner again. She drove past the entrance twice. Since her last visit it had been transformed from a Spanish hacienda into an early-Colonial dwelling. Inside, these days, the house is all white; the walls, the furniture, the grand piano, and the carpets are white, softened by accents of color here and there in paintings, luster, and old glass. Joan has an upstairs sitting room, a dressing room made chiefly of mirrors and shoe closets, and a sleeping porch built around a gigantic four-poster bed. Any guest in the house is instantly taken on a tour, including the kitchen, which is as big as most living rooms.

Joan gives more thought to the meals served in her house than a good many housewives do who have nothing much else to think about. She is one of the few women anywhere who know enough about good food to serve thin cucumber sandwiches with mountain trout. Often, if she has to rush to the studio in the morning without seeing to the menu, she telephones from the set and reminds her cook of what Mr. Franchot Tone [the third of her five husbands] would like to have for dinner, or, perhaps, of a dish which she

JOAN CRAWFORD From dancer to actress: Joan Crawford was the Jazz Age flapper personified in *Our Dancing Daughters* and *Dance, Fools, Dance;* she twirled with stars such as Douglas Fairbanks Jr. (her husband for a time) and Clark Gable, while becoming a star herself. Breaking free of the ingenue trap, she won an Oscar as *Mildred Pierce* in 1945, and her second screen career—as ambitious striver, sufferer (*What Ever Happened to Baby Jane?*), and occasional vamp—seems to have been more like the real Joan.

knows to be a favorite with Helen Hayes, Jean Dixon, Fred Astaire, or whoever happens to be a guest that evening. Joan has four servants —a Finnish butler and his wife, and two maids—and their rooms are decorated as carefully as the average guest room in a country house. Last summer, when the house was done over, Joan made all the draperies and curtains for the servants' rooms. She sews during every available moment and wastes no time on frivolous trifles, preferring something big and serviceable, like a hooked rug or a curtain. The skeptical, who remember Joan as Hollywood's hey-hey girl, may consider such concentration on housewifely duties a little labored. Any hard-boiled cracks can be answered only by the tranquil statement that Joan doesn't have to impress her fans by doing any of those things. Press agents are gifted people, and could easily make the general public conscious of Joan as a housewife by publishing pictures of her with an eggbeater in one hand. The truth is that Joan likes to order meals and to make curtains, and that such chores are doubly important to her because she knows that attractive surroundings created by herself are a long step toward the goal she has set for herself, of being a woman of effortless taste and distinction.

Joan's salary is about $5,000 a week, and she gets—after her income tax and her agent's fee are paid—about $1,800. She is revered by tradesmen as a customer who pays her bills as soon as they are rendered. Except for six or eight cups of coffee a day and about a package of cigarettes, her diet is spartan. She is always conscious of the way that she appears to her public, and is continually concerned about her face and figure. When she is working on a picture, she drinks a cup of hot water when she is called at six o'clock, has fruit juice and coffee for breakfast, a salad for lunch, and dinner without white bread or potatoes. She drinks wine now and then, but no hard liquor. At dinner parties given by Joan and Franchot Tone, the guests gather in the music room before dinner, on stools along the bar, while Franchot goes behind to mix cocktails. Joan wanders around happily enough with a glass of sherry. Once she saw a row of women sitting on stools along a bar, and the contours where each lady met the stool frightened her. Since, she has taken her sherry standing up. □

PARAMOUNT'S BOYS Sylvester Stallone, Michael Eisner, John Travolta As Paramount's president from 1976 to 1983, Eisner—who would take over Walt Disney's empire the next year—was buoyed by his cunning and his boyish exuberance, as well as a brood of stepmoguls whose ranks included Jeffrey Katzenberg, Don Simpson, and Dawn Steel. Typifying his bravado: Eisner paired two fleet-of-foot mega-stars, Stallone (*Rocky*) and Travolta (*Saturday Night Fever*), in *Staying Alive*.

PHOTOGRAPHED IN 1983
BY **ANNIE LEIBOVITZ**

NORMA SHEARER AND **IRVING THALBERG**
An arrival from Canada, Shearer was acting in *The Stealers* (1920) when she was first noticed by Thalberg, who found her again upon becoming the boy wonder at MGM. (According to *Vanity Fair*, 1932, *she* thought *he* was the office boy.) Love, then marriage, overcame this. She went on to master three great roles—Elizabeth Barrett Browning (in *The Barretts of Wimpole Street*), Juliet (in 1936, the year of Thalberg's death), and *Marie Antoinette*; she also shone in ensemble (*The Women*). Pity she turned down the chance to play Scarlett O'Hara and *Mrs. Miniver*: no coming back from that.

PHOTOGRAPHED IN 1932
BY **EDWARD STEICHEN**

MERYL STREEP No actress of her era has been more in demand—or more in command, with 12 Oscar nominations to show for it. You wanted to rush in and save her in *Sophie's Choice* and *Silkwood*. Yet death did not become her, or vice versa, and she proved she didn't need any help in either *Defending Your Life* or *The Bridges of Madison County*. Has been the difficult woman from *Manhattan* to *Kramer vs. Kramer* to *Plenty* to *Heartburn*: puts men on the defensive; makes many just marvel. PHOTOGRAPHED IN 1982 BY **ANNIE LEIBOVITZ**

GLORIA SWANSON G-L-O-R-I-A! By all means. She bewitched Joseph Kennedy, made *Male and Female* for DeMille in 1919, and became a French marquise by marriage. All while the films were still silent. But it's as N-O-R-M-A that we remember her: exiled queen of Billy Wilder's *Sunset Boulevard*, that strip of broken dreams. Having gone bust making *Queen Kelly* with Erich von Stroheim, she lived to prove that the butler did it. The movies didn't really get small. Then again, neither did she.

PHOTOGRAPHED IN 1928
BY **EDWARD STEICHEN**

HOLLYWOOD ISSUE COVER, 1998 From left: Joaquin Phoenix, Vince Vaughn, Natalie Portman, Djimon Hounsou, Cate Blanchett, Tobey Maguire, Claire Forlani, Gretchen Mol, Christina Ricci, Edward Furlong, Rufus Sewell.

PHOTOGRAPHED IN 1997
BY **ANNIE LEIBOVITZ**

GRACIE ALLEN AND **GEORGE BURNS** George used to pull on his cigar to keep his sanity as his wife, Gracie, scattered her brains and malapropisms all over the set. Together they made 13 feature films (including *Love in Bloom* and *College Swing*). She appeared without him in *Mr. and Mrs. North,* and made a daffy presidential run—on the Surprise Party ticket—in 1940. As a result of her death in 1964, it took him a while to be funny again, in *The Sunshine Boys* (his Oscar, in 1975), or funny enough to play the Supreme Being three times thereafter.

PHOTOGRAPHED IN 1933
BY **LUSHA NELSON**

BEN STILLER Comedians changed the kid's diapers (his folks are humorists Jerry Stiller and Anne Meara); laughing jags have rattled his crib ever since. Young Ben (here ministering to a model) directs devilish satire (*Reality Bites, The Cable Guy*). Favoring a slightly fried, post-electroshock look on-screen, he's excelled as the hapless antihero who gets the girl in the end (*There's Something About Mary, Mystery Men*).

PHOTOGRAPHED IN 1998
BY **ROBERT MAXWELL**

CHRIS ROCK Everyone who mourned the retirement of Richard Pryor has cheered up no end at the rise of Chris Rock, who, soaring above such schlock as *Beverly Hills Ninja* and such stereotypes as *New Jack City*, has burst out of the small screen, grabbed the mike and center stage, and, in *Dogma*, challenged the received ideas of, and about, black America.

PHOTOGRAPHED IN 1997
BY **SAM JONES**

183

STEVE MARTIN The Woody Allen of Los Angeles, writing, directing, and producing himself as part clown, part victim, part nuisance, part stand-up. Encouraging symptoms of insecurity and egomania (*The Jerk, The Man with Two Brains, All of Me, Dirty Rotten Scoundrels, Parenthood, Bowfinger*). Able to rework old genres to imaginative effect (*Pennies from Heaven, Dead Men Don't Wear Plaid, Roxanne*). Perhaps too much of a lonely guy to do buddy movies (*Three Amigos!; Planes, Trains and Automobiles*). PHOTOGRAPHED IN 1995 BY **ANNIE LEIBOVITZ**

W. C. FIELDS King of the curmudgeons; famously disliked children and small dogs; brilliantly opted to die on Christmas Day 1946, though not in his preferred Philadelphia. Superb as Micawber in Cukor's *David Copperfield* (1935), Fields generally favored his own vehicles, such as *The Bank Dick*, *It's a Gift*, *My Little Chickadee*, and *Poppy*. Born William Claude Dukenfield and fast with a pseudonym, he was at different times Mahatma Kane Jeeves and Otis J. Criblecoblis.

PHOTOGRAPHED IN 1925
BY **EDWARD STEICHEN**

By Peter Biskind

S"ue Mengers is dead!"

The voice on the phone is deep, sandpaper-rough, too many cigarettes, too many deals. It is immediately recognizable, if you've heard it even once, as the voice of Sue Mengers, very much alive but not feeling all that well, in a worse humor even than usual. This is how it's been since 1996, when her husband of 23 years, Jean-Claude Tramont, died of cancer and she entered a tunnel that led to radiation therapy for cancer of her own on top of quadruple-bypass surgery and then her mother's death—a tunnel from which she has yet to emerge. She's definitely not up to talking, certainly not about herself in the 1970s, when she was famous throughout the Western world as the first "superagent," the agent who could pick up the phone and reach anyone, who could make things happen, and a woman to boot, and funny, very funny. *That's* the Sue Mengers who's dead, ancient history. Why dredge up those stories people have heard a thousand times? And the other Sue Mengers, the one rattling around the house in Beverly Hills, who's interested in her? She rarely goes out, puts off would-be visitors with excuses, lies around reading novels and watching television, rarely even bothering to dress. She was going to write her memoirs, but discovered that calling up the past depressed her even more than she was already. "Memory lane is O.K. if you're currently happy," she mutters. "If you're not, it's a reminder of things that are never going to be again. I'm not feeling good about myself. You got me on a bad day."

"It's always a bad day."

"I'm bored with myself, I'm too fat, I'm going to lose some weight, call me back then."

The "late" Sue Mengers was the anti–Mike Ovitz. Or, rather, Ovitz—who followed in her diminutive footsteps in the 80s, when most of the drugs were flushed and the business finally became a business—was the anti-Mengers. Blonde, zaftig, and abrasive, always a great quote, she was a magnet for the media, a star in her own right, as famous as some of her clients, which eventually became a problem. There was nothing buttoned-down about Mengers. What you saw was what you got. She kvetched, she kvelled, she wheedled, flirted, and threatened like no one else, and she usually got her way. In the prime of her career, a span which lasted a good 10 years before her world crashed around her, she represented nearly everybody who was anybody. As her friend David Geffen puts it, "She had the greatest client list of any agent in Hollywood." Her stable included most of the top-of-the-line actresses of the era, first and foremost among them Barbra Streisand in her glory days, when her voice could make strong men weep; but also Ali MacGraw in hers, before Steve McQueen put her in front of a stove; Cher; Cybill Shepherd; Candice Bergen; Faye Dunaway; and Dyan Cannon; as well as a handful of important male stars such as Ryan O'Neal, Burt Reynolds, Gene Hackman, Tony Perkins, Michael Caine, and Nick Nolte. She also represented many of the blue-chip *auteurs* of the director's decade, men such as Arthur Penn, Peter Bogdanovich, Mike Nichols, Brian De Palma, Sidney Lumet, and Jonathan Demme. "You couldn't do a movie without Sue," says John Calley, who was a top Warner executive throughout the 70s and today heads Sony Pictures Entertainment. "When you'd have a problem, you'd go to her, and she would make it go away. She was the Man."

"The Man." Mengers was the first woman to breach the boys' club that ran the town. "They can talk about Dawn Steel—whatever," says Toni Howard, now an agent at International Creative Management and once a

colleague of Mengers's, "but there is only one woman that broke the ground for women, and that was Sue." The industry's powerful male executives treated her like an equal. She counted among her friends Robert Evans when he headed production at Paramount, Barry Diller when he later ran the same studio, and Calley, who went so far as to take Mengers along on his honeymoon in 1973. She was famous for her parties, which were de rigueur for anyone who was happening or hoped to happen. They were such select, star-studded affairs that Bogdanovich once had to drag Cybill Shepherd by the arm up Mengers's driveway because she was afraid to go in. At one such event, Johnny Carson is reputed to have griped, "God, there are too many stars here, not enough sycophants!"

Larger than life, outrageous, and gifted—some would say cursed—with the tongue of an asp, she became a legend in her own time. According to a chapter about Mengers in the late Paul Rosenfield's book *The Club Rules,* when Sharon Tate was murdered by the Manson family in 1969, Mengers reassured Streisand, "Don't worry, honey, stars aren't being murdered. Only featured players." She once said, "I was so driven I would have signed Martin Bormann." When Sidney Lumet was a hot director she called him at midnight to pitch a client. Lumet told her, "If you're this pushy, I want you to be *my* agent." She was the model for Dyan Cannon's impersonation of a loudmouthed agent in the 1973 film *The Last of Sheila,* a Hollywood whodunit written by Stephen Sondheim and Tony Perkins. Her friends called her a female Billy Wilder.

Naturally, the most acerbic commentator on the Mengers legend is Mengers herself. "Mostly these stories are made up," she complains. "One story David Geffen loves to tell is about when I was a receptionist at the William Morris office and an ape act was brought in and put in the waiting room with me." Geffen does indeed like this story, and, as told to me, it goes like this: The act, famous in its day, was the Marquis Chimps. Their trainer had come to the office with one of his apes to meet with his agent, Harry Kalcheim, who also represented Elvis Presley. In Geffen's telling, "The trainer went to the bathroom, left the monkey, and as he came out he heard Sue saying to the chimp, 'Ooh, little monkey, want to fuck Baby Sue?' He grabbed the chimp, ran into Kalcheim's office, yelling, 'Your receptionist just tried to fuck my monkey!,' and tried to get him to fire her." Thinking about it, Mengers rolls her eyes and exclaims, "Can you imagine?"

The good times, inevitably, came to an end. Bergen walked in the late 70s, so did MacGraw, and in 1981, Streisand left too. After that it was a hemorrhage, and Mengers never recovered. It was Ovitz time. His Creative Artists Associates, with its corporate-lockstep style, would gain a stranglehold on the industry. While Mengers had created a family, he built an empire.

Why Mengers fell from grace when other, lesser agents survived seismic changes in the business and are still working remains something of a mystery. What happened between Mengers and Streisand may never be fully known. Most of her old clients don't call anymore; the only people she seems to see or talk to regularly are Geffen and Fran Lebowitz. She keeps up with the trades and watches the Oscars on television. The small group of intimates

Sue Mengers, the first superagent—and the 70s' bawdiest power broker—relaxed at a Beverly Hills wedding in 1978 with then Paramount chief Barry Diller.

who watch with her has gradually diminished. Last year she watched alone.

Chris Mankiewicz, a former studio executive at United Artists and Columbia and a scion of the famously talented family of writers and directors—he is the son of Joe (*All About Eve*) and the nephew of Herman (*Citizen Kane*)—puts it this way: "I grew up with agents and movie stars, and none of them had the kind of charisma she had. When she walked into a room or when she sat down to talk to you, she was just the best. What happened to her, and why she didn't go on forever, is a story."

Mengers's house is Beverly Hills Georgian, or maybe it's architect John Woolf's L.A. version of Greek Revival—architectural styles are notoriously fungible in Southern California. The house was built in the 1950s in a mini-monumental style that makes it resemble a dressed-up mausoleum. Mengers is a cozy girl, yet her house is anything but. She seems like a stranger among the scattering of Biedermeier pieces. The tall windows at the back of the living room look out on an exquisite oval pool she never uses.

Although it is two o'clock in the afternoon, Mengers looks as if she's just gotten out of bed. She's dressed in a loose-fitting, comfortable, otherwise nondescript garment that could be anything from one of the muumuus she favored in the 70s to a nightgown. She lights a cigarette and solicitously offers me a tuna-fish sandwich, then says, "Do you want to come into my bedroom, big boy? I took out some pictures." She shows me photos of her late husband, adding, sourly, "I guess I must have been happy once."

Then it's into the den to watch a tape of a memorable *60 Minutes* profile of her done in 1975. I'm on the Mengers museum tour. Before she hits the play button, and just as the features of Gloria Swanson in *Sunset Boulevard* are beginning to swim before my eyes, she says, with a noise more like a bark than a laugh, "I feel like I've become Norma Desmond, showing my old pictures." This is very Sue Mengers: in the business or not, healthy or ill, she's always there a beat before you, dead on target.

And then, after a hiccup of video, her image is on the television screen, perky and blonde, with the familiar round face, upturned nose, and signature oversize glasses, 25 years younger and somewhat thinner, charming Mike Wallace and explaining how it was that this kid from the Bronx became the Queen of Hollywood. "I was a little pisher, a little nothing making $135 a week as a secretary for the William Morris Agency in New York," she purrs on the tape. "Well, I looked around and I admired the Morris office and their executives, and I thought: Gee, what they do isn't that hard, you know. And I like the way they live, and I like those expense accounts, and I like the cars.... And I suddenly thought: That beats typing."

It did beat typing, and Mengers made it sound easy, but that was just part of the legend she was weaving around herself. The truth is: It was hard. It cost her.

Sue Mengers was born in Hamburg, Germany, at some point in the 1930s. (She won't say just when.) Both her parents had been well-off. "They never really had to work," she recalls. "They lived the middle-class life." Mengers describes her father as a "spoiled playboy." Like the parents of others who made careers in Hollywood—Bogdanovich and Nichols come to mind—hers fled the Nazis. The family's fortunes reversed, her mother wanted to go to Palestine with her relatives, but "not my father," she continues. "He wanted to go to America, gold in the streets. So they came here, without knowing a word of the language. It was very tough for people who weren't used to toughness. It was too tough for my father. He was a door-to-door salesman."

Mengers's family left Europe in 1938 and joined a small enclave of struggling refugees in Utica, New York. Her mother was distant and proper, rarely affectionate. "She was a very domineering woman," Mengers recalls. "He was a lot more fun than she was." But when Sue was in early adolescence, her father killed himself. "He ran into some money problems, and he was reduced to going to friends, none of whom were wealthy. And rather than face my mother and say, 'I don't have that $100,' or whatever, he went to New York, checked into a Times Square hotel, and the rest is foggy to me. I think it was pills. I don't think he shot himself. He never left a note. Or if he did, I never got it. It must have been such a shock that I blocked it all out. Except I'm getting angrier at him as I grow older. I told Dustin Hoffman that when I went to see him in *Death of a Salesman* I had every intention of going backstage, but I was

so upset by it that I couldn't. My father *was* Willy Loman." She pauses. Then: "God, I hate to talk about myself. How do you like the tuna fish?"

According to the Rosenfield book, Mengers moved with her mother, by now a bookkeeper, to the Bronx. In 1955, she answered an ad for a receptionist at MCA, the powerhouse talent agency run by Jules Stein and Lew Wasserman (which later bought Universal and divested its agenting business). Mengers worked at MCA for a couple of years, until she was unceremoniously given the boot for failing to summon an agent from the men's room to take a call from Tyrone Power. From there she went to the smaller Baum-Newborn agency. Again she was frequently in trouble. Her boss, Marty Baum, "had a roaring temper and Sue was a total fuckup," according to Tom Korman, then a young agent, now a manager. An indifferent typist, she was not cut out to be a secretary, and Baum, Korman told Paul Rosenfield, "must have fired her 50 times. One day an actress, who was our client, was supposed to audition for *The World of Suzie Wong,* and nobody could find her. Sue, only Sue, knew she was having an affair with a married musician. Sue was in sheer panic from Marty Baum screaming at her every three minutes.... Finally she called the musician at home, and a woman answered. Sue said, 'You old sneak! I found you.' Well, of course, it was the musician's wife. And Marty Baum fired Sue once again."

Her next job was as secretary to Charlie Baker, head of the theater department at the William Morris Agency. One of his clients was Gore Vidal, who had a hit on Broadway called *Visit to a Small Planet.* Vidal, who became a good friend of Mengers's and eventually a client, remembers her from those days: "She had an outer office, he had an inner office. She was very flirtatious. One day I popped in to see Charlie, and suddenly I said, 'Oh, I've got to go,' and opened the door to his office, nearly putting her eye out as she was down peeping through the keyhole, or with her ear to the keyhole—I never could get her to admit which it was. In due course, she left the Morris office and went to work for another agent."

The other agent was Korman, who had left Baum-Newborn in 1963 to start his own agency, Tom Korman Associates. That same year he wooed Mengers from Morris by offering her her first job as an agent. Korman's shop started out with only three clients: the fading movie star Joan Bennett; Claudia McNeil, who had appeared in *A Raisin in the Sun;* and the writer-actress Lillian Roth, whose memoir *I'll Cry Tomorrow* had been adapted into a hit movie in 1955. But Korman Associates quickly became known as the Jolly Robbers, for the boldness with which it purloined clients, or, alternatively, the Relative Wrong agency, as in dancer-actress Marge Champion instead of Gower, actress Jocelyn Brando instead of Marlon.

Vidal continues the story: "I believe she took Charlie Baker's Rolodex. She had everybody's phone number, and as she had been listening to everything that was going on, she was perhaps the most knowledgeable agent in the business." She wooed people such as Tom Ewell, who was then a big Broadway star, with *The Seven Year Itch* and a lot of other plays to his credit. In those days, actors would come in early, before their matinees, and have lunch at Sardi's, where Mengers would troll for clients. One afternoon, Mengers stopped by Ewell's table, dropped her business card in his water glass, and said, "Hi, I'm Sue Mengers, I met you with Charlie Baker, I'm now on my own, I just want to be frank with you—I'd love you to be our client." According to Vidal, "Ewell said, 'What can you do for me that [my agent] Abe Lastfogel can't do?' She said, 'Fuck David Merrick!' With that, a star was born. She got him, too."

At the time, Merrick, the powerful producer of such Broadway hits as *Gypsy* and *Hello, Dolly!*, and the film director Otto Preminger (*Laura, Anatomy of a Murder, Exodus*) were "the two most formidable, frightening names to agents," according to Mengers. "But Merrick would take my calls because he knew I would be either amusing or I'd give him a free idea. When *Hello, Dolly!* opened, I called David and gave him a list of replacements, from Ginger Rogers on down, and in fact I tried to get Ginger Rogers to let me negotiate it for her. I thought I would faint on the way up to her suite in the elevator. And there she was, sitting behind a tray, sipping coffee, and she never even offered me a cup. She made me feel—ugh."

In 1967, Preminger was directing *Hurry Sundown,* and Mengers was trying to sell him on one of her male clients. Preminger was a liberal, famous for openly employing blacklisted writer Dalton Trumbo on *Exodus.* As she recalls, "He said to me, 'Miss Mengers, your client is a fairy!' Of course he was, but I said, 'Oh, Mr. Preminger, that's not true—I've been to bed with him.' I would go that far, yes. I wish I could say he gave the guy the part, but he didn't. He may have broken the blacklist, but gay was verboten in movies."

One of Mengers's clients was Constance Bennett, Joan's sister and a fading star in her own right. Mengers knocked herself out to get Bennett into her "comeback" film: *Madame X* (the umpteenth remake of a 1908 French melodrama), which starred Lana Turner and Ricardo Montalban and was produced by Ross Hunter. Instead of being grateful, Bennett complained about her billing below Turner, demanding that her name be set off by a box on the ads and posters. It wasn't. Bennett, who had gotten a hefty salary, refused to pay her commission to the agency. Then, just before the movie came out, she died. Mengers sent Hunter a telegram that said, CONSTANCE FINALLY GOT HER BOX!

Mengers was shameless hustling clients. One of her favorite lines was "Get rid of that asshole your agent." She explains, "What should I have said? 'Your agent's wonderful, stay with him'? I was at times very bombastic, because I thought it was the only way I could get people to listen to me." She had two signature phrases. When she heard something that she thought was off the mark, which was often, she snorted, "HellOHH?!," as if it were the dumbest thing imaginable. Then she'd say, "I looooaathe—" and fill in the name of the movie star.

It was in 1962, while she was still a William Morris secretary, that she met a woman who would become key to her career: Barbra Streisand, then a relative unknown playing New York City nightclubs. A year later, when Mengers went into business with Korman, she began to see more of Streisand through the singer's husband, Elliott Gould, who was a client, and through Martin Bregman, Streisand's business manager, who also handled Korman's insurance. For Streisand and Mengers it was something close to love at first sight. The two had much in common, both bright, angry, ambitious Jewish girls from the outer boroughs, with fathers who had died young. The agent Abe Newborn had famously said of Streisand, "She'll never be a star unless she gets her nose fixed." But in 1964 Streisand became a nationally known figure, starring on Broadway in *Funny Girl*—despite her nose— and Mengers began to dream about signing her as a client. Though brazen with everyone else, she treated Streisand with kid gloves. According to Korman, "She was afraid to upset Barbra." Mengers would instruct her boss, "Now, don't open your mouth until [she] talks to you." Which may be the only recorded instance of Mengers counseling circumspection.

Streisand was represented by Freddie Fields and David Begelman, the co-heads of a scrappy, up-and-coming agency called Creative Management Associates, which later became one of the most powerful in the business. According to Korman, Streisand pressured Begelman and Fields to bring in Mengers to service her. Success has many fathers, however. Both Gould and Bregman say they themselves called CMA and suggested the agency hire Mengers. Fields himself doesn't remember the circumstances.

Mengers has her own, needless to say more colorful, version. Gore Vidal had introduced her to two friends of his she was dying to sign: Paul Newman and Joanne Woodward, both of whom were represented by CMA's John Foreman. Newman was a huge movie star, Woodward a cou-

Flanked by client Faye Dunaway and producer Robert Evans (who cast Dunaway in *Chinatown*), Mengers attended the 1975 Golden Globe Awards.

ple of rungs lower on the ladder, but the couple's hearts, if not their pocketbooks, belonged to Broadway. Right away Mengers recognized how she could appeal to their vanity and make trouble for their agent. "I was zetzing them all the time in my fantasy, thinking I'd get them as clients. 'Oh, Paul, you should do Strindberg. Call up Tennessee, have him write a play.' That's half of what agents do to get new clients, is to make them unhappy with their current representation. So John Foreman had to spend his time explaining to Paul and Joanne why he can't call Arthur Miller and have him write a play. Finally, John went to Freddie Fields and said, 'Will you hire that broad, what's her name, that little agent, Sue Mengers. She's driving me crazy—she keeps telling Paul and Joanne they should do theater.'" However it happened, around 1966 Mengers ended up at CMA, where she would begin her 10-year reign.

CMA was considerably less tightly wrapped than the Morris agency, its main competitor, and would come to represent most of the big stars of the 1960s and early 70s. Geffen worked there as a young agent. So did Mike Medavoy, who went on to become an executive at United Artists and Orion, then head of Tri-Star, and most recently chairman of Phoenix Pictures; Alan Ladd Jr., who later ran Twentieth Century Fox, where he gave *Star Wars* a green light; and Guy McElwaine, who headed Columbia Pictures in the 1980s. Jeff Berg, now chairman of ICM, was a trainee.

"With Freddie Fields you got the straight story," says Korman, "you always knew where you stood. David Begelman was hail-fellow-well-met, then he'd turn around and bury you." Begelman later became notorious for embezzling money when he headed Columbia Pictures in the mid-70s, and eventually he committed suicide, but in those days he was riding high, known for his golden tongue and imperial habits, rich even by Hollywood standards. (He had the detailing on his Rolls polished with a toothbrush, and in later years he was reputed to have had one of the first penile implants in Beverly Hills, of which he was immoderately proud.) Begelman knew movies and had charisma to burn. In CMA's London office he'd hold forth from behind his desk to the likes of Richard Burton, Richard Harris, Stanley Baker, Michael Caine, Roger Moore, all sitting on the floor at his feet, spellbound.

There was no better place for Mengers to learn the business than CMA. "David put a lot of time and effort into her and so did I," says Fields. "We did everything to support her and made her an important woman in the movie business. With great pride, by the way." Mengers started in the agency's New York theater department, then moved out to Hollywood in late 1968. "I loved it," she remembers. "I saw Fred Astaire walking in Beverly Hills my second day. People you just dreamed about—Lana Turner, Rita Hayworth, Glenn Ford. I was in heaven." It was a great time to be there: the giants of the studio era were still walking and talking, while a new golden age, the 1970s, was in its infancy. Right away, she was a hit. "Talent responds to enthusiasm, and I was genuinely enthusiastic about these people," she says. "They could sense that." Her secret weapon was her relationship with Streisand, who by that time not only was a huge recording and Broadway star but had also hit it big in Hollywood with the 1968 movie version of *Funny Girl,* for which she won an Oscar. "I loved her," Mengers says. "She was like family. Barbra schlepped me around when she was invited someplace, so I was given a golden opportunity to meet people, which is half the battle. You can't sign them till you meet them."

Mengers signed a young Peter Bogdanovich after seeing his debut feature, *Targets,* a zero-budget thriller he directed for Roger Corman in 1968. But her first real coup at CMA was landing Ryan O'Neal, then best known for his role as Rodney Harrington on TV's *Peyton Place,* just before the release of a picture he did for Robert Evans at Paramount called *Love Story.* Evans persuaded his new flame, Ali MacGraw, to leave her agent and sign with Mengers, too. Thus, when *Love Story* became the year's biggest hit upon its release in 1970, she found herself repping two of the hottest stars in Hollywood. That same year, Mengers shoehorned Gene Hackman into William Friedkin's *The French Connection.* Recalls Richard Zanuck, who was then president of Twentieth Century Fox, which financed the movie, "I didn't think Gene was totally right for the part. I was hoping to land a bigger star, because at that time he was a secondary player, and Billy [Friedkin] felt the same way. Sue single-handedly got him this job. She would call me three times a day, she was a relentless bird dog on this issue. I'd never been campaigned in my entire career like she campaigned for that role. She beat up on us, and we just couldn't take it anymore, so we did it. And how right she was. The picture won an Academy Award"—as did Hackman—"and he became a huge star. Gene should have a shrine [to her] in his house that he kneels before."

Bogdanovich's second feature, *The Last Picture Show,* an elegiac deconstruction of small-town life in Texas, opened in 1971 to wild critical acclaim and strong box office, which put him among the pack of Young Turk directors then challenging the Hollywood establishment. Mengers signed his girlfriend, Cybill Shepherd, a stunning former model who had made a splash in the film. Recalls Shepherd, "When our relationship began, Sue would talk to me very slowly, as if my brain was blond. She might have told me, 'Don't talk too much in an interview.'"

Mengers had finessed an early screening of *The Last Picture Show* for Streisand, who was anxious to do something serious, something "significant." She loved it, and immediately signed on for the director's as-yet-to-be-determined next feature, to be produced at Warner under Calley, which she imagined would be something in the same vein. To Streisand's dismay, Bogdanovich developed a script for a screwball comedy, an homage to films such as Howard Hawks's *Bringing Up Baby.* The actress had one foot out the door, but Mengers and Bogdanovich talked her into staying with the project, which was eventually titled *What's Up, Doc?* when it was released in 1972. "Barbra and I saw it together at the first screening, and we both thought it was a disaster," recalls Mengers. "Her manager, Marty Ehrlichman, hissed at me after the screening, 'Are you satisfied? You've ruined her career.' I flew to Klosters for Christmas. I remember Calley calling me there, saying, 'It's a smash.'" Indeed, it was—Bogdanovich's second consecutive triumph. Not that that caused Mengers to alter her opinion: "I still don't think it's so funny."

After *What's Up, Doc?,* which co-starred Mengers's client Ryan O'Neal, the agent was white-hot. As Richard Benjamin, another client, remembers, "You wanted to be with her, because she seemed to be at the center of everything." She went from score to score. Nineteen seventy-three's *Paper Moon* was Bogdanovich's third hit in a row; it also starred O'Neal, as well as his daughter, Tatum, another Mengers client (who won an Oscar for the part). Mengers secured the title role in the 1974 version of *The Great Gatsby* for Robert Redford over Jack Nicholson by convincing Evans, who was looking for a male lead to pair with MacGraw, then slated to play Daisy, that casting two brown-haired stars would make for a boring film. (Mia Farrow would eventually be Redford's co-star, leaving Evans with two blonds.) Mengers got Faye Dunaway the role of Evelyn Mulwray in Roman Polanski's *Chinatown* by telling Evans, who preferred Jane Fonda, that Dunaway was about to take an Arthur Penn film—a lie. As Mengers recalls, "Of course we got Evans's offer for Dunaway, and at the end of the conversation I said, 'Bobbee, there is no Arthur Penn picture.' And he said, 'You cunt!'"

Mengers thought it would be good for Paula Prentiss if she worked with Alan Pakula—who had had a big hit with *Klute*—and insisted she woo the director for a part in *The Parallax View,* the 1974 political thriller starring Warren Beatty. Recalls Prentiss, "Sue said, 'Hon-eee, go to lunch with him and wear very, very tight pants,' which I did. She said it was the way they do it at MGM, which is that they sew them to your underwear."

Mengers's efforts made Michael Caine a household name. In the 60s he was known for English films like *The Ipcress File* and *Alfie;* in the 70s he began to appear in Hollywood fare like Neil Simon's *California Suite.* "She was trying to get me accepted in America as being a Brit," he remembers. "Now I am kind of accepted as an American who talks funny, and that's based on Sue. Just smashing through. She was a bulldog with charm."

In 1975 she got a then astronomical $1 million for Gene Hackman to do the ill-fated *Lucky Lady* opposite Liza Minnelli and Burt Reynolds. That same year she rescued Cybill Shepherd's career after the disastrous opening of Bogdanovich's musical, *At Long Last Love,* in which Shepherd, Reynolds, and Madeline Kahn warbled Cole Porter tunes. (At the time, Gene Shalit said, "Cybill Shepherd cannot walk or talk, much less sing.") Mengers got her a part in Martin Scorsese's *Taxi Driver.* "At that time, she had icicles forming on her body," explains Mengers. "She needed to work with a director of that cachet."

Mengers had clawed her way up in the pre-feminist era, and she had no qualms about playing the gender card. One minute she would be batting her eyelashes and burbling baby talk, and in the next breath she would say something like "Fuck yourself, you little kike!" She could kill you in a negotiation, and then scold you for not opening the car door for her. She herself never thought her gender created problems for her. But younger women whom she nurtured professionally disagreed. Toni Howard, the ICM agent who represents Samuel L. Jackson and Christina Ricci, was Freddie Fields's secretary when Mengers first arrived in L.A. She recalls, "It was like Little Sue and 'the guys.' The guys tried to hold her back, not particularly Freddie. Somebody would sign some kind of ordinary person, and everybody would go, 'Oh, how fabulous!' And Sue would sign Ali MacGraw and Ryan O'Neal, and she didn't get the kind of attention somebody else would have gotten."

As cutting as Mengers could be to others, she often made herself the butt of her own jokes. If she wasn't getting enough sex, she'd complain, "Sue's cooze is cold." Recalls manager Michael Black, who worked with her at CMA and ICM, its successor, "She would be the first to make fun of her size, make fun of the fact that here is this Jew—she would refer to herself as 'this Jew'—sitting down at lunch with, say, Jacqueline Kennedy." Black regarded such extravagant displays of self-immolation as a business strategy. "If someone were likely to dish her, it undercut them if she said it about herself first," he continues. "And for someone who was intimidated by her, it relaxed them, made it easy to bond with them, get information."

She was so entertaining that Bob Sherman, the agent whose office was next to hers at CMA, used to put a water glass to the wall to eavesdrop on her conversations. He discovered that her usefulness to her clients far exceeded career advice. One day he overheard her tell someone, "You don't have to come *every* time." Says Dick Shepherd, one of the original CMA partners and Mengers's titular boss there, "She marched to her own drummer. She'd do what her instincts told her to do, and if it was done wrong, she would expect somebody to bail her out. I always said to her, 'Your instincts are perfect, but your execution sucks.'" The problem was that Mengers ignored the nuts and bolts of agenting. She would nail down a great salary, but leave the fine points of negotiating, the minutiae of the contract, to others.

Nor was she much of a team player. There was a staff meeting every Wednesday morning at CMA, which Shepherd chaired. Mengers was always late and "obstreperous," he recalls. One Tuesday night he ran into her at a black-tie function on the Warner lot. In front of a group of people, he instructed her, "Just do me a favor—try to get to the meeting on time tomorrow, nine o'clock." The next morning, 40 or so people, including several clients, were gathered in the conference room when Mengers arrived, promptly at nine, still wearing her gown and wrap from the previous night. Trying mightily to maintain his dignity, Shepherd was damned if he was going to laugh. But she dropped into the seat next to him, looked down into his lap, and said in a voice loud enough for the whole room to hear, "Dick, your fly's open."

Mengers may have been a diva, but, adds Shepherd, "she made a huge difference. A lot of the people whom we represented became clients or stayed with the agency because Sue was fun to be around. She held on to certain people that I don't think Freddie [Fields] could have kept, like Barbra. No matter how sloppy she was in her agentry work, at the end of the day, she could make things happen. I never knew anyone quite like her."

Mengers was so quotable that people dined out on delicious Sue-isms. Stevie Phillips, one of the few other female agents at CMA and a rival, was the opposite of Mengers in every respect: prim, proper, and reserved. One afternoon at someone's home—the particulars have been lost to time—Mengers was chugging along in the pool, swimming stark naked, when out of nowhere, the story goes, appeared the Greek actress Melina Mercouri, famous for her hit 1960 film, *Never on Sunday,* and her husband, blacklisted director Jules Dassin (*Naked City*). Even Mengers was embarrassed, but she stepped out of the pool with aplomb, shook off the water with a toss of her blond mane, and without missing a beat said, "Hi! I'm Stevie Phillips!"

As Vidal remembers her in those years, "she was a bit lax in the flattery department, which was interesting because that's where agents usually shine. So she was something of a relief from those agents who were always telling their clients, 'You're the greatest, baby, you're the greatest.' She would be saying, 'Take it. You may never get another offer.' Joan Collins was turning middle-aged, with children, a broken marriage, going through a bad patch. Sue said to Joan, 'Give it up. You've got enough money to live on, you've got children to raise, just settle down, forget the business.' With that, Joan left Sue and got *Dynasty,* I think just to show her up."

Mengers was her own best press agent. She couldn't resist sharing a good story. As she recalls, "A couple of days before New Year's Eve 1973, Bob Evans called me and said, 'You cannot tell anybody, this is top-secret, but Kissinger is coming here for New Year's Eve and you have to bring Candy [Bergen].' I said, 'I can't get Candy to go out with Kissinger.' 'You gotta do it, you gotta do it, he wants to see Candy.' So I called Candy. I said, 'Candy, look, it's history. The secretary of state ... we'll be with you, nothing's gonna happen.' So we prevailed upon Candice, and Bob kept saying, 'You cannot tell anybody, this is top-secret.' Well, I wasn't *not* going to tell people that I had New Year's Eve with Henry Kissinger, *intime* dinner, six people, so I called Joyce Haber, the gossip columnist at the L.A. *Times.* 'Joyce, I just want you to know on New Year's Eve ... ' Little did I know that Kissinger had told his fiancée, Nancy, that he was going to Hanoi or someplace, and that it was only when it was in the paper that she found out he was spending New Year's Eve with Candice Bergen at Bob Evans's house. That is when Nancy said to Henry, 'Marriage, or bye-bye.' So Henry called Bob, said, 'Bob, I want to thank you for helping me get married.'"

Mengers's own parties were all business. "I ran those parties like—if my mother had been outside in the rain, she wouldn't have been able to get in," she continues. At one dinner she put Ann-Margret together with Mike Nichols, who then cast her in *Carnal Knowledge.* She introduced Burt Reynolds to Alan Pakula, who cast him in *Starting Over,* a hit 1979 romantic comedy, opposite Bergen and Jill Clayburgh. Paul Schrader met Lauren Hutton and used her to play one of Richard Gere's clients in the 1980 film *American Gigolo.* Michael Black remembers taking Hutton to that particular party. "When I picked her up at the Chateau Marmont, she was wearing a long, white gauze skirt, and no underwear. I gave her my drawers and I said, 'Darling, it's one thing to walk into Sue's party and try to get this role in *American Gigolo* and look fabulous and sexy. It's another thing to give a floor show with your beaver.'"

But all work and no play makes even movie stars dull boys and girls, and, after all, it was the 70s. "The big thing was grass," Mengers remembers. "It was like a ceremony. People sat on the floor, you'd smoke a joint. Darling Annette Funicello was there one night. I thought, How great, if I can turn her on, and I handed her the joint, and she looked at me, and she laughed and said, 'Not a chance.' I turned Billy Wilder on once. He had a Thanksgiving dinner at his house/apartment. I sat between him and George Burns, and I lit a joint. Billy was always against all that stuff. He took one or two tentative puffs. And now, when I see him, I talk to him as if he were Tim Leary."

The only cloud on Mengers's horizon in the mid-70s was Jon Peters, the hairdresser who became Streisand's boyfriend in 1973. Streisand was a difficult client even on a good day. "Barbra was demanding, and it was impossible to get her to read scripts," says Mengers. "She was one major star whom you had to force into committing to a movie. The wonderful thing about her was you could say anything to her—'I don't like the way you look in this movie'—and she would listen. She wouldn't do what you wanted all the time—she was offered *Cabaret,* and I begged her to do it—but she didn't get annoyed. She only wanted the truth."

But by 1974, Peters became Streisand's de facto manager and agent (and eventually producer, beginning with the 1976 remake of *A Star Is Born*). Streisand had passed up parts in *Klute* and *Cabaret*—for which Jane Fonda and Liza Minnelli, respectively, had won Oscars—in favor of roles in pictures such as the 1972 dud *Up the Sandbox.* Peters, a full-service Svengali, took advantage of this to persuade Streisand that she wasn't receiving good enough advice. As Mengers remembers it, "I was very possessive of Barbra, and I felt Jon had a lot of self-interest [in the relationship], because he wanted to establish himself, so there were a lot of bloody battles, and Barbra let us fight them out." It didn't help that Streisand had set her heart on adapting an Isaac Bashevis Singer short story called "Yentl," which she wanted to star in—playing a boy, yet—and direct. Mengers was less than enthusiastic, not to say openly discouraging, as only she could be. "I thought of her, not as disorganized, but I was always concerned about her attention span, and [*Yentl*] was a hard, hard period picture. I never thought it would get off the ground, and it didn't, until she announced she was doing it as a musical, and you figure when that throat opens, you're home free. The minute I heard the word 'musical,' I thought, Oh, great, that's money in the bank. And I did love the picture," which was eventually made in 1983. But in the late 70s it had been an issue between them.

In the summer of 1970, Mengers had met Jean-Claude Tramont at a dinner party at the home of Henry Ford's daughter Charlotte. Tramont was a screenwriter (*Ash Wednesday,* the 1973 film in which Elizabeth Taylor gets a face-lift) and director of Belgian extraction. He was a striking man—"this tall, elegant borzoi or Russian-wolfhound-looking kind of guy, immaculately turned out," in the words of Chris Mankiewicz, who knew Tramont well and spent a lot of time with the couple.

"I was not at all interested in him," Mengers recalls. "Too good-looking. I've never liked handsome men. My attitude was: Gotta be something wrong with them. And it wasn't hard, because they didn't come calling, ya know? I think Jean-Claude was intrigued that this short, fat Jewess didn't pay attention to him.

"About a week after the dinner, he called, and I didn't recognize the name. It was the only time in my entire life that a man pursued me. And I was no chicken. I was gettin' way up there in my 30s. He's the first man who ever—not wanted me, because I had my share—who wanted *me.* He came over for a drink, and that was it." This was in June. By September they were living together.

Mengers used to tell a story about the early days of their relationship: When Tramont spent the night with her, in the morning he would complain about her snoring. She replied, "I don't snore."

"You do snore."

"I don't snore." He put a tape recorder under her bed, and, lo, when he played back the tape, the sounds of Mengers's honking filled the room. She thought, "Oh God, and he still loves me—I have to marry him! There's nobody else who would put up with that snoring."

A few months after they met, Tramont proposed to her during a flight from New York to L.A. He pretended to be drunk, said, "Why don't we get married?" She replied, "Don't be ridiculous!" That's where the matter stood until a few years later, when Calley invited them to accompany him to Greece on his honeymoon. One night, before the trip, when Mengers and Tramont were in the middle of a fight, she said to him heatedly, "If you think I'm gonna go on John Calley's boat on *his* honeymoon and not be married, you're crazy."

So in May 1973 the couple wed at Ventana, a Big Sur resort popular among the hipper elements of Hollywood. Gene Hackman was shooting a film up there, and Mengers, who was always working, even on the day of her nuptials, felt she might as well be near him in case he needed anything. The bride and groom had planned to fly up to Big Sur for an anonymous service by themselves, "like two orphans, two sad souls," as Mengers recalls. "We arrived at the airport, and suddenly Streisand showed up, a total surprise, with her then beau." This was a few months before she took up with Peters. "She became my maid of honor," Mengers continues, "and this strange guy that Jean-Claude had never met was his best man. But the whole ceremony was about Streisand. The justice of the peace, who looked exactly like Spencer Tracy, kept staring at Barbra, and the music they played was 'People.' And that night, our wedding night, Streisand and her beau joined us for dinner. She looked more like a bride than I did, and when they brought out the wedding cake, they put it in front of her! I could feel Jean-Claude's anger building. My poor husband, what he went through. But Barbra gave us the most unique wedding present. She taped German lieder for me, love songs, and, on the other side, French songs for Jean-Claude. That was so unbelievable, such a lovely, personal gift."

Once married, Mengers and Tramont did indeed accompany Calley to Greece, though he insists that the trip was actually Sue's honeymoon. In any event, Calley had recently married a Czechoslovakian former actress, and as Mengers recalls, "Olinka would get up every morning looking like Miss Czechoslovakia, the most gorgeous girl in a little bikini, and I was like Jeannie Berlin in *The Heartbreak Kid* [the 1972 Elaine May film in which newlywed Charles Grodin dumps Berlin on their honeymoon for Cybill Shepherd]. I'd come out wrapped in a towel, and my husband would look at Olinka, and then he'd look at me, just like Chuck Grodin. Olinka would jump off the boat and swim, and I'd still be huddled there."

("She's forgetting a big part of it," Calley says when I relay Mengers's account to him. "It was like word had gotten from island to island that Sue was coming, because when we pulled into port, there would be, like, 50 Mustache Petes waiting for a shot at her. She was a bit heavy, but Greek guys like their women slightly heavy, and she would put on her transparent schmatte and walk along the beach and have a line of guys following her, apparently playing with their worry beads but actually playing pocket pool, trying to get behind her so they could look through this garment into the sun, see her outline as she jiggled along in her high-heeled shoes.")

Mengers and Tramont were an unlikely match, a union of opposites if ever there was one. "Jean-Claude was this kind of aristocratic, very sophisticated, incredibly witty, incredibly cultivated person," says Chris Mankiewicz. "He was embarrassed by shows of emotion and affected considerable dislike for the vulgarity of Hollywood. He loved to talk about world affairs, which never interested her at all. She just loved Hollywood movie stars and loved all the gossip. He was this Catholic aristocrat and she was like the maid, almost, in terms of how she looked. She would like to hang around in her bathrobe, the quintessential Jewish hausfrau. What they had in common was this extraordinary sense of humor."

"My husband was a very witty guy," says Mengers, offering the ultimate compliment: "He made me sound dumb." Tramont gave vent to one of his more notorious lines while he was watching the Academy Awards on TV. Noticing that yet another Holocaust documentary had won an Oscar, he said, "There's no business like *Shoah* business!" On another occasion, a party for Sue's mother's 85th birthday, he surveyed the guests, her mother's friends, all women of advanced years, 85, 90, with their walkers, all Holocaust survivors, and exclaimed, "Schindler's B-list!" Adds Mengers, "He had me believing for a while he was half Jewish, until I found out he was full of it. But he had that kind of angry Jewish humor. He was anti-everything. It was because he wasn't being paid enough attention, because in this town you walk into a room, you're immediately judged by your accomplishments. So he became a provocateur to get attention." Eclipsed by her notoriety, he suffered from being Mr. Sue Mengers.

"Nick and Nora Charles were nothing compared to Sue and Jean-Claude," says Mankiewicz. "On a good night it was like watching two of the greatest swordsmen of France thrusting at each other with rapiers, because they were both incredibly quick, witty, and funny. [On a bad night] he was, at times, cruel to her. Sue likes to cuddle. She gets to be like a little girl at home, and she loved Jean-Claude, and she loved to snuggle up to him—she called him Moojie. And he'd say, 'Sue, stop it! Stop it!' and they'd yell and scream. He would say, 'You kike!' There were times when she was hurt by him, and she would either start crying or she would just leave. And be really pissed off."

Most of their friends were her friends, and some of her friends, the ones who loved her, didn't like the way he spoke to her. He'd say, "You're a lazy cunt," and she'd say, "Yeah, I am." But others understood that this was part of their dialogue, just the way they were together. Mankiewicz: "Once Jean-Claude and I wanted Sue, whose idea of exercise is to get out of bed and call her housekeeper to bring her some Häagen-Dazs, to work out more, so he and I set off to get a treadmill for her at a sporting-goods store. The man came over, asked, 'Are you looking for anything in particular?' And Jean-Claude looked at him and said, 'Well, yes, have you got one of these Isadora Duncan models?' I just started screaming with laughter, because the whole image was of Sue's scarf getting caught in the treadmill. It was like, how many ways can you murder your wife?

"There were a lot of women in this town who would have thrown themselves at Jean-Claude's feet if he ever left Sue. And people kept thinking, Why does he stay with her? She hasn't done much for his career. But I don't think it was ever the case that he really wanted that. This was not a marriage of convenience from his point of view. He really loved Sue, really adored her."

During an interview with Mengers in 1987, Paul Rosenfield remarked on the fact that Mengers had represented several couples—Ryan O'Neal and Farrah Fawcett, Bogdanovich and Shepherd, Prentiss and Benjamin, Jacqueline Bisset and Michael Sarrazin—and wondered whether she had been using her work to look for a family. "Don't forget," she responded, "I had no brothers or sisters, no cousins, for a long time no boyfriend, no husband. *This* was family." In Tramont, despite his caustic wit, she finally found the warmth she had lacked growing up. "He was willing to become my daddy," she says. "He was willing to take care of me. It wasn't his looks, it was the compassion that he had."

On January 27, 1979, Tramont got a collect call from Mengers's mother—"'Collect call' were the only English words she learned," says Sue—informing him that his wife's L.A.-to-New York flight had been hijacked. A woman who claimed she was wired with nitroglycerin was holding the plane hostage on the ground at J.F.K. According to Joe Armstrong, who was also on the plane—he was then the editor in chief and publisher of *New York* and *New West* magazines and is now vice president of Talk Media—the passengers were terrified. "People were on their knees praying, you saw people with their hands in their faces in fetal positions on the floor. We thought a big ball of fire could come roaring down that aisle. Except Sue. She kept saying, 'I'm keeping Candy waiting at Elaine's.' The rest of us are thinking, 'We're gonna die any minute!'"

The hijacker wanted Charlton Heston to read a largely incoherent statement on television. When Mengers heard this, she was flabbergasted. Recalls Armstrong, "Sue said, 'Charlton Heston!??'—like he's a B actor—'I can get *Barbra Streisand!*'" Adds Mengers, "But she wanted fucking Charlton Heston, no substitutes. With my luck Streisand would have said no anyway. 'Blow her up!'

"Meanwhile," Mengers continues, "Jean-Claude didn't feel like talking to my mother, so she screamed at the operator, 'She's been hijacked!' So then Jean-Claude had a dilemma. Should he fly in? If it was gonna explode, I was already dead, so who did he call for advice? Bob Evans [the marriage expert]! Bob said, 'What if she doesn't die? You gotta keep your marriage going, you better go.' So, begrudgingly, he got on a plane, figuring he'd either bring me home or my ashes."

After five, six, seven hours, in Mengers's words, "I realized, This could be serious. I'm gonna fuckin' die here, and I thought, I'm not going to go without being stoned. So I lit up a joint. Theodore Bikel, who was on the plane, took his guitar and started striding up and down, singing, 'Hava Nagila, hava Nagila' . . . There is nothing worse than Theodore Bikel. Nothing. And so I was thinking, I'm gonna die listening to Theodore Bikel, and he wouldn't fuckin' sit down and shut up. Like he's consoling us with these songs." Finally, after eight hours on the ground, an F.B.I. agent was able to overpower the hijacker and disarm her; the bomb turned out to be a phony. As the passengers disembarked, Armstrong noticed 80-odd stretchers, with bottles of plasma, waiting in a hangar while ambulances stood outside. Mengers went off to Elaine's with some of her fellow abductees, "having the best time," she adds, "and when I got to the hotel at two in the morning, there was Jean-Claude, livid."

Mengers had a great run at CMA under Begelman and Fields. But by the mid-70s, agents were leaving the business in droves, becoming studio executives and producers. "A lot of those guys just looked down the road and said, 'It's not how I want to grow old,'" Mengers explains. "Being an agent is like being in the gulag. A lot of them didn't want to spend their lives being beat up, which is what you are most of the time. I never thought of being an agent as a stepping-stone. It was the ultimate, a calling from God. I was written about so much, and made such a fuss over, I really began to believe I knew everything, and that if I ever left the business, it would collapse. I thought I was the most important person in the entire industry. It never occurred to me that the clients I really cared for could leave me. Or that they'd get old. I was totally an idiot." Begelman left to go to Columbia Pictures in 1973. Mengers, too, got offers to go to the studios. She adds, "But Freddie Fields threatened them. I may have wanted to, but I couldn't." ("I wasn't in a position to threaten any studio," counters Fields. "It was not like today. You didn't go in and say, 'You're not going to get so-and-so.'")

In 1975, Marvin Josephson's International Famous Agency bought CMA. The new mega-agency became ICM. Fields soon left for a producing deal at Paramount. At the same time, five obscure agents led by Michael Ovitz left William Morris to form CAA. With all the fire and smoke surrounding the ICM deal, no one really noticed, but an era had ended. The agency business would become considerably more regimented. Armani would replace muumuus.

Mengers had enjoyed a love-hate relationship with Begelman and Fields. "They were wonderful to me," she says, "but why not? They had a genius

Mengers, with Barbra Streisand, right—the most favored star in the agent's Hollywood stable—and Fred Glaser, then Streisand's hairdresser, in 1969.

agent working for them for scale. I was like a little puppy, I was so thrilled to be doing what I was doing. They screwed me pretty good when it came to money. There were a lot of promises, I never had stock, I was always told, 'Don't worry about it. If we ever sell the company, we'll take care of you.' Of course, they didn't, and those were my good years, so I have no love lost. If I never see Freddie again, it'll be too soon."

Says Geffen, "She really had no clue. She so completely trusted them. They always said they were going to take care of her, and they didn't. By the time they sold the agency, she had virtually no money. On some level, Sue was her own worst agent." "Sue has always been bitter about [the sale]," says Fields, "but she was unrealistic. I didn't get rich, David didn't get rich, no one got rich. The company didn't sell for that much." He adds: "Sue was treated equally with her peers."

By the late 70s, several of Mengers's oldest and biggest clients were in the grip of career crises that she was powerless to ameliorate. First there was MacGraw, still in thrall to McQueen. "As Jon and I fought over Barbra, Steve and I fought over Ali," she recalls. "They only had one telephone line in the house. I would say to my secretary, 'Get Ali MacGraw,' and the line would be busy for hours. And then, finally, the phone would ring and Steve would pick up, and my secretary would say, 'Miss Mengers calling Ali MacGraw.' He'd say, 'If she wants to talk to Ali, let her dial the phone herself!' And hung up." Eventually, MacGraw left her.

She and Bogdanovich also parted company. Bergen left after 1979's *Starting Over,* which was a hit. "She was annoyed with me because she wanted the Jill Clayburgh part, I was too negative, I was this, I was that, I was pissed," Mengers remembers. "A star is the star. They don't want their agent to be a star. And they're right. I wouldn't want to read about my lawyer and his life. But on the other hand, when you've been an unknown all your life, it's very flattering to have people call you up. It was wonderful to talk about myself. But I don't think it helped." Says Michael Black, "Historically, when Sue lost a star, she would re-sign someone two weeks later that was just as big. All of a sudden she had departures and she wasn't re-signing bigger stars to take their place."

The way Mengers treated Cybill Shepherd says a lot about her complacency in this period, not to mention her bluntness. Despite the plum role in *Taxi Driver,* Shepherd at the end of the decade had returned to Memphis (where she grew up), married a local man, and had a baby, effectively leaving the business. Then she tried to get her career back. "I couldn't get a job in TV or movies," she recalls. "The only jobs I had were singing in small jazz clubs and doing regional theater, and I was kind of desperate. So I called Sue, and I said, 'Well, Sue, would you represent me again?' She said, 'Cybill, you've been gone so long you might as well be dead.'" (When Shepherd hit it big with *Moonlighting* a few years later, Mengers approached her, but Shepherd turned her down. "I have tremendous affection for Sue Mengers," Shepherd says, "but I was already represented by someone I was very satisfied with, and I wasn't going to leave.")

Still, there was Streisand. As Black puts it, "Sue never considered Barbra a client, she considered her a sister. Even though others would come and go, she and Barbra would always be in business together." Then, in 1981, Mengers finally secured a feature for Tramont to direct, a Universal picture called *All Night Long,* an offbeat comedy about an unhappy drugstore manager with Gene Hackman in the lead, opposite Lisa Eichhorn, a promising actress who had appeared in *Yanks* and *Cutter's Way.* But several weeks into production, Eichhorn was gone, and Streisand took her place as the neglected housewife and aspiring singer with whom Hackman's character has an affair.

Tongues wagged. To Mengers's enemies, the people whose calls she never took, the people she steamrollered, the people she wounded with her tongue, the people who were just plain envious of her power, it looked as if she had strong-armed Streisand into saving Tramont's picture. People said Mengers had finally lost it. Indeed, prodding your biggest client and best friend to prop up your husband's movie could have been dangerous, even suicidal, if that is what happened. Her friends warned her that it smelled bad, but she looked at them as if they were crazy—for someone who was such a savvy agent, Mengers could be unbelievably naïve, especially where relationships were concerned. She loved Tramont, she loved Streisand, and that was enough.

According to the film's screenwriter, W. D. Richter, Hackman from the start had had his heart set on Streisand, who read the script and turned it down. Hackman was inconsolable, and made Eichhorn, Tramont, and everybody else miserable. Then Streisand changed her mind. As one source who is familiar with the players observes, "Barbra did it not for Sue, because Barbra would not do something for somebody else in a million years. She did it because she wanted to do it." Mengers negotiated a very rich deal for her: $5 million, plus 10 percent of the gross, for five weeks' work—a stunning amount at the time. Richter says that Streisand was so pleased with her compensation that she figured out how much she was getting by the hour. Also, according to Richter, she seemed quite content, required no script changes, and got along well with Tramont.

But after the production wrapped, Streisand fired Mengers, who has always denied that the movie's eventual failure had anything to do with the breach—for one thing, the call from Streisand came before the movie opened. Instead, Mengers detected the hidden hand of Jon Peters. "*All Night Long* caused a lot of strain between Barbra and Jon," she says. "Because it was the first thing Barbra had done where Jon wasn't involved. He liked to get producer credit—and this one announced to the industry: She's a free agent. Producers didn't feel, 'Oh my God, if I bring that script to Streisand, I'll have to bring in Jon Peters.' I think it was wearing her down, living with a man who hated her agent and closest friend. So ultimately she made the choice. You know?" Streisand and Peters both declined to comment for this article.

"When Barbra called to tell me that she was leaving, I was livid," Mengers says, "because I felt I had been an impeccable agent for her. And she then said, 'But we can still be friends!' My reaction was anger: 'Of course we can't be friends. You've rejected what I do, you've announced to the world I'm not good enough.' And her reaction was: 'Oh my God, she only cares about me if I'm her client.' She couldn't understand, and it hurt her for a long time. I don't think we talked for over three years. For me it was not just, 'Oh, well, I've lost a client,' which would upset me under any circumstances. But Barbra was and is very special to me. She was the jewel in the crown. Not only did I love her, I was proud to be representing her. While I was working with her it was the joy of my life, even though she never expresses gratitude or even acknowledgment of anything you may achieve. It's such a thin line an agent walks between friendship and a work relationship. You can never forget, no matter how close you are to a client, you're the employee." But in those days this was a reality Mengers didn't want to acknowledge.

In any event, by the time *All Night Long* opened, Mengers and Streisand were not speaking. Tramont's picture is a winning, underappreciated gem, but it is a small film, European in sensibility, character-driven rather than tightly plotted. It might have done well in the early 70s, but by 1981 it was too late for films like that. It flopped, unable to compete with movies such as *Raiders of the Lost Ark.* Two years later, Hackman left Mengers, too.

Mengers had always had difficulty controlling her anger. After she lost Streisand, her foot came off the brake. When clients were having difficulty finding work, she blamed them. She'd tell them to lose weight, do fewer pictures. As Geffen puts it, "Sue was famous for her 'Let's-face-it conversations.' And a lot of people don't want to face it. Sue felt she was being honest, and without intending it, she became insensitive. It was because she was so hurt herself." As Mengers once put it, "Looking over my career, I see negativity as probably my major fault." She became increasingly bitter. "None of the actors who received Oscars because of what I did ever wanted to acknowledge that I helped them get a gig," she says. "Never. Never."

In 1986, Mengers ankled ICM, as the trades would put it. "It wasn't burnout, it was blackout," she explains. "When Streisand left, I already wanted to stop working. I knew it was over. I just knew that my marriage needed more time, it was going south, and I was dispirited. I had lost more clients than I wanted to, ever, and watched other people lose theirs. Anyone else, a normal person, would have said, 'Well, Barbra left, too bad, on to the next.' I really let it affect me. And then Hackman—I didn't want that pain. I felt I was too good."

After she finally left ICM, Mengers spent the next two years getting to know her husband, enjoying the extended honeymoon she had always been too work-obsessed to have. The couple split their time between Beverly Hills and their apartment in Paris. They were good years. She had even patched things up with Streisand.

But in the end Mengers couldn't stay away from the business, and in 1988 she succumbed to the blandishments of the Morris agency, whose once potent movie division was in trouble, having been surpassed by its more forward-thinking competitors at CAA and ICM. (The famous line was "I don't have an agent; I'm with the Morris office.") Morris was the worst place she could have chosen. Hidebound, clubby, and paternalistic, it was a bastion of the golf-and-cigar culture of old Hollywood. The board members were the kind of men who put their initials on their license plates and called the female agents "girls." "I went back because I wanted the money," Mengers explains, "and I thought, Maybe I was too hasty. I'm still a young woman. But I knew I had made a mistake from the first day. You can't go home again."

While she was there she served as mentor to a group of women agents who today are among the most powerful in the business, including Toni Howard; Elaine Goldsmith-Thomas, who represents Julia Roberts, Susan Sarandon, and Tim Robbins; Risa Shapiro, who represents Rosie O'Donnell and David Duchovny; and Boatie Boatwright, who represents Norman Jewison and Joanne Woodward. Says Goldsmith-Thomas, "I learned a lot from her, because she'd always preface everything by saying, 'Don't make the same mistakes I did. I used to beat them up, I used to talk like the guys, and they hated me for it.'"

But Mengers continued to cling to old habits. For instance, she had come to prefer established stars to young talent. As Goldsmith-Thomas recalls, "When she first came in, she looked at my client list and went, 'Who's this Julia Roberts?' I said, 'Oh, she's great. She's got the lead in this movie, *Steel Magnolias,* with Sally Field, Shirley MacLaine, Daryl Hannah, Olympia Dukakis.' And she said, 'HellOHH? Do you notice a pattern? They're all well known, she's not. She's an unknown—drop her!' When I said, 'This guy Tim Robbins, whom I'm working with, is great—he wants to be a filmmaker—' 'HellOHH? Please, actors can't direct!' She now writes him notes, 'Dear Kurosawa . . .'"

Nevertheless, Goldsmith-Thomas insists, "Sue was incredibly helpful." One day, the younger agent recalls, she and Julia Roberts were at the office discussing her next film, *Pretty Woman,* with the actress insisting she wouldn't do any nude scenes. As Goldsmith-Thomas remembers it, "She had no advance warning about Sue, was not prepared for her. Suddenly Sue came in and said, 'Hello, Sue Mengers, no need to stand!' And without taking a breath, she said, 'Let me give you a little hint. This is a movie about a hooker.' Julia said, 'What do I say to my mom?' 'Tell her you're working for Disney, she'll be fine.' Julia just went, 'Uhh,' and Sue looked at her and said, 'What do you have to hide? If I had your body I'd be walking down Wilshire Boulevard [naked].'"

As entertaining as ever, Mengers was nevertheless unable to rebuild her old power base. She had expected that her former clients would flock back to her—as the Morris office had hoped when it hired her—but they didn't. "That was shocking to me," she says. "People like Sidney Lumet, we'd had such a wonderful relationship, and Nolte, and Demme, the whole list of them." Though the breach with Streisand had been repaired, she was another who stayed away. According to Chris Mankiewicz, even in this period,

"Sue and Barbra talked all the time.... Barbra couldn't wait to ask Sue about everything, including getting a date. Jean-Claude, who called Barbra the 'Jewish camel,' was deeply unhappy that she did not go back to be with Sue, given the fact that Sue really needed a couple of names to shore up her position at William Morris."

Even a maverick agent like Mengers is more effective as part of a team, and Morris didn't have the depth that either CMA or ICM had had. "The system that she went into at Morris was not supportive," says Fields, contrasting the agency to what he says was a more collaborative ethos at CMA. "That's what she missed. She lost touch with who was out there." At the same time, with a blizzard of new ancillary markets such as home video and cable, the business had changed dramatically. Says producer Cary Woods, who was an agent at the Morris office at the time, "When Sue was in her prime, the deals were less sophisticated. Like the other big agents, she would ask for as much money as she could get up front, and didn't really get into back-end deals. When she returned, she walked into a different business." Says Mengers, "I had lost it. I could not find that old excitement. I knew too much, having seen how callously people leave the agent that started them. So it's harder to give them that dedication, because you're steeling yourself against being hurt." Mengers finally resigned in 1991.

Says Goldsmith-Thomas, "When Sue left, it felt like the halls were empty, like the creativity got sucked out. I felt I had lost a wealth of information."

Mengers hasn't worked since.

There's a parlor game to be played with the names of people who were too smart for Hollywood and suffered for it. But that's not quite accurate. There are a lot of smart people in Hollywood, most of whom do quite well; it's more the loose cannons who lose out, the people who don't have the stomach for the bullshit, who can't or won't keep their mouths shut, who aren't politic or careful. Mankiewicz is certainly on this list, and so are people like Vanessa Redgrave, Sean Penn, Alec Baldwin, Alex Cox. Mengers and Tramont as well.

"This is a business that is ruled by fear and insecurity," says Mankiewicz. "So I admire courage and guts and honesty almost more than anything else. Sue and Jean-Claude were both fearless, and in the end it probably cost them both their careers. She didn't make it because she knew somebody or she was related to somebody or because she got a break or blackmailed somebody or fucked somebody. She made it because she was simply fucking brilliant, and terrific at what she did. She earned every penny she got in this business. She was the last of the great gunfighters, the people who could walk into a town and make deals happen. At the end of the day, that's not a bad epitaph."

Five years after Mengers left William Morris, in the fall of 1996, Tramont called Mankiewicz from Paris. Following an exchange of pleasantries, Jean-Claude confessed, "I'm not well, I'm having trouble walking up the stairs, I have this thing on my spine." It was a tumor. Tramont and Mengers returned to Los Angeles, where he was treated with radiation. Mankiewicz went out of town for Christmas, and just before he left he spoke to Tramont in the hospital. Jean-Claude said, "I'm coming home in a day or two. When I get a little bit better, I'll see you, and we'll talk." Mankiewicz recalls, "Five days later I came back, and he had died. I was just devastated. He was the

Hollywood's reigning agent at the time, Sue Mengers worked the phones from her International Creative Management office in the mid-1970s.

closest friend I had in the world." The funeral was small and private, a requiem Mass at a Catholic church in L.A. Among the attendees were Mankiewicz; Bergen; Sidney Poitier and his wife, Joanna Shimkus; Marcia Diamond, Neil Diamond's ex-wife; and, of course, Sue.

"Without him, nothing really interests me," says Mengers, three years later. "I don't like to shop, I don't like to go out. Maybe it's a stage, maybe I'm still in mourning. Sometimes when I get depressed I think, Maybe I should have had a kid. But I remember panicking at the thought of having to give up any of my time. The baby to me seemed extra. But if I had it to do all over again, with hindsight, I would have worried less about the clients and more about a baby."

Says Boatie Boatwright, the agent and a lifelong friend of Mengers's, "We finally gave up thinking that she's going to get up one morning like the rest of us and try to live a normal life. Thank God for Geffen. At least he gets her out of the house."

So many relationships in Hollywood revolve around who you are in the business—can you help me?—that when people leave, no matter how powerful they are or have been, they cease to exist. There's a well-known story about John Calley at a party right after his exit from Warner. An actress went up to him and asked, "Are you John Calley?" Calley replied, "I was." Pointing to his successor, who was standing nearby, he added, "That's the man you want."

It is testimony to Mengers that it didn't happen to her. Even clients who had dropped her were supportive and compassionate. She says, "When my husband died, I was astounded at the letters I got from people I perceived weren't that fond of me. I've [even] had a sort of rapprochement with Jon Peters. It's only taken 20 years."

On occasion, she's almost cheerful. "I found myself very comforted by just being here quietly," she continues. "It's wonderful not to have to wake up with an alarm, just when I feel like it. My todays are what I want them to be, quiet, divided between reading, watching TV, and sleeping. And I love it. Everyone said, 'Oh, you'll miss working.' Never. When I hear the anxiety in the voices of the people that *are* working, and I'm lying in bed reading the *National Enquirer*—joke—I think to myself, How was I able to do it?"

But for all her protestations to the contrary, the business is too deep in her bones for her to shrug it off entirely. She can't help playing virtual agent in her mind: "I like this Vince Vaughn. Julia Roberts. She's of an age now where she can really do some interesting things. Cameron Diaz is enchanting. Parker Posey. She's a great comedienne. Very versatile. Christina Ricci. I love her. She's hot. I kind of like Drew Barrymore. In certain scenes she can look ravishing, and then she doesn't. I also love Michelle Pfeiffer. Janeane Garofalo, love her."

Directors?

"Paul Thomas Anderson. I loved *Boogie Nights.*"

Tarantino?

"I loved *Pulp Fiction.* Because Tarantino had the imagination to bring back Travolta. Who would pick Travolta to play a punk killer? He was out of the business. I tried to sign him every minute I was an agent. He's one of the ones that got away. I think the reason I didn't get him is he once saw me smoking marijuana at a party, and I saw his face, and I thought, Uh-oh."

Mengers pauses, her face breaking into a mischievous grin. "If Tom Cruise, Tom Hanks, and 10 or 20 people of my choosing said, 'Sue, we're signing lifetime contracts with you that stipulate that we cannot fire you until you die, but you can fire us'—*then* I would be an agent again." □

SHAFT, PAST AND PRESENT Samuel L. Jackson, Richard Roundtree, Gordon Parks, John Singleton Parks had vision to go with the guts. Artist and writer, composer and photographer (for *Vogue* and *Life* and the Farm Security Administration), he tried his hand at directing in 1969 with *The Learning Tree,* and then, in 1971, brought a slick, powerful African-American character to the screen, in the form of Detective John Shaft (played by Roundtree). More violence, higher octane figured in the 21st-century remake, *Shaft* redux (directed by Singleton, starring Jackson).

PHOTOGRAPHED IN 2000
BY **NORMAN JEAN ROY**

STARS AGLOW ON OSCAR EVE Superagent Irving "Swifty" Lazar used to throw *the* Academy Awards–night event. Since his passing in 1993, at age 86, *Vanity Fair* has assumed the role of Hollywood's foremost host, inviting the glittering A-list of the industry—many bearing shiny statuettes of gold—to its legendary do at Mortons restaurant in West Hollywood. As these pages attest, *Vanity Fair*'s gathering is the capstone to Oscar night, drawing the incomparable (Cruise and Kidman, De Niro and DiCaprio, Ali and Arnold, Oprah *and* Uma), the mogulian (Diller, Eisner, Geffen, Kerkorian, Redstone, Turner, et al.), the sensual and consensual (Anna Nicole, Pamela, Monica, Heidi), and the fabulous (Madonna, Madonna, Madonna). Pundits have called it "the titan of all Oscar parties," "a fantasy elixir of undiluted stardom" replete with a paparazzi gauntlet that triggers "an almost narcotic thrill."

PHOTOGRAPHED BY **PETER BEARD,
JONATHAN BECKER, ALAN BERLINER,
LARRY FINK, DAFYDD JONES, SAM JONES,
PATRICK McMULLAN,** AND **HERB RITTS**

Gwyneth Paltrow, Elle Macpherson, and Uma Thurman

Dominick Dunne, Joan Collins, and Kirk Kerkorian

Jay Leno, Meryl Streep, and her daughter Grace.

Hollywood in vine: an Oscar-esque topiary.

Goldie Hawn and Kurt Russell

Shirley MacLaine and Nancy Reagan

Cher

David Geffen, left, cheers fellow billionaire Ted Turner, while Jane Fonda, center right, amuses Sally Field.

Annette Bening and Warren Beatty

Kevin Spacey and Edward Norton

Alma and General Colin Powell

Kirk Douglas, Michael Douglas, and Ronald Perelman

Senator Bob Kerrey, Shirley MacLaine, Debra Winger, Barry Diller, and Diane Von Furstenberg

Jennifer Aniston and Brad Pitt

The tented room attached to Mortons, moments before the post-awards party.

Kim Basinger with her 1998 best-supporting-actress Oscar for *L.A. Confidential.*

Christopher Ciccone and Madonna

Catherine Deneuve

Sharon Stone and Ellen Barkin needle the 19-year-old, pre-*Titanic* Leonardo DiCaprio.

Tom Ford and Faye Dunaway

Ellen DeGeneres, Anne Heche, and Sigourney Weaver

Mel Gibson brandishes two 1996 Oscars for *Braveheart.*

An ivy-league V.F.

Kelly Lynch in the line of fire.

Barbara Walters and Oprah Winfrey

Elisabeth Shue

Patrick Whitesell, Ben Affleck, and Matt Damon

Fran Lebowitz

Tom Cruise, right, high-fives his *Jerry Maguire* co-star Cuba Gooding Jr., who won the 1997 Academy Award for best supporting actor, as Jim Carrey and Lauren Holly, among others, look on.

Bob Colacello and Lynn Wyatt

Ronald Perelman, Barry Diller, and Cynthia Carter

Charlton and Lydia Clarke Heston

Robert De Niro and Kirk Douglas

Meg Ryan and Dennis Quaid

Andie MacDowell

Francesca Annis, Ralph Fiennes, and Gabriel Byrne

Queen Latifah

Tom Cruise and
Nicole Kidman

Shakira, Michael, and
Natasha Caine

Sandy Gallin

Goldie Hawn and
Steve Martin

Cary Elwes and
Jim Carrey

Charlize Theron

Arnold Schwarzenegger
and Walter Cronkite

Jack Nicholson on V.F.'s 1998
Sunset Boulevard billboard.

Mick Jagger and
Madonna

Jill Vanden Berg, Tony Curtis, Betsy
Bloomingdale, Connie Wald, Denise Hale,
and Prince Egon von Fürstenberg

Audrey and Billy Wilder

Brian Grazer, Annie Leibovitz,
and David Hockney

THE
HOLLYWOOD

A beaming Buster Paltrow shows off his Oscar-winning granddaughter, Gwyneth, and her 1999 best-actress prize for *Shakespeare in Love*.

A spotlit table brims with roses flown in from Holland.

Nigel Hawthorne and Anthony Hopkins

Luise Rainer

Quincy Jones and Stevie Wonder

Liam Neeson, Alex Kingston, and Ralph Fiennes

Nicole Kidman, Tom Cruise, and Liz Smith

David Hockney and Sir Ian McKellen

Minnie Driver and Charlize Theron

Clockwise from left: Martin Scorsese, Helen Morris, Ronald Perelman, Fran Lebowitz, Diane Von Furstenberg, Barry Diller, and Cynthia Carter.

Brian Grazer, Bryan Lourd, and David Geffen

Kevin Spacey and Nicolas Cage, wielding their 1996 Oscars, accompanied by Cage's wife, Patricia Arquette.

Artie Shaw and Kirk Douglas

Jim Threapleton and Kate Winslet

Celebrity gridlock encircles Mortons as guests greet 100 members of the media covering the party.

Fran Lebowitz and Candice Bergen

John Cleese and Steve Martin

Diana Ross and Angie Dickinson

Matt Damon clutches his 1998 best-original-screenplay Oscar for *Good Will Hunting*.

Sean "Puffy" Combs and Oliver Stone

Cher, k. d. lang, Madonna, and Joni Mitchell

Kurt Russell, Robert Zemeckis, and Tom Hanks

Gore Vidal and Anjelica Huston

SEAN CONNERY Scotland's entry in the 1953 Mr. Universe contest took a while to catch on south of the border, but when the former Edinburgh laborer impersonated the suave English spy in *Dr. No* (1962), he evoked the most resounding "Yes," instantly bonding with a global audience. Quitting the Bond market and tossing aside the rug, while staying with the rugged, Connery showed bald brawn and grizzled charm in *The Man Who Would Be King* (1975), *The Wind and the Lion,* and *The Untouchables* (for which he won a bald trophy). He just gets older and better and, like his beloved Scotland, more and more independent.

PHOTOGRAPHED IN 1998
BY **MICHAEL O'NEILL**

MICHAEL CAINE As Maurice Micklewhite, his given name, he could have made *The Swarm*, but not *Zulu*; *Beyond the Poseidon Adventure* but not *The Ipcress File*; *Blame It on Rio* but not *The Man Who Would Be King* (with old mate Connery) or *Hannah and Her Sisters* or *The Cider House Rules*. It took Michael Caine to do those: the real, diamond-in-the-rough, *Alfie*-portraying, *Sleuth*-plotting, Rita-educating Michael Caine. Took his surname from a famous mutiny: bountifully rewarded.

HOLLYWOOD ISSUE COVER, 1999 From left: Adrien Brody, Thandie Newton, Monica Potter, Reese Witherspoon, Julia Stiles, Leelee Sobieski, Giovanni Ribisi, Sarah Polley, Norman Reedus, Anna Friel, Omar Epps, Kate Hudson, Vinessa Shaw, Barry Pepper.

PHOTOGRAPHED IN 1998
BY **ANNIE LEIBOVITZ**

TIM ROBBINS AND **SUSAN SARANDON**
First couple of liberal Hollywood, and of
Bull Durham (1988), scene of his first pitch
to her. (He later perfected the "pitch"
motif, in Robert Altman's *The Player*.) She,
graduating from *The Rocky Horror Picture
Show*—and from mammaries with a twist in
Atlantic City—became her own woman in
Thelma & Louise, and a compassionate sis-
ter in *Dead Man Walking*. Together again
in *Bob Roberts*, with a cameo for Gore
Vidal, godfather of their children.

PHOTOGRAPHED IN 1995
BY **ANNIE LEIBOVITZ**

WILL SMITH AND **JADA PINKETT** Here is Mr. Smith, with his fresh princess, Jada Pinkett (a point of light in *Menace II Society*; Ms. Purty in *The Nutty Professor*). A monster-masher, Smith came from a rap background (and from *Six Degrees of Separation*) to fend off aliens in *Independence Day* and *Men in Black*, which together grossed $1.4 billion. Was his own menace to society's forces of corruption in *Enemy of the State*; rode a blazing saddle in *Wild Wild West*.

PHOTOGRAPHED IN 1997
BY **ANNIE LEIBOVITZ**

DOUGLAS FAIRBANKS This "candid caricature" purported to show the suave, cavalier Mr. Fairbanks, producer, Hollywood host, and film swashbuckler, "chatting in his own impressive French, to the small man in a homburg hat who stopped to shake his hand" in front of Ciro's nightclub. His power-couple partner was Mary Pickford, with whom he formed United Artists, made millions, ruled the City of Angels, and built the cutely named "Pickfair" love nest in Beverly Hills.

ILLUSTRATED IN 1924
BY **MIGUEL COVARRUBIAS**

COVARRUBIAS

MARY PICKFORD *Vanity Fair* once wrote that "if she were to call at your home, the entire household, from the scullion to the lady of the house, would probably recognize her immediately." Between them, the scullions and the nobs forced Pickford, although born in Canada, to go on being "America's sweetheart." (She portrayed *Pollyanna* well into her 20s.) When she rebelled and did *The Taming of the Shrew* with Fairbanks in 1929, those who had loved her golden curls turned fickle. Her revenge was to grow up and become a successful woman of business, thus ascending from playing *Cinderella* to having scullions of her own.

PHOTOGRAPHED IN 1934
BY **EDWARD STEICHEN**

CATE BLANCHETT Pale yet incandescent. "Ethereal," said her *Elizabeth* director, Shekhar Kapur, remarking on "a certain fire in her eyes" as she assumed the role of the budding Queen of England. Cate Blanchett, smoldering out of Australia, is an actress on the verge. Having brightened *An Ideal Husband, Pushing Tin,* and *The Talented Mr. Ripley,* she has also stoked our hearts as an itinerant kisser, making out quite convincingly with both Ralph Fiennes (in *Oscar and Lucinda*) and his brother Joe (in *Elizabeth*).
PHOTOGRAPHED IN 1999
BY **ANNIE LEIBOVITZ**

By P. G. Wodehouse

The school which I propose to found for the benefit of a small but deserving section of the community will have as its object the education of moving-picture villains in the difficult art of killing moving-picture heroines. The scheme deserves, and will doubtless command, public sympathy and support, for we all want moving-picture heroines killed. Is there one amongst us who would not have screamed with joy if Pauline had perished in the second reel or the Clutching Hand had massacred that princess of bores, Elaine? But these pests carried on a charmed life simply because the villain, with the best intentions, did not know the proper way to go about the job.

You and I, gentle reader, when circumstances or some whim compels us to slay a female acquaintance, just borrow a revolver and a few cartridges and do the thing in some odd five minutes of the day when we are not at the office or watching a ball game. We don't worry about art and technique and scientific methods; we just go and do it. But the villain suffers from a fatal ingenuity. Somewhere back in the past the old folks at home must have told him that he was clever, and it has absolutely spoiled him for effective work.

Ingenuity is a good thing in its way, but he overdoes it.

He is a human Rube Goldberg cartoon. A hundred times he maneuvers his victim into a position where one good dig with a knife or a carefully directed revolver shot would eliminate her forever, to the great contentment of all, and then, the chump, he goes and spoils it all by being too ingenious. It never occurs to him to point the pistol at the girl and pull the trigger. The only way he can imagine doing the thing is to tie the girl to a chair, erect a tripod, place the revolver on it, point it at her, tie a string to the trigger, pass the string round the walls of the room till it rests on a hook, attach another string to it, pass this over a hook, tie a brick to the end of the second string, and light a candle under it. He has got the whole thing reasoned out. The candle will burn the string, the brick will fall, the weight will tighten the first string, thus pulling the trigger, and there you are. Of course, somebody comes along and blows the candle out.

The keynote of the curriculum in my proposed school will be a rigid attention to simplicity and directness. The pupil will start at the beginning by learning how to swat flies. From this he will work up through the animal kingdom in easy stages till he arrives at movie heroines, and by the time he graduates, the Elaines and Paulines will be climbing trees and pulling them up after them to avoid the man, for by then he will be really dangerous.

The great difficulty will be to exorcise that infernal ingenuity of his. His natural impulse, when called upon to kill a fly, would, of course, be to saw away the supports of the floor till a touch would break it down, tie a string across the doorway, and send the fly an anonymous letter urging him to come to the room at once in order to hear of something to his advantage—the idea being that the fly, hurrying to the room, would trip over the string, fall on the floor, and tumble with it into the depths, breaking his neck. That, to the villain's mind, is not merely the simplest—it is the only way of killing flies, and the hardest task facing the instructors at the school will be to persuade him that excellent results may be achieved with a rolled-up newspaper.

Once, however, he has grasped it, his progress ought to be rapid. Should he by chance succeed in slaying Pauline or Elaine or Genevieve or Gladys, he knows the gratitude which will pour out toward him from a million hearts which are aching to have the infernal serial finished and get on to the Charlie Chaplin stuff.

But we must not be too optimistic. Success, however desirable, is at present far away, and can only be reached with patience. A villain with those ideas will not learn in a day that the quickest method of killing a heroine is to decoy the girl down a dark alley and lean a couple of feet of gas pipe against her Irene Castle bang, but he may come to learn it in time, and it is with that hope that I am founding my school. □

CHARLES LAUGHTON The World (Senator Cooley—his last role—in *Advise and Consent*), the Flesh (Gracchus in *Spartacus*, the title role in *The Private Life of King Henry VIII*), and the Diabolic (Captain Bligh in *Mutiny on the Bounty*, Earl Janoth in *The Big Clock*, Inspector Javert in *Les Misérables* of 1935). Most of all, the Flesh: his wet-lipped, voluptuous bulkiness defined him as a magnificent grotesque, from Quasimodo to the solicitor in *Witness for the Prosecution* (opposite his wife, Elsa Lanchester) to *Ruggles of Red Gap*.

PHOTOGRAPHED IN 1935
BY **EDWARD STEICHEN**

By Dorothy Parker

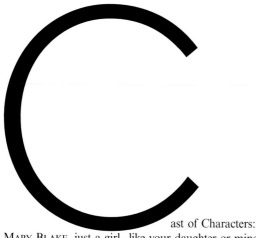

Cast of Characters:

MARY BLAKE, just a girl—like your daughter or mine.
MRS. BLAKE, her widowed mother.
JOHN MURDOCK, a man's man.
HARFORD NEVILLE, a wealthy millionaire.
VERA LA TOUR, one of Those Women.
GUNMEN, THIEVES, GAMBLERS, KIDNAPPERS, SECOND-STORY WORKERS, WHITE SLAVERS, INEBRIATES, DRUG FIENDS, MAGDALENS, ETC.

CAPTION: "Mary Blake—one of God's sweetest flowers, blossoming in the pure sunshine of mother love, all unknowing the bitter winds of men's evil passions that rage outside of the sheltered garden of her life." (Suggested decoration for caption: crossed Easter lilies.)

Close-up of Mary, taken on a windy day, against a background of apple trees in full bloom. She is bending down one branch and chatting vivaciously to an unresponsive pigeon balanced on the end of it. Slow fade-out.

The Blakes' house—respectable poverty indicated by shopworn furniture, oil lamps, and stained wallpaper, but the impression of a cultured and artistic taste conveyed by the chenille portieres, the ribbon rosette on the canary's cage, the reproduction of *The Soul's Awakening* over the mantel, and the lace tidies on the footstools. Mrs. Blake is lying on a sofa with a shawl over her, registering extreme ill health. Mary runs in, excitedly waving a newspaper. She drops to her knees beside the sofa, and lovingly thrusts the paper in her mother's face.

Close-up of the lower half of a help-wanted page in the *Evening World.* In the middle is pasted an advertisement—in type three times as large as that surrounding it: "Young lady wanted for important position in refined office. Must be young and attractive. No previous experience necessary. Apply to Harford Neville, Wall Street." Mrs. Blake and Mary embrace rapturously, and Mary rushes to get ready. She runs to the mirror and begins to unbutton her dress. Immediate change of scene.

Neville's outer office—his tremendous business interests are shown by tickers, stock reports, insurance calendars, revolving chairs, hordes of clerks rushing in and out, wearing pencils on their ears, and three stenographers strumming on typewriters. A large glass door bears the sinister legend HARFORD NEVILLE, PRIVATE. Mary enters timidly and speaks to the office boy. He motions languidly to the glass door, and she falteringly approaches it.

CAPTION: "Harford Neville—rich and powerful, waiting his chance to cruelly spring on the helpless ones that relentless Fate sends across his path." (Suggested decoration for caption: bag of gold, on which sits a long-tailed devil.)

Close-up of Neville, a large and heavily built man, with hair touched with talcum at the temples, nervously chewing the end of a thick black cigar.

Neville's inner, or private, office. He is sitting in a large leather chair before an impressive desk, frowning at a pile of letters. He glances up impatiently as Mary enters, then looks amazed, and springs up to meet her. He brings a chair for her and they talk, Mary gradually losing her shyness. Finally she rises and grasps his hand in impulsive gratitude, then runs happily from the office. He goes to the door and stands looking after her, registering lust.

CAPTION: "And so Mary became Neville's private secretary, little thinking, as the busy days slipped by, that he whom she so trusted in was but biding his time, craftily spinning the trap in which to someday snare her." (Suggested decoration for caption: a spider and its web.)

Neville's private office. Mary is improvising on the typewriter, while Neville sits at the desk, watching her. She looks at the clock, which registers 4:50, and springs up to put on her hat and coat. Neville follows her, and puts a hand on her shoulder.

CAPTION: "Will you not dine with me this evening, Miss Blake? I am very lonely, and you will be doing me a great favor by giving me the pleasure of your company. I will escort you home at an early hour—your mother will not worry." (Suggested decoration: bottle and overturned glass of wine.)

Mary stands a moment in doubt. A flash of her mother, lying on the sofa, wearing an expression of intense suffering, appears on the upper left-hand corner of the screen. Mary puts her hand over her eyes as if to shut out the vision, then squares her shoulders, tosses back her curls, and nods at Neville.

Close-up of Mary and Neville in Neville's limousine. He is leaning close, talking to her, while his arm rests on the cretonne upholstery behind her. Mary sits very straight, as far from him as possible.

CAPTION: "The White Light restaurant—the heart of the nightlife of the pleasure-crazed metropolis, where many a fluttering moth has had her frail wings singed in the dizzy whirlpool of folly." (Suggested decoration: girl dancing on table.)

Private room in the restaurant. Table set for two, mostly with glasses. A waiter hovers. The door opens, admitting Mary and Neville, followed by a headwaiter. Mary gazes delightedly around the room, registering, "So this is Paris." While she isn't looking, Neville draws the headwaiter aside and gives him a small vial, making elaborate gestures of secrecy. The waiter bows reassuringly and tiptoes over to the serving table, looking nervously around him.

Close-up of slightly soiled hand holding vial, the contents of which drop slowly into the half-filled cocktail glass, causing a succession of evil-looking bubbles to rise slowly to the top.

Mary and Neville sit at the table, and the waiter serves the cocktails, giving Mary the drugged glass. (This is done very slowly and carefully, so that everyone in the audience can get it—without a struggle.) Mary at first refuses to drink, then, as Neville urges her, she raises the glass. A small trick picture of Mrs. Blake (tossing feverishly about on her sofa) appears in the glass. Mary puts the glass down hastily. She and Neville argue, for about 100 feet of film, to prolong the suspense; then Mary recklessly drinks the cocktail. She instantly becomes dazed, bewildered, then falls in graceful unconsciousness on the table. Neville carries her out of the room.

CAPTION: "John Murdock, reporter on the *Daily Sphere.* Unheard of in the gay life of the metropolis, because he is not one of its so-called aristocrats or society idlers, but a member of the nobility of toil." (Suggested decoration: an acorn and a sturdy oak.)

Close-up of John Murdock, wearing the conventional belted coat and fedora hat. He carries a pad and pencil, thus showing that he is a reporter. He looks fearlessly into the camera and rapidly raises and lowers his chest, registering virility.

The exterior of the restaurant. John is just passing when Neville comes out, carrying the unconscious Mary. John sees them, stops, and watches Neville and his burden get into a taxi. He waits till the taxi starts, to make it more difficult, then takes a running jump and hangs on to the back of the cab.

CAPTION: "Vera La Tour, a product of the metropolis—a creature without soul or shame, in whose gilded halls such men as Harford Neville find ready welcome." (Suggested decoration: a coiled serpent, rearing its head.)

Close-up of Vera La Tour, lying, in curves, on a divan which is covered with tiger skins. She is leaning on her elbow and flaunting the movie badge of shame—a cigarette. Picture fades slowly into . . .

The Den of Iniquity. Vera La Tour's apartment—a place evidently about the size of the Grand Central Palace. A large, high-ceilinged room, caked with furniture of the late Robert E. Lee period, and lined with paintings and mirrors. Glimpses may be had of adjoining rooms with men and women in evening dress crowding about a roulette wheel, and of other depraved creatures shamelessly dancing the two-step and the old-fashioned waltz. Powdered footmen pass in and out, carrying bottles of synthetic champagne.

Neville enters, carrying the still-unconscious Mary. Vera looks at him in languid surprise, laughs contemptuously, and flicks the ash from her cigarette. She rises and leads the way to a smaller room (which is thrown on the screen in a gruesome green light). The room is poorly furnished and contains a cot. Neville places Mary on the cot, and he and Vera leave the room. The moment they leave, she regains consciousness.

Close-up of Mary, registering, "Where am I?" Flash of Mrs. Blake, lying on her sofa, pathetically watching the clock. Close-up of a clock registering 9:25.

Neville re-enters the room, smiling wickedly at Mary, who backs away from him in terror. He locks the door lingeringly, meaningly puts the key in his pocket, and approaches her. She struggles with him desperately—her clothes tear in all the most becoming places. She at last breaks away from him and rushes to the window. Close-up of her face, with plump tears of glycerine sliding slowly down her cheeks. Flash of John Murdock in the street below, registering Nobility of Purpose. He sees Mary's face at the 12th-floor window, immediately flings down his fedora hat, tears off his girdled coat, revealing a Byronic shirt, and begins to douglasfairbanks up the outside of the house.

Neville sneaks up on Mary, and the struggle begins again. He slowly overpowers her. The entire picture is about to be stopped by the National Board of Censorship when John appears on the outside of the window. He leaps into the room, landing on Neville. They battle—one of the great moments of the film. Chairs and tables are overturned, and both men bleed dark paint profusely. John's shirt tears picturesquely, but nothing interferes with the glistening perfection of his coiffure. Mary conveniently faints again. The fight looks like a draw when it is interrupted by Vera La Tour, pounding furiously on the outside of the locked door.

CAPTION: "For Heaven's sake, unlock the door. The police!!!!!!!" (Suggested decoration: handcuffs, held together by festoons of heavy chains.)

The fight ceases abruptly. Neville, cursing visibly, staggers to the door and unlocks it, admitting Vera. All register excitement except Mary, who goes right on fainting. The scene changes abruptly to . . .

The Raid. The Big Scene. Here is the chance for the director to show his real stuff. Battalions of policemen swarm all over the apartment, completely surprising the roulette players and the waltzers. General panorama of the

conflict, interspersed with close-ups of hand-to-hand struggles. Grimly realistic notes are given by flashes of policemen penetrating dark corners and bringing blinking drug fiends into the light, and close-ups of wild women at bay. At this point a gang of gunmen arrive, through a back passageway, almost overpowering the police. (This not only makes things more exciting, but it brings in the requisite touch of the underworld, and also gives employment to innumerable supers.) At the critical moment, however, a fresh battalion of police arrive and efficiently clean up the place.

The scene reverts to Vera, Mary (who is now regaining consciousness), Neville, and John. Vera, who has not registered the least surprise at seeing John in the room, turns furiously on Neville.

CAPTION: "For me has come the end, for I can never face the darkness of the prison cell. But, before I go, Harford Neville, I shall send you back to the Hades from which you came, for it was you who made me the thing you now see before you." (Suggested decoration: tigress about to spring.)

Vera draws a pearl-handled dagger from her bodice and stabs Neville in the heart. He dies—for 50 feet or so—and finally sinks to the floor. Then, without even cleaning the dagger, Vera kills herself. Mary registers terror, and clings to John, who puts a strong arm around her.

CAPTION: "Come, little girl, this house of horror is no place for you and I." (Suggested decoration: same handcuffs as before, but this time with all the festoons of chains hanging broken.)

John climbs up to the windowsill and helps Mary up beside him. A telegraph wire is conveniently stretched from the window to the roof of the house opposite. John turns his back on Mary; she clasps her arms around his neck. With Mary clinging tightly to him, John grasps the wire and works his way along it, hand over hand, to the opposite roof. (There is no special reason why they shouldn't go right through the front door and walk quietly out into the street, but the picture has to live up to its advertisements.) John's hair remains absolutely unimpaired. An open automobile passes below them. John takes Mary's hand and they leap, landing neatly in the tonneau.

Close-up of them both in the speeding automobile, showing that John's hair still retains its original glistening order.

The Blakes' house, again. Mrs. Blake and Mary are embracing while John stands benignantly above them, his arms folded, the torn shirtsleeves displaying the muscles admirably. Mary turns shyly to John.

CAPTION: "How am I to ever thank you for saving me from a fate far worse than death? Although I do not even know you, my deathless gratitude is forever yours." (Suggested decoration: a wreath of orange blossoms.)

John looks at Mary, who shyly drops her eyes. Mrs. Blake turns discreetly away.

CAPTION: "But Gratitude is very close to that purest of all God's gifts to us—True Love." (Suggested decoration: Cupid shooting at a winged heart.)

John holds out his arms and Mary walks into them. They embrace—at great length. Then, still embracing, both turn their backs on the camera for the first time in the entire production. Fade out as slowly as possible . . .

The word "Finis" flashes upon the screen.

Then, without a pause, follows the announcement in red, yellow, and green: "At This Theatre, Next Wednesday and Thursday Positively—Theda Bara, in the Six-Reel Drama of Thrills and Passion, *The Love Drunkard.*" □

ALL ABOUT EVE The cast from the Joseph L. Mankiewicz classic stride across the Twentieth Century Fox lot: Gary Merrill, Bette Davis, George Sanders, Anne Baxter, Hugh Marlowe, Celeste Holm. PHOTOGRAPHED IN 1950

THE MGM GIRLS Louis B. Mayer's Metro musical starlets from the 40s and 50s—Jane Powell, June Allyson, Ann Miller, Cyd Charisse, Gloria DeHaven, and Marge Champion represent a fair sampling—made 250 films, which grossed more than $400 million. PHOTOGRAPHED IN 1998 BY **SAM JONES**

RICHARD GERE Goodbar … gigolo … gentleman: Gere stayed in the key of G to make his name, trading up, by way of His Holiness the Dalai Lama, to the high register of *Pretty Woman*. The B's and C's—*Breathless, Beyond the Limit, The Cotton Club*, Cindy Crawford— have been supporting players in the evolution of an unarguably alpha male. PHOTOGRAPHED IN 1990 BY **HERB RITTS**

ROBERT MITCHUM To have been Philip Marlowe twice (in *Farewell, My Lovely* and *The Big Sleep*) is to have earned those bags and that mackintosh. Busted for dope before it was fashionable; twice did time—once on a Georgia chain gang. Slow, wry, tough, and boozy: his smoky voice was the subtext of *The Sundowners, Cape Fear,* and—lazier yet—*Ryan's Daughter.* Nominated for an Oscar for *The Story of G.I. Joe* (1945); ideally cast as a shabby, two-timing hood in *The Friends of Eddie Coyle.*

PHOTOGRAPHED IN 1995
BY **ANNIE LEIBOVITZ**

GRACE KELLY As collected and resourceful in *Rear Window* as Jimmy Stewart was (she always had class written all over her), she drove a fast car in Monaco for Hitchcock the following year in *To Catch a Thief* (1955), then steered Rainier to the altar a year after that. Her high-society high noon as princess of that Ruritania was intense, with intimations of Grace under pressure; it ended on a hairpin bend on the same Riviera in 1982.

PHOTOGRAPHED IN 1955
BY **LEO MIRKINE**

WALTER HUSTON Yet another Canadian gift to the United States, Walter Huston didn't hit the screen until he was 46, and was soon old enough to appear in movies made by his two-time Academy Award–winning son, John—taking a minor part in *The Maltese Falcon* and a 1948 Oscar for *The Treasure of the Sierra Madre*. (John won an Oscar, as well, for directing the picture.) Popular hit in the eponymous role of Sinclair Lewis's *Dodsworth;* man enough to be D. W. Griffith's *Abraham Lincoln* in 1930.

PHOTOGRAPHED IN 1934
BY **LUSHA NELSON**

ANJELICA HUSTON It goes on: Anjelica Huston took her time to emerge from her father John's aura, and her beau Jack Nicholson's. Even *Prizzi's Honor*—in which she first shone and won an Oscar—was her dad's work; same with *The Dead*, his final film. But with *The Grifters* and *The Golden Bowl*, and as director of *Bastard out of Carolina* and *Agnes Browne*, she got back on that horse and went from canter to gallop.

PHOTOGRAPHED IN 1985
BY **ANNIE LEIBOVITZ**

THE REDGRAVE WOMEN (clockwise from bottom left) Natasha Richardson, Joely Richardson, Rachel Kempson, Vanessa Redgrave Britain's royal family of theater and screen players, the Redgraves were led by the late Sir Michael (*The Lady Vanishes, The Captive Heart*) and commanding matriarch Rachel Kempson (*Out of Africa, Tom Jones, Georgy Girl*—the last of which also featured daughter Lynn Redgrave). From cradle to stage to moving picture, their headstrong Vanessa has lately reigned—compelling and rebellious—from *Blowup* and *Julia* to *Girl, Interrupted* and *Cradle Will Rock*. With director Tony Richardson, she started Act III: daughters Natasha—Mrs. Liam Neeson—a Broadway mainstay with Hollywood credits (*The Handmaid's Tale, The Parent Trap*), and Joely, who has been a waitress (*The Hotel New Hampshire*), a princess (*King Ralph*), and that lady in *Lady Chatterley's Lover*.

PHOTOGRAPHED IN 1986
BY **ANNIE LEIBOVITZ**

KIRK AND **MICHAEL DOUGLAS** The fabulous Douglas men. Captain Kirk has four sons, all Hollywood boys, but his Dauphin is Michael (something, maybe, about the chin). Colonel Dax (*Paths of Glory*), van Gogh (*Lust for Life*), Charles Tatum (*Ace in the Hole*), "Last Hero" Burns (*Lonely Are the Brave*), and *Spartacus* are hard personalities to follow: Michael has done just fine. A sometime producer (*One Flew over the Cuckoo's Nest, The China Syndrome*) and full-tilt actor, he has run the gamut from *Wall Street* baron to *The American President*, braving dangerous liaisons with Kathleen Turner (*Romancing the Stone, The War of the Roses*), Glenn Close (*Fatal Attraction*), and Sharon Stone (*Basic Instinct*). Quite a wonder boy.

PHOTOGRAPHED IN 1995
BY **ANNIE LEIBOVITZ**

THE BOX-OFFICE BOYS Arnold Schwarzenegger, Tom Cruise, Tom Hanks Each commands more than $20 million a picture. Each is a mini-industry, having separately spearheaded upwards of $1.4 billion in domestic box-office receipts. Each excels at playing the lone wolf or the single-minded renegade who triumphs over adversity, often against great odds. Each, in his own way, owns the town. "Every little boy," explains Hanks, "wants to play a cowboy." To each his own.

PHOTOGRAPHED IN 1994
BY **HERB RITTS**

THE FAMILY FONDA Jane Fonda, Henry Fonda, Peter Fonda Papa Hank cut his teeth in *Way Down East* (1935), then moved on from *Mister Roberts* (1955) to *On Golden Pond* (1981) and, in between, blessed some of the screen's best directors with his sheer nobility—Fritz Lang (*You Only Live Once*) and John Ford (*The Grapes of Wrath*), Alfred Hitchcock (*The Wrong Man*) and Sidney Lumet (*12 Angry Men, Fail Safe*). Daughter Jane, perpetually reincarnated in film and in fact, fairly eclipsed her dad with seven Academy Award nominations, netting two Oscars (*Klute, Coming Home*); son Peter slipped Hollywood a dose of the radical 60s in *Easy Rider*. And it goes on: *his* daughter, Bridget, has been in more than 30 features, from *Single White Female* to *A Simple Plan*.

PHOTOGRAPHED IN 1978
BY **FRANK EDWARDS**

MADONNA Madonna Ciccone—*seven* times a *Vanity Fair* cover subject and in this regard a recordholder—has over time justified love, sex, bisexuality, motherhood, and, through it all, celebrity. From MTV to MP3, *Desperately Seeking Susan* to *Evita*, she has been the High Priestess of Image in our image-filled age.

PHOTOGRAPHED IN 1986
BY **HERB RITTS**

STEVEN SPIELBERG The ever evolving Spielberg. Harmlessly haunted the bedtimes of children with *Jaws* and *E.T.,* and of adolescents with his dinotopian *Jurassic Park;* went on to express an adult's take on warfare's waking nightmare in *Saving Private Ryan.* Not since Disney, though, has childhood, on celluloid, been so extensively, expensively evoked. Reality checks—*Amistad* and his masterly *Schindler's List,* which earned him dual Oscars for best picture and direction in 1993—were comparably authentic. And, oh yes, this co-founder of the DreamWorks studio first disturbed our slumber when he was all of 21, directing a 1969 horror segment for TV's *Night Gallery.*

PHOTOGRAPHED IN 1994
BY **ANNIE LEIBOVITZ**

THE GANGSTER AND THE GODDESS

By Patricia Bosworth

t rained in Beverly Hills that Good Friday, April 4, 1958. Rain pelted against the elegant white colonial mansion that movie star Lana Turner had just rented at 730 North Bedford Drive. Upstairs, in her lavish, pink-carpeted bedroom, a violent quarrel was going on between the petite blonde actress—barefoot in a white blouse and black silk pedal pushers—and her darkly handsome lover, Johnny Stompanato, a former bodyguard of the mobster Mickey Cohen.

At 37, Turner was one of America's three archetypal sex goddesses, along with Rita Hayworth and Ava Gardner. Four times married, always in the gossip columns, and with more than 40 films to her credit, Turner reveled in being a movie star and gave herself over to the Hollywood myth-making machine. But she had always guarded her glittery image with steely determination.

For months she had been trying to break with Stompanato, even as they carried on a passionate affair. Because of his underworld connections, she had refused to be seen in public with him. "Johnny was madly in love with Lana," says a fellow actress, "but there were so many mixed messages, so much game playing. When they were together, Lana seemed crazy about him. She showered him with presents; she'd phone him up to six times a day. But she wouldn't even go out to a coffee shop with the guy. He got confused. He felt deballed. He started roughing her up, and things got increasingly ugly." After she wouldn't allow him to escort her to the Academy Awards on March 26 (she'd been nominated for an Oscar for *Peyton Place*), he beat her savagely.

About nine o'clock that Good Friday evening, Turner said they were finished and ordered him to leave the house. Stompanato defied her. "You'll never get away from me," he threatened angrily. "I'll cut you good, Baby.... No one will ever look at that pretty face again."

Out in the hall, Turner's tall, gangly 14-year-old daughter, Cheryl Crane, listened to the argument, terrified. After a few seconds, she ran down to the kitchen. Turner's Mexican maid, Carmen Cruz, who has never been interviewed before and who appears in no earlier account of the story, says that as she was passing from the foyer to the living room that night she saw Cheryl enter the kitchen and come out with a butcher knife in her hand. Then Cheryl vaulted back upstairs.

The argument was continuing full blast. "I've had just enough," Turner cried, and Stompanato yelled, "Cunt! You're dead!"

Cheryl pounded on the door. "Let me in! Let me talk to both of you!"

There are many versions of what followed. In 1982, Turner wrote her autobiography, *Lana: The Lady, the Legend, the Truth,* and in 1988, Cheryl Crane published her gritty, powerful memoir, *Detour: A Hollywood Story,* which she co-wrote with author Cliff Jahr. There are also the coroner's inquest transcript and various newspaper stories.

From these, one can piece together the following: The door to the pink bedroom was opened by Turner. Stompanato was behind her, his arm raised. Like a zombie, Cheryl moved forward and plunged the knife into his gut, piercing the liver, the portal vein, and the aorta.

The gangster stared at her in horror. "My God, Cheryl, what have you done?" he managed to choke out before falling on his back on the pink carpet, making awful gurgling noises in his throat. Cheryl put the knife on the marble dressing table and ran screaming from the room.

It was 9:20 P.M.

urner later testified that she hadn't noticed any blood at first, because of the way Stompanato had fallen, but then she saw the red, wet knife. She lifted up his sweater, saw the wound—just a slit—and realized that he'd been stabbed.

She picked up the knife, carried it into the bathroom, and dropped it in the washbasin. Returning with a towel, she screamed, "Cheryl! Come quickly! You've got to help!"

Her daughter didn't respond, because she had run to her room to call her father, Stephen Crane, whose restaurant, the Luau, was just minutes away.

Turner was too distraught to remember her doctor's number, so she phoned her mother. Mildred Turner asked her what was wrong, but Lana said only, "Please call Doctor Mac immediately. It is an emergency. Tell him to come at once."

Just then Cheryl appeared in the doorway, whimpering. Turner asked her to get some fresh washcloths from the bathroom to put on Stompanato's forehead.

Turner bent down to speak to him, but he didn't answer. She slapped his cheeks and gave him mouth-to-mouth resuscitation. She was so intent on saving her lover's life that she didn't hear the doorbell ringing. Suddenly her ex-husband Stephen Crane was in the bedroom, staring at the blood-soaked towels.

"Oh, my God," Crane muttered.

Only then did Turner glance up. "Stephen! Why are you here?" she cried, and she ran forward, as if to block the view.

"I did it, Daddy, but I didn't mean to. John was going to hurt Mommy," Cheryl said, sobbing, as Turner put her arms around her.

Crane dragged Cheryl away from her and into the hall. "Everything will be all right," he told her.

The doorbell rang again, and minutes later the gaunt, severe Mildred Turner was upstairs, demanding, "Lana! Lana! What happened? Where's my baby?" She ran to Cheryl's bedroom, where the girl was crying convulsively. Mildred Turner wrapped her arms around her granddaughter and rocked her back and forth.

he doorbell began to ring incessantly. It was John McDonald, the family doctor, known as Doctor Mac, who had taken care of Turner's every sniffle for years. He hurried up to the pink bedroom, flung off his jacket, saw Stompanato on the floor, and gave him a shot of adrenaline. He ordered Turner to dial 0 for emergency and get an ambulance. He phoned for another doctor and put a stethoscope to Stompanato's chest. "Lana, I can't get a heartbeat," he said. Then he told Turner, "Call Jerry Giesler."

Giesler was the most powerful criminal lawyer in Hollywood. His clients ranged from gangster Bugsy Siegel to Charlie Chaplin. Turner reached him at a dinner party, and he said he would be there right away.

Outside in the rainy darkness sirens wailed. Stephen Crane later testified that he had run outside to move the four cars parked in the driveway. There were no keys in any of them, so he helped push the vehicles—which included Stompanato's white Thunderbird—into the street just as an ambulance screeched to a halt.

Lights began popping on in houses on North Bedford Drive, and people

In 1957, Lana Turner ventured out on a rare public foray with gangland escort Johnny Stompanato. He would be killed a few months later.

FROM THE PAGES OF *VANITY FAIR,* APRIL 1999

in bathrobes came out onto the sidewalk to gawk as medics, ambulance attendants, and police poured into the mansion.

James Bacon, now 84, was then a respected A.P. correspondent. He remembers "moving right along with the cops," telling whoever answered the door that he was "assistant to the coroner." He'd heard about the murder from a photographer friend who had a two-way police radio. "I'd done a lot of interviews with Lana Turner, ever since she made *Honky Tonk* with Clark Gable back in 1941.

"So there I was in Lana's big blue floral living room," Bacon continues. "I just marched right up to the second floor. Nobody stopped me, and I walked right into Lana's pink bedroom and saw the dead body of Johnny Stompanato lying on the pink carpet.... But there was no blood. The room was pristine clean, but it was filling up with people—cops swarming around with tape measures and notebooks, a photographer snapping pictures of Stompanato with his sweater pulled up so they could document the stab wound."

Bacon thinks he saw the detective Fred Otash nosing around. "Giesler, who was there too, probably brought him. They often worked together on cases." Otash was the private eye who later helped obtain men to put wiretaps in Marilyn Monroe's house when she was involved with J.F.K.

About 10:50 P.M., Clinton Anderson, the chief of the Beverly Hills Police Department, arrived at the crime scene. One week earlier he had received a phone call from Mildred Turner, who said that her daughter, Lana, was worried about Johnny Stompanato's increasingly violent behavior, and asked what she should do. He told her to have Lana report it to the police department immediately. But she never did.

Stompanato's reputation was notorious. The wavy-haired ex-Marine used aliases such as John Valentine and was known as an extortionist. Anderson had once kicked Stompanato out of a Beverly Hills hotel after he became abusive during a police investigation. Stompanato had been arrested at least twice, and had had numerous run-ins with the law, but had never been jailed. Married and divorced three times, with a 10-year-old son, John III, he had, at various times, sold cars, owned a pet shop, and run a furniture store to make ends meet, but mainly he preyed on wealthy women. He was known in Hollywood, according to one actress, as "a great lover with a big dong."

Anderson conferred with the medics and detectives. Then he noticed James Bacon and "blew his stack," Bacon says. And when he spotted Giesler and Otash, "he practically goes ape. The fact that the press, a private eye, and the attorney Giesler were at the murder site before he was really upset him."

Bacon recalls watching Anderson take Turner, "looking mighty calm under the circumstances," into a corner of her dressing room while a fire-department resuscitation crew worked on Stompanato's lifeless body. "I heard her asking, 'Can I take the blame for my baby?' or some such thing, and Anderson tells her, 'Not unless you actually committed the crime.' And Lana bows her head and says, 'O.K., Chief, it was my daughter.'"

Anderson then went to Cheryl's bedroom to hear her version of the story. A year earlier the rebellious teenager had run away from boarding school and had been picked up by police on skid row. Since then she'd been shuttled between her mother and her grandmother. Anderson and Cheryl's father were good friends, but Anderson was "direct and official" with her that night, she would recall. The words tumbled out. "I'm so sorry, Chief. I didn't *mean* to do it. Johnny said he was going to hurt mother." Afterward, Anderson would report that mother and daughter told virtually identical stories.

At midnight, Turner and her daughter were driven to the Beverly Hills police station, a few blocks away. Stephen Crane followed in another car. News photographers were allowed to snap pictures of Cheryl and Chief Anderson in his office, while Turner and her ex-husband sat on the sidelines. In another room, Giesler told reporters, "This was justifiable homicide. There is no justification for a trial."

After the press left, Giesler joined Cheryl as she gave a statement to the police, which was in part: "He was threatening mother ... to kill her and to hurt Daddy, Granny, and me ... so I rushed into the room and struck him with the knife."

Then, between sobs, Lana Turner spoke. She had been afraid of Stompanato, she said. She admitted having given him thousands of dollars, "not counting the tabs I picked up for him." She said the argument that night started because he had lied about his age.

Cheryl learned one important fact. She had thought that when her mother opened the door, Stompanato was behind her with his arm raised as if to strike. Actually he was holding up "a jacket and a shirt" on hangers. Years later, Cheryl wrote, "Would I have raised the knife if John's arm hadn't been raised? ... I don't know.... I believe that, in my fright, I jabbed at him with the knife out of a split-second impulse to scare him.... I knew little of knives. Indeed, the autopsy revealed that the blade had been inserted upside down, that is, sharp side up."

Once the statements were given, Cheryl was led away by a police matron. "Where is she going?" Turner asked, and Anderson explained, "She'll be spending the night here."

Turner screamed, "Oh no! I want my baby home with me." Suddenly the enormity of what had happened dawned on her. Bolting from the office, she ran after Cheryl, down a long, garishly lit hall, only to see the barred door to the holding cell shut. "That vision is one that will never go away. My child's face behind bars," she wrote later. "Open that door!" she ordered the matron.

The matron did, and Turner ran in and embraced her daughter. Together they sank down on the narrow cot, and Turner tried to reassure her that they would get her out the next day. Shortly after that, Cheryl was booked on a holding charge of suspicion of murder.

About one A.M., Jerry Giesler took Turner home in his limousine. As they pulled up, attendants were wheeling Stompanato's sheeted body out the door and into a coroner's wagon.

Turner let out a keening cry. Giesler pushed her down on the floor of the car. Then he jumped out of the limo as flashbulbs exploded, and told the journalists Turner had gone somewhere else to rest, so they could all leave.

The remaining reporters took off after the ambulance, and Giesler led a sobbing Lana Turner into her house, where close friends were waiting to comfort her. Del Armstrong, her trusted makeup man, was there, as was Glenn Rose, her press agent. Rose and Armstrong had worked on Turner's most recent movie, *Another Time, Another Place,* so they'd both known Stompanato. "Everybody knew Johnny," Rose says. "He never left Lana alone."

That night, Rose recalls, "She started climbing the walls. She kept shrieking at Jerry Giesler, 'Why can't they let me take my baby home?'"

At the morgue, gangster Mickey Cohen, almost in tears, identified Stompanato's body, and said he would arrange for the burial in Stompanato's hometown of Woodstock, Illinois. (Accompanying the body might have been a problem, since Cohen was under indictment for assaulting a federal agent.) "I don't like the whole thing," Cohen yelled. "There's a lot of unanswered questions about how Johnny was killed. I'm going to find some of these answers—no matter what happens."

Calming down slightly, he told a reporter, "Johnny's been around for a long time. But if what they tell me is true, he made no effort to dodge the knife. It just doesn't jell with me.... When I heard how Johnny was killed, cold chills went through me. It's a fantastic way for a man like Stompanato to die."

Police emptied Stompanato's pockets and found tenderly inscribed photographs of Lana Turner, as well as a lock of her platinum-blond hair. They also removed from his left wrist a heavy ID bracelet engraved in Spanish: "Daddy John my sweet love, this recalls a piece of my heart which will be with you always, and remember, Guido, my life for you for all time. Lanita."

By four A.M. the atmosphere in Turner's house had become so charged, Glenn Rose recalls, that he suggested to Lana that she "sleep over at my place." She agreed, and when they arrived at his apartment in Beverly Hills, "Lana fell into a doze in my spare room."

Over in Westwood, Fred Packard, a clerk at the Del Capri Hotel, where Johnny Stompanato rented a suite, heard about the stabbing. Packard grabbed a passkey and let himself into Stompanato's apartment. He found the lights on, and the bathroom window had been jimmied. A maid later said that a leather shaving kit was missing from its place above the washbasin. It had been stuffed with letters, she said.

By the next morning, everyone knew about the gangster's violent death. Newspapers, radio, and TV broadcast the crime around the world. It was the biggest scandal to hit Hollywood since the 1920s, when another lurid incident ended the career of silent-screen star Fatty Arbuckle, who was accused, but acquitted, of raping a young starlet who subsequently died.

Dominick Dunne heard about the stabbing right after it occurred. "My wife and I lived a block away from Lana. On the night of the murder we were giving a dinner party, and we got a phone call alerting us about it just as coffee was being served."

Dunne admits to joining the crowd milling around Turner's home the next morning. "It was like a circus. By the end of the day, entire families were crammed into their cars ogling, and there were people literally hanging from the trees with binoculars. For weeks there was a constant traffic jam. The public just couldn't get enough of all the gory details, and I was frankly fascinated, too. It had all the ingredients of a sordid detective thriller. I mean, the gangster and the movie star—what could be better than that?"

At 7:30 A.M. on April 5, Turner and Stephen Crane were back at the police station with breakfast from a local drugstore for their daughter. But Cheryl refused to eat.

A daylong conference with the police and lawyers followed. Giesler represented Cheryl, and Lana was represented by Louis Blau. Crane had hired a lawyer for himself, Arthur Crowley, who had once defended *Confidential,* the scandal magazine. When attempts to have Cheryl released into the custody of her grandmother Mildred Turner failed, she was taken to Juvenile Hall.

District Attorney William Mc-Kesson refused to break with customary procedure and release her in less than 72 hours. Lieutenant William Richey of the Beverly Hills police had submitted a petition to the court stating that Cheryl Crane had not been properly supervised. The teenager would remain in jail, pending a hearing to decide whether she should stand trial for murder. As a minor she would not be subject to the death penalty.

The following day was Easter Sunday. "Still raining," Glenn Rose recalls. "Lana received permission to visit her daughter early. Parents of other kids at Juvenile Hall stood around in the rain complaining very loudly," Rose says, as the movie star and her ex-husband glided up to the door in separate Cadillacs. There were press reports of special treatment.

"The police were bending over backwards to stand tough," Rose adds. "They did not want to be accused of going easy on celebrities. Cheryl would not be released until after the coroner's inquest." Cheryl later wrote that when her parents visited her in jail, "between silences we talked of trifles.... I didn't tell them how awful the place was."

Turner took her daughter some soap, and Crane gave her a box of candy. Cheryl didn't talk about the runaways and unwed mothers she was meeting in jail, or about the girl who had cornered her in the day room and yelled, "I bet you didn't do it. I bet your mother really did it." Cheryl had found herself screaming back, "*I did it! I did it! I did it!*"

Lana Turner remained in seclusion until the coroner's inquest, set for a week after the stabbing. Nobody gave her the newspapers, so she didn't see her love letters to Stompanato splashed on the front pages. In the letters, in which she described their lurid romance in intimate detail, she cautioned "*Cuidad*" (Be careful), and she referred to Stompanato as Daddy.

The morning after Stompanato's slaying, the *Los Angeles Times* plainly stated that Turner's daughter, Cheryl Crane, had wielded the knife.

One letter read, "I'm your woman! I need you, my man!" In another, Turner wrote, "Phones are great, yes, but I need to touch you, feel you, feel your tenderness and your strength. To hold you in my arms so, so close—to cuddle you sweetly—and then to be completely smothered in your arms and kisses, oh, so many many kisses!!!"

The letters had been sneaked to *The Los Angeles Herald & Express* by Mickey Cohen, who insisted he had received them from Stompanato before his death. He denied having had anything to do with the break-in at the Del Capri Hotel. He said that he'd allowed the letters to be published because "it's been said he was chasing Lana and she was afraid of him. The letters show they were deeply in love with each other."

When Turner learned about the publication of the letters, she felt ashamed. But ironically the contents revealed not a wanton woman, as she was portrayed in the press, but a hopelessly naïve romantic. That only heightened her appeal with fans. Favorable mail poured in at an astonishing rate.

Meanwhile, Stompanato's 45-year-old brother, Carmine, a barber, arrived in Los Angeles from Woodstock, Illinois, to claim the body. He told the press that he did not believe Cheryl's story, and he demanded a full investigation, including a lie-detector test for Turner. How, he wanted to know, could an ex-Marine be killed by a 14-year-old who had never wielded a knife before? He suggested, "Maybe he was asleep when he was stabbed."

On April 8, Carmine Stompanato flew back to Woodstock, and his brother's body arrived on a separate plane. Because Johnny Stompanato was an ex-Marine, he was buried in a flag-draped coffin with full military honors. His stepmother, Verena Stompanato, told reporters, "We're not vindictive," but she said she believed that her son had been slandered. "They are saying things that couldn't be possible. I don't believe the real truth is known.... Any cold-blooded murder should be investigated. I don't believe there is such a thing as justifiable homicide." Lana Turner had wanted to marry Johnny, she said, and had even considered sending Cheryl to school in Woodstock under an assumed name. She said she had destroyed most of the letters Johnny had written her because they were very damaging.

"Damaging to whom?" a reporter asked her.

"Lana Turner."

Del Armstrong, Turner's makeup man, held down the fort at North Bedford Drive. Retired today and in his 80s, Armstrong began his career at MGM doing makeup on *The Wizard of Oz* and ended it more than 50 years later. He remembers that he didn't leave Turner's house for three days. "I manned the door and answered the phone. It was absolutely crazy outside. Cars honking in the street. Reporters, photographers clamoring to see Lana. I let very few people in. Frank Sinatra was among the first to pay a visit. He stayed about 15 minutes with Lana. Long ago they had been lovers. They were still close friends." Armstrong says he used to be "Lana's 'date' when Frank was separated from his first wife, Nancy. I'd bring Lana to Frank's concerts, and then I'd walk her backstage and leave her with him."

Armstrong had been doing Turner's makeup since *Marriage Is a Private Affair,* in 1944. "Oh, God, was she beautiful. What a face! Perfection.... We traveled all over the world together on location. After work we used to get drunk together and talk 'guy talk.' Very basic stuff. We knew a lot about each other. I'd do anything for her, and she'd do anything for me. The only thing we hadn't done is go to bed together.... Once or twice we talked about hopping into the sack, but I'd say, 'You have too short a concentration span,' and she'd laugh, but it was the truth. She'd say, 'I want that one,' and she'd get him. She was always the aggressor. But once she slept with a guy, she'd lose interest, except with Tyrone Power.

"The week after the murder, Doctor Mac kept Lana sedated. After three days, she kind of woke up and asked to see me," Armstrong says. "I ran right up, and there she was in that huge pink bedroom. As soon as she saw me, she began to cry....

"I'd been through a lot with her. When Tyrone Power broke her heart, and when Fernando Lamas beat her up so bad she had to call Sinatra, and Frank gave her his house in Palm Springs to hide out in until her face healed, I was there.

"So that afternoon I let her cry, and then I lit her cigarette, and then she said, 'I've got to tell you exactly what happened.' She'd never lied to me, and I'd never lied to her.... She told me that she and Johnny were having one hell of a fight and she told him to get out, and that's when he began threatening her and saying he was going to beat her up. She was aware Johnny was dangerous. We all were. He was a very sinister man. Cheryl wanted to defend her mother. She was terrified he was going to kill her. He'd tried to before.

"Lana told me, 'Cheryl walked into this bedroom, and Johnny and I turned around, and said something like "Oh, no, not now," but Cheryl just kept going. And Johnny walked right into the knife and dropped like an ox.'"

There was already another theory swirling around Hollywood—that Lana Turner had stabbed Johnny Stompanato because he was fooling around with her daughter and she was jealous. Armstrong calls this theory "preposterous. Neither Lana or Cheryl ever deviated from the fact that Cheryl had stabbed Stompanato because he was trying to hurt her mother. I *knew* Johnny Stompanato, and he *was* trying to kill Lana. Besides, nobody could make up a story as complete as Lana and Cheryl told and stick to it if they were lying. It is all so crazy it has to be true."

Esther Williams, the champion swimmer who became one of MGM's biggest stars and had a dressing room next to Lana Turner's, says, "We all heard the different versions of the murder. It was the No. 1 topic of conversation in 1958." She adds, "Nobody will ever know the entire truth. The bottom line is, there have always been cover-ups here, because Hollywood protects its own."

The writer Jill Robinson, daughter of Dore Schary, head of MGM in the 50s, says she wouldn't be surprised if Stompanato had tried to fool around with Cheryl, and Lana found out. Robinson went to school with Cheryl and remembers her as a "fragile, damaged, frightened kid."

As the day of the coroner's inquest approached, Glenn Rose attempted to handle the press—"a three-ring circus of yellow journalists." It was impossible to tell from some of the news features whether Cheryl was on trial for stabbing Stompanato or Lana Turner was on trial for her loose morals. "The fans were overwhelmingly in favor of Lana," Rose says, but *The Hollywood Reporter* stated, "The town's sympathy is with Steve Crane and his daughter."

Rose says that Giesler told him they were all on the firing line together. "'Don't show emotion,' he would tell us, 'and, for Christ's sake, don't panic. Best advice: shut the fuck up.'"

Rose ignored Giesler's orders only once, when he got into a fight with the columnist Walter Winchell outside the nightclub Mocambo. "Walter had some love letters from Lana to Johnny that he planned to publish in his column, and I told him to give them back to me, they weren't his property. At one point we're pushing and shoving each other on the sidewalk, and Walter is yelling, 'You can't talk to me that way. I'm God!'" (Later, Winchell wrote a thousand-word column about Lana, telling her fans to "have a heart for a lady with a broken heart.")

After that incident, Rose says, he managed to "stay cool." "The image of Lana Turner as the distraught, concerned mother, speechless with grief and shame, was the best image to play," so he kept pushing that.

On April 11, the morning of the inquest, Lana Turner rose at dawn to be made up and coiffed. Del Armstrong says, "I couldn't be there, because I was working on another film, but I knew she was prepared. Giesler had coached her for hours. It was the most important performance of her life."

Hundreds of fans lined the sidewalk to watch Turner, severely elegant in a gray silk Italian suit, with her hair cropped mannishly short, enter the Hall of Records building in downtown Los Angeles and go up to the eighth-floor courtroom on the arm of Jerry Giesler.

More fans and 150 reporters from around the world jammed the courtroom. The local affiliate of ABC was filming and taping the inquest, with orders to make the recordings available to other radio and television stations.

Cheryl Crane was not present. She had been excused from testifying because she was a juvenile, and, Giesler said, because she had already "gone through enough." Her statement was read into the record.

The first witness was Mickey Cohen. Asked if he had identified the body as Stompanato's, he said, "I refuse to identify him as John Stompanato Jr. for the reason that I may be accused of this murder." After that he was hastily excused.

Next, Chief Anderson took the stand and confirmed that he had identified Stompanato's body.

About 10 A.M., Lana Turner testified, and for 62 minutes she held the courtroom spellbound. She underplayed, speaking very carefully and very slowly, and always calling Johnny "Mr. Stompanato." Every so often she clasped one white glove, which she kept in her lap, and she took occasional sips of water.

She described how "he kept swearing and threatening me, and he had a jacket and a shirt hanging in the closet.... He walked back to me and was holding the jacket on the hanger in a way that he was going to strike me with it. I said, 'Don't ever touch me again. I am absolutely finished. This is the end, and I want you to get out.' And after I said that, I was walking toward the bedroom door, and he was right behind me, and I opened it, and my daughter came in.... I truthfully thought she had hit him in the stomach. As best as I can remember, they came together and they parted. I still never saw a blade."

Turner would write in her 1982 memoir, "It was a humiliating ordeal to explain on the witness stand what I barely understood myself—to confess before the cameras that strange helplessness that bound me to John for so long."

After her testimony there was a 15-minute recess. Cheryl Crane would later write that reporters clustered around Turner and she suddenly felt faint. "Jerry, could we go somewhere for a few minutes?" she murmured, but Giesler stumbled, and Turner had to catch him by the arm. "Who's helping who?" she said dryly.

Reporters later quoted a bystander as saying, "What an act she's putting on!"

After the break, the inquest continued. Police and other witnesses moved on and off the stand, "providing puzzling forensic details that would raise questions for years to come," Cheryl Crane has written.

No identifiable fingerprints on the knife. No blood in the bedroom, except for "spots the size of a ten-cent piece alongside of the body," Chief Anderson testified. Later he wrote, "The most ironic angle of the Stompanato investigation was the refusal of the underworld to believe that this 'tough' ex-Marine could have been killed so easily by a 14-year-old girl.... Here's how it happened. Surprise and accident brought about tough, muscular Johnny's sudden death. The distraught child caught him off guard."

The medical examiner was among the last to testify. He described the fatal wound, adding that during the autopsy he had discovered that Johnny Stompanato was suffering from an incurable kidney disease and would not have lived more than another 10 years.

At the end of the inquest, one spectator jumped up and shouted, "Lies! Lies! All lies! This mother and daughter were both in love with Stompanato. He was better than any of them.... Johnny Stompanato was a gentleman!"

After 25 minutes, the jury returned with a verdict of "justifiable homicide," but Cheryl was ordered to be kept in jail pending a Juvenile Court hearing two weeks later. However, District Attorney William McKesson made it clear he would not be inclined to prosecute her without further evidence.

Turner said she cried every night while Cheryl was in jail and could barely sleep. One night Doctor Mac, dropping by the mansion to give her a sedative, suddenly realized that only days earlier a horrible death had occurred in that room, inches away from the bed where she lay. "My God!" he cried. "What have I done to you? You can't continue to stay here." He picked her up in his arms and carried her out of the house, to her mother's apartment nearby. The next day Turner rented another house, sight unseen, on Roxbury Drive, and she never set foot in the pink bedroom again.

Before Cheryl Crane's Juvenile Court hearing, an investigation was launched into Turner's private life. Her four marriages and lavish lifestyle were examined. The *Los Angeles Times* ran a scathing editorial chastising Turner for her self-indulgences and saying, "Cheryl isn't the juvenile delinquent; Lana is." *Life* magazine ran photographs of Turner's trial scenes in *The Postman Always Rings Twice* and *Peyton Place,* comparing the cinematic images with her pathetic breakdown at the inquest.

On April 24, Cheryl was temporarily made a ward of the court, the judge decreeing that she would live with her grandmother Mildred Turner for 60 days and have visits with her parents no more than once a week without special permission. (By December this arrangement had been made indefinite by the judge because neither Turner nor Stephen Crane objected to it.) Afterward, Turner faced reporters and bravely told them, "I am pleased with the decision."

Then she fled to Giesler's limousine, clutching a summons from the Stompanato family, which was filing a wrongful-death suit against her and Stephen Crane for $752,500. The suit charged Turner with parental negligence and with falsely alleging that Stompanato was going to disfigure her, which had "incited" Cheryl Crane "to inflict the wound."

In the weeks that followed, Turner grew increasingly anxious. In debt to her lawyers and MGM, she was terrified that the scandal had ruined her career. "But Lana never looked back," says Del Armstrong. She pushed herself to go on, because she had her mother and her daughter to support. If she couldn't work, how would she survive?

"You know those little toys, the ones that bounce back when you hit them?" Turner had once said. "That's me!"

Lana Turner was born Julia Jean "Judy" Turner on February 8, 1921, in the mining town of Wallace, Idaho. She was the only child of John Virgil Turner, a good-looking miner who loved to gamble, and Mildred Frances Cowan, his teenage wife. When Judy was six, the Turners picked up and moved to Stockton, California. Soon after, Mildred and Virgil separated, and Mildred eventually supported herself and Judy by working in a beauty parlor.

From an early age, Turner was shadowed by violence. When she was nine, her father was robbed of money he'd won in a crap game in San Francisco and was bludgeoned to death. After Virgil's funeral, Mildred boarded her daughter with friends in Stockton, who one day beat the child black-and-blue. Mildred found out and took her to another family, in Lodi. She stayed there until Mildred could rent an apartment for them in the Richmond district of San Francisco.

To forget their troubles, they'd escape to the movies. Mildred memorized outfits she saw on the screen, and she cleverly mended and accessorized the few dresses they had. Her obsession with appearance rubbed off on her daughter, and after she became a star she had entire rooms filled with suits, dresses, furs, and hundreds of pairs of shoes.

In 1936, at the height of the Depression, the two arrived in Los Angeles in an old rattletrap. They were soon sharing a cramped house with a friend.

The killing occurred on Good Friday, April 4, 1958. The next day, a photographer took this shot of Turner's Beverly Hills house, at 730 North Bedford Drive.

Mildred got a job in a beauty parlor; Judy enrolled at Hollywood High.

At 15, Turner was five feet three and voluptuous, with perfect features, big blue eyes, and creamy dimpled skin. She had the habit of hugging herself and then laughing. "She was absolutely ravishing," says a classmate.

One morning she cut a typing class and ran across the street to the Top Hat Café to buy a Coke. As she sipped it at the counter, she noticed a dapper man with a black mustache staring at her. The counterman introduced her to him; he was Billy Wilkerson, the publisher of *The Hollywood Reporter* and owner of several nightclubs, including the Cafe Trocadero. "Would you like to be in the movies?" he asked Turner, who calmly replied, "I'd have to ask my mother."

The rest is history. Wilkerson took her to the talent agent Zeppo Marx, whose associate got her an audition at Warner Bros. with Mervyn LeRoy. The director was casting a movie called *They Won't Forget* and looking for someone to play a sexy teenage student who gets murdered. LeRoy remembered Turner as "so nervous her hands were shaking." But she was so beautiful and appealing that he gave her the part and signed her to a contract at $50 a week. When Turner received her first paycheck, she told her mother excitedly, "You'll never have to work again." And she never did.

LeRoy changed Turner's first name from Judy to Lana. They would both claim credit for the name change later, and she liked to tell reporters, "That's Lana as in 'la-dee-da,' not 'lady.'"

Turner appeared in only the first 12 minutes of *They Won't Forget.* In one scene she walked quickly down the street, shoulders back, in a tight skirt and sweater. LeRoy orchestrated the soundtrack—an upbeat version of "Dixie"—to go along with her bouncing breasts and swaying hips. At the preview, the audience went wild, whistling and catcalling. After the movie opened, Warner press agents nicknamed her "the Sweater Girl."

By 1938, LeRoy had moved to MGM, taking Turner with him. She was cast in low-budget films such as *Love Finds Andy Hardy* and *Calling Dr. Kildare.* She invariably played luxury-loving bad girls, and as her roles got bigger her hair changed from auburn to blond. She posed tirelessly for publicity stills and gave dozens of interviews. Voraciously ambitious, she was always cooperative.

By 1941, Turner was earning $1,500 a week, after having perfected her slow, imperious walk in *Ziegfeld Girl.* Playing a showgirl whose head is turned by celebrity and money, she gave a critically acclaimed performance. It was the first time she was taken seriously as an actress, and the role connected with what the public had been reading about her private life. Articles usually depicted her as a nightclub queen, decked out in jewels and sables, on the town with a different man every night. While still a teenager, she had had an affair with Greg Bautzer, the flamboyant, 30-year-old lawyer for MGM, and had married and divorced bandleader Artie Shaw. Early in her 20s, she became briefly involved with billionaire producer and aviation executive Howard Hughes.

The 1940s were golden years for Turner. "She was the bridge between Jean Harlow and Marilyn Monroe," film historian Jeanine Basinger writes in her book *Lana Turner.* MGM carefully crafted her image and built her up as one of its biggest stars, pairing her with Clark Gable, Robert Taylor, and Spencer Tracy. Critics dismissed her as limited, but the public adored her soft voice and sexy magnetism. "Turner's career did not abound in great films, but it did abound in great screen moments," Basinger goes on, "her walks in *They Won't Forget* and *Ziegfeld Girl,* her mad scene in *Johnny Eager,* her execution in *The Three Musketeers.*" During World War II she was a favorite pinup, along with Betty Grable. Her exquisite face and upswept hairdo appeared in hundreds of fan magazines.

In 1942 she married an impoverished but charming man-about-town named Stephen Crane. Soon after she became pregnant, she discovered Crane's divorce from his first wife was not final, so she got an annulment. Eventually she remarried Crane, not because she wanted to, but because he pleaded with her until he finally wore her down.

Cheryl was born on July 25, 1943. She was an Rh-incompatible baby and had to have numerous blood transfusions. When the infant was finally able to go home, Turner continued to concentrate on her career. Growing up, Cheryl would sneak into her mother's closets and breathe in her distinctive perfume, Tuberose. "The scent made me long to be with her," Cheryl later wrote, but she rarely saw her. Instead she was raised by nannies and by Mildred: "My beloved Gran gave me the only warm nurturing I knew."

In 1944, Turner divorced Stephen Crane. Meanwhile, the MGM publicity department was frantically trying to keep her romantic life hidden, particularly her on-again, off-again liaison with Frank Sinatra.

She and her mother fought constantly. They were sharing a house in Bel Air, and Mildred disapproved of her daughter's increasingly reckless lifestyle. Turner retaliated by moving Mildred into an apartment of her own.

Her reputation as an offscreen sex symbol of wanton allure was becoming as powerful as her on-screen image, especially after she starred in the film based on James M. Cain's *The Postman Always Rings Twice* in 1946. Turner gives her most celebrated performance in it. Who can forget the image of her standing in a doorway in white shorts, white halter, and white turban, applying lipstick to her insolent, pouty mouth as John Garfield watches, lusting?

In 1947 she fell in love with her dream man, Tyrone Power, who had the dark, sexy good looks she was always attracted to. He was intelligent and cultivated besides. "In my memory we will always be an especially beautiful couple," she would write. "Tyrone, so stunningly handsome, was majestic, and I wanted so to be his equal."

According to Fred Lawrence Guiles, Power's biographer, Turner suffered from frequent bouts of melancholia and took amphetamines to keep her spirits up. She had irrational mood swings and often seemed out of control, which frightened Power. She became increasingly possessive of him. Whatever happened—and that included aborting his child—Turner was never quite the same after Power left her to marry Linda Christian. Esther Williams says, "Ty was the love of Lana's life. She never got over him."

By the 1950s, Turner had become one of the most popular stars in the world, earning $5,000 a week and living in a 15-room mansion in Holmby Hills with a soda fountain, a beauty parlor, a swimming pool, a tennis court, and 10 servants. She drove a white Cadillac monogrammed with her initials. Her dressing room at MGM was the grandest on the lot, with a 10-foot dressing table and a young woman whose only duty was to put records on the phonograph so that Turner could hear soothing music as she was being made up for movies such as the legendary *The Bad and the Beautiful.* In that film she gives her most sustained performance, as Georgia Lorrison, superstar and sometime lush. Turner was proud of her hysterical car scene, in which she dug deep into her own feelings about her "bitter experiences with love."

Behind the scenes, however, her life was chaotic. Her third husband, millionaire Bob Topping, whom she had married in 1948 on the rebound from Power, became violent when he drank. Her two pregnancies with Topping ended in a stillbirth and a miscarriage. In 1951 he left her, and Turner slashed one of her wrists. Del Armstrong recalls that during the filming of *The Merry Widow* a special bracelet was designed to cover her scar.

Aside from Del Armstrong, Helen Young, her hairdresser, and Alyce May, her stand-in, the only person Turner really trusted was Carmen Cruz, her Mexican maid. Cruz had gone to work for her in 1947, she says, "when I was 24 and Lana was 26." She often called Turner "Lanita." "When she spoke to me for the first time, I knew she was a sincere person. I was hired to be her personal helper.... Lana paid very well and took care of my every need.... I was her confidante at home." Carmen's first duty was to care for the rooms and rooms of clothes. Even after Turner's staff was reduced to two by the early 60s, Cruz remained with her. For 48 years Cruz served Turner

devotedly and traveled all over the world with her. "I never dreamed I could work for so long with all that was going on," Cruz says.

By the 1970s the two women had established a ritual. When Turner wasn't working, they would sit together most afternoons, watching television, drinking coffee, and talking. Turner seemed at her happiest and most relaxed then. In time Cruz would learn everything about Mildred Turner's sense of futility, about Cheryl's desperate need for love, and about Lana's lavish spending on Cheryl and her friends. "For my marriage, the birth of all my children, and even the death of my husband," Cruz says, "Lana would take care of everything. My kids would come swimming at the Malibu house all the time. Lana was very much involved in the upbringing of my kids.... Lanita had three stillbirths—little tragedies." In time the Cruzes became Turner's surrogate family.

In 1953, Turner married her fourth husband, Lex Barker, the former Tarzan, a beefy, handsome man with an easygoing manner, whose family was in the *Social Register.* For a while they were happy together. They tried to have children, but she had a stillbirth at seven months. She then became despondent and started drinking again. Barker wanted her to stop, but she refused.

"She liked her booze," recalls reporter James Bacon. He remembers once when they were on their way to a cocktail party in a limousine and she was drinking vodka from a silver flask. "I said, 'Lana, you're going to have a drink in 10 minutes,' and she said, 'That's 10 minutes without a drink.'"

In 1957, Cheryl let her mother know that Barker had been sexually molesting her. Barker denied it, but Turner said she could no longer go on living with him after such a horrifying accusation. When the couple broke up, Barker described Cheryl as "very strange," and it was reported that he had warned Turner her daughter "would end up in ... great trouble." Until he died in the 1970s, he insisted that Cheryl had lied about him.

After her divorce from Barker, Turner grew edgy. Her most recent pictures had done poorly at the box office, and her contract at MGM was up. After 17 years as one of the studio's top stars, she decided to go independent. Burdened with tax debts, she sold her mansion and looked for a house to rent, staying at the Bel-Air Hotel when she was in town. She was hoping to spend the summer of 1957 with Cheryl when producer Jerry Wald cast her in *Peyton Place.* The role of a prim, repressed mother in a small town, with an emotional teenage daughter, was unusual for her, but Turner attacked it with gusto. It was one of the best performances of her career, but when Cheryl saw it she said she felt slightly ill, because "Mother was acting in the movie the way she behaved with me in real life."

Johnny Stompanato began telephoning Turner in mid-1957, calling himself John Steele. He deluged Turner with flowers and gifts. "How did he know what music to send me?" Turner wrote. "He knew how to get things done. He had mysterious ways of obtaining information and access, as I was to learn at my bitter cost.... His cunning at finding things out about me should have made me cautious."

They began a passionate affair just before Turner started filming *Peyton Place.* Their trysts always took place in her apartment. Johnny was tender with Turner at first, and kind to Cheryl. He would take her for drives in his Thunderbird and tell her, "I really care for your mother." "With his dark good looks, stealthy movements, watchful eyes, and deep baritone," Cheryl wrote, "it's not hard to see the mystery he held for restless women."

She couldn't understand how he could keep showering her mother with expensive presents when his only source of income seemed to be the small gift shop he ran in Westwood Village. Cheryl worked there for a while, for 25 cents an hour. She found the place unimpressive—"inexpensive pieces of crude pottery and wood carvings displayed as though they were art.... John spent all his time in a brightly lit back office and store room, speaking on the phone in low mumbles. Two or three men came to see him each day." Cheryl was asked to mail packages at the post office. She suspected that they didn't contain pottery.

When a friend informed Turner that the man she was so crazy about was not John Steele but Johnny Stompanato, who was "associated with Mickey Cohen," she confronted him. He told her, "So my name is Johnny Stompanato. So what?" She said she couldn't see him anymore, because he had lied to her. He just laughed. "Lana darling, just try and get away from me!" he said. After a while, whenever he phoned, Turner hung up on him. She also began dating other men and locking even the bedroom door of the apartment she was renting.

One night she left the door unlocked, and Stompanato sneaked in and began smothering her with a pillow. Before she blacked out, he pulled the pillow away and tried to kiss her. Although she threatened to complain to the authorities, "almost the last thing I would consider was calling the police, and John knew it," she wrote. "I was paranoid about what people used to say or write about me. There was another reason . . . his consuming passion was strangely exciting."

She was about to start filming a new movie, *Another Time, Another Place,* with Sean Connery in London. It would be her first production for her company, Lanturn. In the meantime she continued her affair with Stompanato.

"I remember Johnny accompanying Lana to all the fittings she had for *Another Time,*" recalls Moss Mabry, who designed the costumes. "He would just melt sitting there, watching Lana standing straight as a little soldier, scrutinizing her gorgeous reflection and his in the floor-to-ceiling mirror. . . . He was utterly charming and likable—beautiful manners, very seductive, terrific-looking too. He wore clothes beautifully. A real ladies' man." Mabry discovered that "he'd been keeping company with one of my seamstresses, a very proper lady who had a nest egg. How Johnny found out about it I don't know, but he spent a lot of time with this lady while he was sleeping with Lana. And he apparently got money out of her too."

Turner flew to London with Del Armstrong. Because of union laws he could not do her makeup, so she made him associate producer on the film. Turner had planned to break totally with Stompanato, but she was restless. She phoned him regularly and wrote him passionate letters. Within weeks she sent him a one-way ticket.

Their reunion was "joyful," Turner writes in her autobiography. Stompanato bought her a little black poodle named Gypsy, and they settled down in a house Turner had rented in Hampstead Heath.

Soon the fights started again. He wanted her to pay $1,000 to option a story called "The Battered Bride," which he hoped to produce with her. Turner said no. She was already giving him a weekly allowance.

More fights ensued, and once he nearly strangled Turner to death. The next morning Lana could not speak. "Her vocal cords were damaged," says Glenn Rose, who was doing the publicity on the movie. "We told the press she had laryngitis." For three weeks she could do only scenes without dialogue.

At Armstrong's urging, Turner told Scotland Yard that Stompanato had threatened her life and should be deported. Within 24 hours detectives hustled Stompanato out to the airport and walked him onto a plane. Armstrong recalls, "John set the Mob against me after he found out I'd helped kick him out of England. Then Lana found out and warned him she'd spill the beans about all his criminal associations. So he shut up about doing something to me."

Cheryl Crane, then 14, Lana Turner, and attorney Jerry Giesler, standing, center, appeared at Crane's juvenile-court hearing.

In January 1958, Turner finished the picture, but she was a nervous wreck. She arranged for a vacation in Mexico. When she changed planes in Copenhagen, a smiling Stompanato was waiting on the tarmac, and reporters and photographers were in the terminal. Against her will, he accompanied her to Acapulco, where they stayed at the luxurious Villa Vera. He continued to slap her around, because she refused to make love to him, she wrote, until he held a gun to her head. Teddy Stauffer, the manager of Villa Vera, remembered, "She appeared to be anxious to see my wife and me alone, but it didn't work out. Stompanato was always around."

One day her agent, Paul Kohner, phoned to tell her she had been nominated for an Academy Award for *Peyton Place.* After Kohner's call, she cut her trip short and returned to Los Angeles, where she began looking for a house to rent. "[Johnny] insinuated his presence into my every act, even to the point of criticizing every house we saw." Finally she chose a big white mansion in a very exclusive part of Beverly Hills, on North Bedford Drive. It was spacious, with two huge bedroom suites and a tennis court.

Stompanato wanted to escort Turner to the Academy Awards, but she told him she was going with her mother and Cheryl and Glenn Rose. That evening, Stompanato glowered as he watched Turner get dressed in a skintight white lace mermaid sheath over a deep tan slip and put on a glittering diamond necklace that Bob Topping had given her. "She looked magnificent," Glenn Rose remembers, "but she seemed jittery. Something was eating her."

As she dressed, Stompanato shadowed her, trying to bully her into taking him. Hours after she returned—she lost out as best actress to Joanne Woodward for *The Three Faces of Eve*—Stompanato beat her brutally. The following week she sobbed in her daughter's arms, confessing that he had thrown her against a wall, punched her, and blackened her eyes. The 14-year-old tried to comfort her.

On April 1, Turner and Cheryl moved into the North Bedford Drive mansion. On Good Friday, April 4, it rained. "Real gloomy," Del Armstrong remembers. He dropped by the Bedford mansion for a drink, with "Bill Brooks, who we'd met in Hawaii when Lana was doing the John Wayne movie [*The Sea Chase* (1957)]. . . . We were sitting around drinking gin and tonics and shooting the breeze when Johnny walked in. He was very civil to me, and he didn't have to be, but I'd never been intimidated by him and I guess he knew that. Anyhow, Bill gives him the glad hello. They obviously knew each other. Johnny gets uncomfortable. Then Bill announces they'd gone to military school together in Missouri.

"I could tell Lana seemed surprised," Armstrong adds. "Johnny makes some kind of excuse, then leaves. Then Lana asked Bill, 'When did you go to school with John?' and he says, 'We graduated in 1943.' And Lana says, 'I thought Johnny was 43 years old.' Bill says, 'Hell, no, he's my age, 33.' Then he warns Lana, 'That Johnny is no good, bad news. He got into terrible trouble at school stealing.' Lana is fit to be tied."

Armstrong and Brooks asked Turner to join them for dinner, but she refused. She said she had to keep on unpacking. As soon as they left, she called Cheryl downstairs and started crying. "Johnny's lied to me about something else," she said, and she told her Bill Brooks's story, ending with "I'm going to get rid of him tonight."

At 8:30, Stompanato returned to the mansion, and he and Turner began fighting in the living room. She told him she would not tolerate his lies. Cheryl could hear their raised voices as she sat in her room upstairs, trying to do her homework. When the fighting seemed to get worse, she tiptoed out into the hall and leaned over the railing. "Mother! What's going on?" she called, so that Stompanato would know she was there.

A few minutes later the gangster and the movie star continued their quarrel in Cheryl's bedroom.

"He seethed," Cheryl writes. "He clearly hated her. It was controlled anger, but his neck veins stood out, and he breathed from one side of his mouth."

"You're not going to get rid of me so easy, Miss Moviestar!"

"I don't want to argue in front of the baby!" Turner cried. Then she announced, "I'm going downstairs for a drink." When she came back upstairs, she went to her room and locked herself in. Stompanato went after her and rammed his shoulder against the door. "Open up this motherfucker!" Then Cheryl heard the click of the lock, and he disappeared inside.

The fighting continued, punctuated by shouts and hysterical sobs. Finally Cheryl could stand it no longer, and she ran over and knocked on her mother's door. "Please, Mother, can I see you for a second?" To her amazement, Turner told her to come in. Stompanato was standing with his back to her, leaning against a wall. He was trembling with rage.

Cheryl reached out her hand, and Turner clasped it. Her fingers were icy. Together they walked down the hall. "Why don't you just tell him to go?" Cheryl whispered. "You're a coward, Mother."

Turner, her blue eyes very wide, whispered back, "You don't understand. I'm deathly afraid of him."

"Don't worry. I won't leave you," Cheryl assured her. "I won't be far away."

Turner seemed to gain strength from that remark. Squaring her shoulders, she marched back into her bedroom to face her lover. Amid more threats and curses, Turner ordered Stompanato to get out. Cheryl heard him shout, "You'll never get away from me! Wherever you go, I'll find you ... I'll cut you good, Baby! You'll never work again. And don't think I won't also get your mother and your kid."

Cheryl dashed down to the kitchen and grabbed a carving knife from the counter. Carmen Cruz says that she saw her leave the kitchen and run upstairs.

After the judge placed Cheryl in the custody of her grandmother, Turner remained in seclusion in her newly rented house. There were threats on her life, menacing phone calls, and ugly mail. A police car circled the house day and night. Stompanato had often warned her that if anything happened to him the Mob would get even.

During the summer of 1958, producer Ross Hunter persuaded Turner to star in the remake of *Imitation of Life,* a tearjerker based on Fannie Hurst's novel. The plot blatantly exploited the Stompanato murder, concerning as it did a self-involved, beautiful star who alternately spoils and ignores her daughter. "The movie even pandered to the ugly rumors that there had been a romance between Stompanato and me," Cheryl wrote in her memoir.

Imitation of Life revitalized Turner's career. It was one of Universal's biggest box-office hits at the time. Lana later wrote that she had made a deal for half the profits. She became a millionaire.

She was briefly on top again, and some of the other movies she made in the 60s, including *Portrait in Black* and *Madame X,* also reflected her personal scandals. There was an undercurrent of violence in these films which seemed linked to her sex appeal.

Turner's renewed success didn't alleviate her daughter's agonies. Cheryl writes, "I was destined to travel an odyssey through the depths of the juvenile justice system." She spent 11 months in reform school, and then returned to live with her mother.

Meanwhile the Stompanato family's $752,500 suit was still going on. It suggested that doubt existed over whether it had been Lana or Cheryl who wielded the knife with which Stompanato was stabbed in the stomach. If the case had gone to trial, facts might have emerged to explain why there were no identifiable fingerprints on the knife, and why it took so long for the police to arrive. A lawyer for the Stompanato family contended that Johnny had been stabbed as he lay on Turner's bed. He claimed

that if Stompanato had been standing up, he would have doubled over and fallen forward.

Turner believed she could win if the case went to trial, but she considered her daughter's welfare and privacy worth more than the settlement. In 1961 the suit was settled for $20,000 and the money was paid to John Stompanato III, who lived in Hammond, Indiana, with his mother.

During the 1960s, Cheryl ran away four times and ended up at the Institute for Living, an elite sanatorium in Connecticut. Told by her mother—incorrectly, as it turned out—that the court had extended her wardship by a year, she attempted suicide. She credits the humor and encouragement of a fellow patient, comic Jonathan Winters, with helping her regain the will to live.

Her mother continued to make headlines by getting married again, and again—to Fred May, a racehorse breeder who adored her; to Robert Eaton, an attractive gentleman much younger than Turner, who she said introduced her "to the real fulfilling pleasure in sex." Both marriages ended in divorce.

Her seventh and last husband, whom she married in 1969, was a nightclub hypnotist named Ronald Dante (né Peller). Within six months he'd defrauded her of $35,000 and stolen $100,000 in jewelry, at a time when she had other problems as well. *The Survivors,* a TV series she'd pinned her hopes on, didn't pan out. She was now close to 50, and movie roles had stopped coming. She started touring in shows such as *Forty Carats,* playing in dinner theaters all over the country. It was a brutal existence, but she endured it for a while because she could make more than $17,000 a week.

In 1971 a handsome blond hairdresser and former dance instructor for Arthur Murray named Eric Root met Turner. "We liked each other instantly," he says. "She thought I resembled her father, Virgil. We used to go dancing a lot. Virgil had taught her to dance."

Root began doing Turner's hair, and gradually he became her regular escort, bodyguard, and confidant. In time, Root says, he persuaded Turner to "lay off the booze." He took her to his holistic doctor, who helped her get on a healthy diet.

For the next 14 years, Root and Turner traveled extensively. "All Eric wanted was some peace and happiness for Lana," says Karen Cadle, another friend of Turner's in those last years. "He became Lana's main connection to the outside world. Along with Carmen, he took care of her and really loved her, and she loved him back."

In 1982, when Lana Turner published her autobiography, she stated unequivocally that her daughter had killed Stompanato. In April 1985, however, Root says, Turner confided in him that she—not Cheryl—had stabbed her lover. "I killed the son of a bitch and I'd do it again," he says she told him. She made him promise, he adds, to "tell the truth so I can rest in peace. Don't let my baby take the rap all her life for my mistake."

Root says he never pressed for more details, but when he wrote *The Private Diary of My Life with Lana,* after she died, he maintained that he had been able to piece the story together with the help of Raymond Strait, detective Fred Otash's biographer. According to Otash's unpublished recollections, Jerry Giesler took Otash to the mansion before the police arrived. Together they persuaded Turner to let her daughter take the blame for the stabbing. Otash "wiped the prints off the knife and replaced Lana's prints with Cheryl's." (The police reported only smudged prints on the knife.) "The bed looked as if a hog had been slaughtered in it," Root quotes Otash as saying.

When questioned about this version of the murder, Cheryl Crane answers by telephone from her home in Palm Springs. "Liz Smith had the ultimate comment. She said, 'The Egyptians got it right. They buried their servants with their masters.'" She goes on to say, "This idea that Root had in his book is so far-fetched.... You know, everybody has something they want to sell. I guess it was the only way he could get his book published."

Months earlier, Crane explained to me why she would not speak in depth about Stompanato or her mother. "I said it all in my book." Her memoir also describes in harrowing detail what it was like to grow up as the child of a driven, self-centered star.

When *Detour: A Hollywood Story* was published, Cheryl was 44, and had more than gotten her act together. "She is one brave, smart lady," says Jill Robinson. For 15 years she helped her father, Stephen Crane, run his chain of Kon Tiki restaurants. They made millions. When he sold them in 1978, she became a successful real-estate broker in Hawaii and San Francisco. She also created a happy, stable private life for herself with her companion, Joyce LeRoy, a willowy brunette whose nickname is Josh. The two women are still together. Josh told Cheryl early on in their relationship, "I think it was a very brave and noble thing to go to your mother's defense."

Crane writes that she was astounded. "No one had ever said that what I had done was anything but monstrous. . . . My life changed." She contends that Josh encouraged her to have an honest and open relationship with Lana Turner.

However, according to Eric Root, meetings between mother and daughter were few and far between. "Lana and I had dinner with Josh and Cheryl a couple of times," Root recalls. "It was tense. Sometimes Lana would act dismissive about Cheryl's accomplishments in life. Once she reduced Cheryl to tears. Later I asked her, 'How can you say that? She's your flesh and blood.' And Lana yelled, 'That's not my blood!' I said, 'What do you mean?' and she told me, 'When Cheryl was born, they removed all of my blood from her body and replaced it with someone else's blood. God only knows whose!' "

Carmen Cruz says, "Lana was very upset with Cheryl after she stabbed Stompanato. She used to say to me, 'How could she have done such a thing? She defended me, yes, but if she was capable of such violence, what else is she capable of?' She got more and more scared of Cheryl as time went on." Crane disputes this. "I never heard that," she says. "There was a bond between my mother and me. It was never broken."

Cheryl Crane is somewhat more equivocal in *Detour:* "I both hated and adored my mother. . . . Deep down, I had always loved my mother, even been obsessed by her."

By the 1990s, Lana Turner had become a virtual recluse, rarely leaving her luxurious condominium in Century City, which she called "my ivory tower." She watched TV, sometimes all day. She became fascinated with the O. J. Simpson trial. "He'll get off," she predicted. Occasionally she'd stay up late and rerun her old movies. She often went to bed at dawn.

The main constant was Carmen Cruz. "My darling Carmencita," Turner called her, vowing that they would always be together. Carmen assured her that she would never leave, and they continued their ritual of coffee every afternoon.

By then, Carmen's children were grown and had children of their own, but they still dropped by to see Lana Turner, and sometimes she would spend holidays with them. She once spent Thanksgiving with Eric Root and his sister, Harriet, who did her nails. She says, "Lana Turner was the loneliest woman I've ever known."

Sometime in the 1950s, Turner realized that Cruz was taking the bus to and from work and offered to buy her a car. From that time on, she provided the maid with a series of automobiles. Late in Turner's life she bought Cruz a Ford Escort, and the two women began taking drives together out to Malibu, because Turner loved the ocean. They would walk slowly over the dunes, the frail, aging movie star in dark glasses, swathed in scarves, arm in

arm with the diminutive Mexican lady, who sometimes wore Turner's cast-off finery and one of her elegant little hats.

In 1992, Turner was diagnosed with throat cancer and began chemotherapy and radiation treatments. "She suffered a lot," Karen Cadle says, "but she was very gallant. She found religion. She read the Bible; she talked about God. She always believed she would get better."

Cadle thinks Turner's finest moment came when she was invited to accept a lifetime-achievement award at the San Sebastián International Film Festival in Spain in September 1994. It was her last public appearance. "Cheryl hadn't wanted her to go," says Cadle.

"Because I was worried about her," Crane responds. "We all were."

Cadle encouraged her and went with her. She produced and directed Turner interviews for a segment of *Lifestyles,* which Robin Leach hosted. Cadle recalls, "Lana was no more than 85 pounds, but she seemed suffused with energy and high spirits. On the show she talked to Robin about the wonders of life. She positively radiated peace of mind."

Turner wore a gorgeous red Nolan Miller ensemble to the festival, and was driven through the streets of San Sebastián in an open car with Cruz sitting next to her. Crowds cheered all along the way to the huge theater, where the actor William Hurt introduced her and clips of her legendary films filled the screen.

On June 29, 1995, she breathed her last. Cheryl Crane, who was with her mother every single day during Turner's final illness, told *Daily Variety,* "She was doing fine. This was a total shock. She'd completed seven weeks of radiation a short while ago, and it looked like she was fine. She just took a breath and—she was gone."

Later, Cruz confided to Eric Root, "Lanita died in my arms." Root adds, "Carmen took to sleeping on the floor next to her bed for months."

Turner in her will left Cheryl $50,000. Everything else she left to Carmen Lopez Cruz, "close friend and longtime employee."

The producer Elliott Martin is videotaping Cruz's recollections about Turner, which he hopes will serve as background for a movie and book entitled *Lana's Secret Diary.* Martin says that in the last months of her life Turner scribbled an epilogue to her memoir. Five days before she died, she gave it to Cruz, who also has things Johnny Stompanato gave her to keep for him. Martin says that there will be a section in both the film and the book about the stabbing.

But whose version?

"Carmen's," Martin says flatly. And Cruz adds, "I was there."

To which Cheryl Crane responds, "That's totally untrue. My God, Carmen wasn't even the maid. The maid who was my mother's maid was Arminda. Carmen was like a second, who would come in. And Arminda had gone home for the evening [the night of Stompanato's killing]."

"But Carmen Cruz was close to your mother?" I ask.

"Oh, yeah," Cheryl Crane says. "But she was just not there [that night]." Cruz was never questioned by the police or the coroner about the killing, and no one who was at the house that night can remember having seen her.

Cheryl Crane is the only one who really knows what happened in that pink bedroom so long ago. "I said it all in my book," she repeats. "I don't want to relive the horror. But I stand by my story."

And so, apparently, does everyone else in this power struggle of competing narratives. Probably we will never arrive at the total truth. Maybe that's why this tale of the movie star and the gangster has inspired novels such as Harold Robbins's *Where Love Has Gone* and *films noirs* such as *L.A. Confidential.* Because this is much more than a thriller. It's a mystery that continues to grow in its endless complications. □

Within a week of the crime, Turner, a veteran of movie trial scenes, testified at the inquest, carefully measuring her words between sips of water.

MALIBU BEACH, 1933 *Opposite*, first row, from left: Miriam Hopkins, Lilyan Tashman, Mae West, Edmund Lowe, Maurice Chevalier (with hat), Kay Francis, Joan Crawford, Leslie Howard, Adolphe Menjou, Dolores Del Rio. Reclining in front: Constance Bennett, Joel McCrea. In enclosure: John Barrymore, Ethel Barrymore, Lionel Barrymore, George Arliss, Helen Hayes. To right of enclosure: Joseph Schenck, Samuel Goldwyn, Joan Blondell (seated), Douglas Fairbanks Jr. (arms in air), Sylvia Sidney, Douglas Fairbanks (arms folded), unidentified sunbather, Oliver Hardy, Stan Laurel. *This page*, first row: Mary Pickford, Norma Shearer (with guitar), Louella Parsons, Ernst Lubitsch, Wallace Beery. Second row: Gary Cooper, Marion Davies, Charlie Chaplin, George Raft, Howard Hughes, Harpo Marx, Jean Harlow, Clark Gable. Third row: Claudette Colbert, Cecil B. DeMille (finger to brow), Fredric March. Fourth row: Edward G. Robinson, Marie Dressler, Katharine Hepburn, Marlene Dietrich, Greta Garbo. Fifth row: Gene Fowler, Nancy Carroll (with beach ball), Jimmy Durante.

ILLUSTRATED IN 1933
BY **MIGUEL COVARRUBIAS**

MALIBU BEACH, 1995 First row: Diane Keaton, Tom Hanks, David Geffen, Steven Spielberg, Jeffrey Katzenberg, Michael Ovitz, Roseanne, Bob Hope, Sophia Loren, Jane Fonda. Second row: Larry Fortensky (shirt with green collar), Elizabeth Taylor, Michael Jackson, Bette Midler, Cher, Barbra Streisand, Richard Gere (behind Streisand), Johnny Depp, Demi Moore, Keanu Reeves (behind Moore), Bruce Willis, Arnold Schwarzenegger (with machine gun), Kevin Costner, Marlon Brando (facing ocean). Under red-and-white umbrella: Robert De Niro, John Travolta, Sharon Stone, Eddie Murphy, Madonna (reclining in black swimsuit), Sylvester Stallone. In distance, at shore: Meryl Streep (pulling raft), Johnny Carson (with binoculars). In water: Shirley MacLaine, Whoopi Goldberg, Sean Connery, Michael Douglas.

ILLUSTRATED IN 1995
BY **RISKO**

BUSTER KEATON The childhood pratfall may have been apocryphal, but to have been christened Buster—so Keaton claimed —by Harry Houdini (who saw him roll downstairs, unscathed, at the age of six months) is to have had, and have been, a lucky star. Arguably Chaplinesque before Chaplin (with whom he finally made a joint appearance in *Limelight* in 1952), Keaton was the dreamy-eyed Pierrot—*Sherlock Jr.* being his best-executed comic reverie— and a uniquely brave stuntman to boot. As a director he could have been famous for *The General* alone.

PHOTOGRAPHED CIRCA 1920

BOB HOPE The old trouper's comic timing is legendary; so, too, his million-gag "joke vault," revealed here, at his home in Toluca Lake, California. Before we had road pictures we had *Road to Singapore* (and to Morocco, and to Hong Kong—seven destinations in all, including Utopia), in which Hope was a global wisecracker, playing off Bing Crosby and Dorothy Lamour. Dedicated holiday entertainer of American forces overseas, even as Vietnam cast a pall. The act became big business, with a staff of quipsmiths, but also a slot machine of money for charity.

PHOTOGRAPHED IN 1995
BY **ANNIE LEIBOVITZ**

SOPHIA LOREN The *bella figura* of Sophia Loren has outlived her onetime co-star Marcello Mastroianni (last seen with her in *Prêt à Porter* in 1994). It has also outlasted the condemnation of the Vatican, which in the early 1960s denounced her as a concubine and her marriage to producer Carlo Ponti as bigamous. Cary Grant met her on the set of *The Pride and the Passion* in 1956 and swiftly proposed. By 1995, *Grumpier Old Men* proved she retained the same allure. Shall we ever forget her in *The Millionairess, Lady L*, or *Arabesque*? Or with Marcello in *Marriage Italian Style*? Her Oscar for *Two Women* in 1961? Even now, there is only one Sophia.

PHOTOGRAPHED IN 1990
BY **ANNIE LEIBOVITZ**

PRESTON STURGES, urbane writer-director (*The Great McGinty, The Palm Beach Story*), donated a lap to Claudette Colbert; Joel McCrea supervised.

FRANK CAPRA (*It Happened One Night, You Can't Take It with You*) was directing's ultimate idealist. He gave us Gary Cooper's Mr. Deeds and Jimmy Stewart's Mr. Smith.

Vanity Fair called **ERICH VON STROHEIM** silent film's most meticulous director: for authenticity, he once made his cast wear military-issue underwear.

Filmmaker supreme **BILLY WILDER**—right, with actor William Holden on the set of Wilder's 1950 masterpiece, *Sunset Boulevard*—created *Double Indemnity, Some Like It Hot,* and *Sabrina.*

JOHN FORD, with Tim Holt in '39 while filming *Stagecoach* (one of Ford's 21 films with John Wayne), directed 140 pictures, securing six Oscars, two for wartime documentaries.

SERGEI EISENSTEIN, Russia's titanic director, made the classic *Potemkin.*

Director **OLIVER STONE** (*Wall Street, JFK, Nixon*) has always courted controversy.

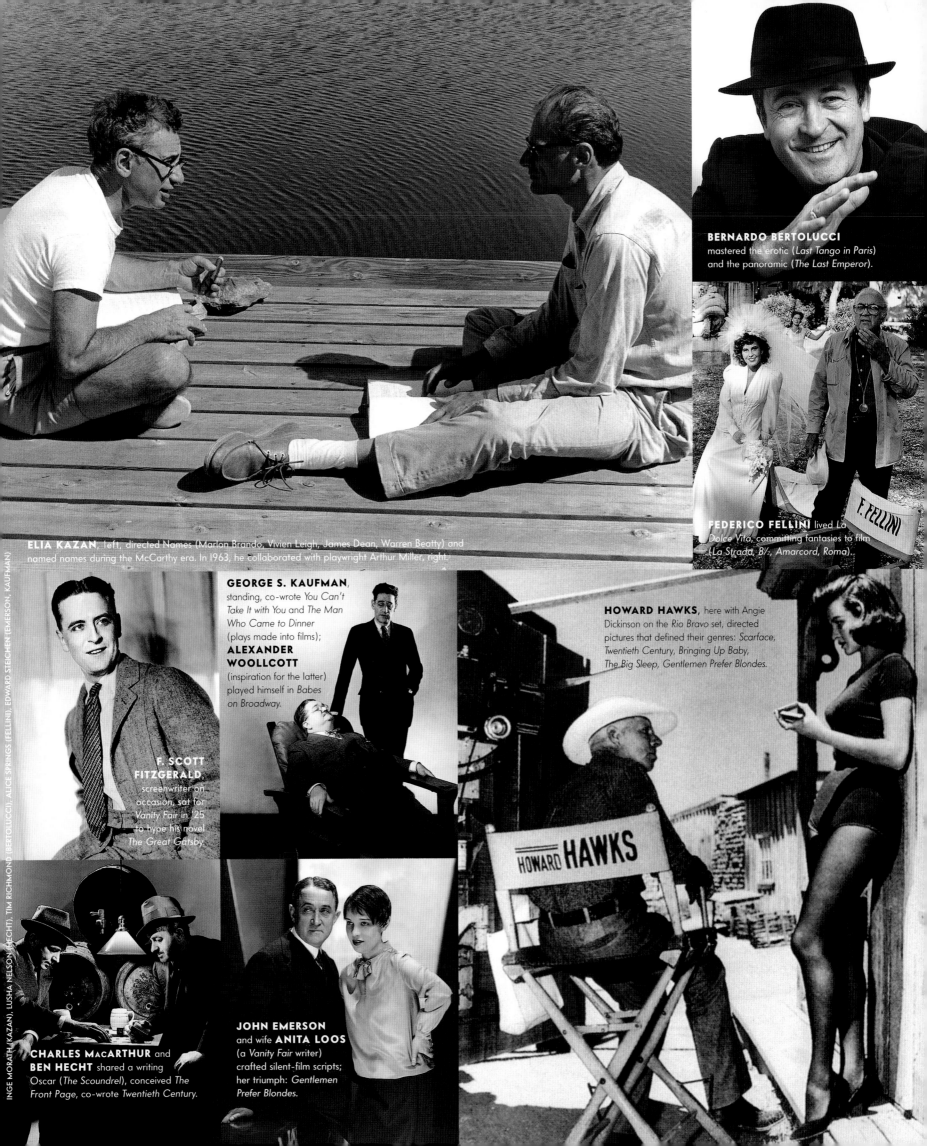

BERNARDO BERTOLUCCI mastered the erotic (*Last Tango in Paris*) and the panoramic (*The Last Emperor*).

FEDERICO FELLINI lived *La Dolce Vita*, committing fantasies to film (*La Strada, 8½, Amarcord, Roma*).

ELIA KAZAN, left, directed Names (Marlon Brando, Vivien Leigh, James Dean, Warren Beatty) and named names during the McCarthy era. In 1963, he collaborated with playwright Arthur Miller, right.

GEORGE S. KAUFMAN, standing, co-wrote *You Can't Take It with You* and *The Man Who Came to Dinner* (plays made into films); **ALEXANDER WOOLLCOTT** (inspiration for the latter) played himself in *Babes on Broadway*.

F. SCOTT FITZGERALD, screenwriter on occasion, sat for *Vanity Fair* in '25 to hype his novel *The Great Gatsby*.

HOWARD HAWKS, here with Angie Dickinson on the *Rio Bravo* set, directed pictures that defined their genres: *Scarface, Twentieth Century, Bringing Up Baby, The Big Sleep, Gentlemen Prefer Blondes*.

CHARLES MacARTHUR and **BEN HECHT** shared a writing Oscar (*The Scoundrel*), conceived *The Front Page*, co-wrote *Twentieth Century*.

JOHN EMERSON and wife **ANITA LOOS** (a *Vanity Fair* writer) crafted silent-film scripts; her triumph: *Gentlemen Prefer Blondes*.

ERNEST LEHMAN The words, yes, the words. They do lead to images, you know. It was Ernest Lehman ("perhaps the greatest screenwriter in history," *Vanity Fair* asserted) who persuaded Hitchcock to hound Cary Grant with that crop duster in *North by Northwest*—on this very patch of farmland in Ventura County, California. For Billy Wilder he co-wrote *Sabrina*. He adapted *Sweet Smell of Success* from his own novella. And for those who like words with their tunes, Lehman dashed off *Hello, Dolly!*, *West Side Story*, and, for good measure, *The Sound of Music*.

PHOTOGRAPHED IN 1998
BY **ART STREIBER**

JOHN BARRYMORE Greta Garbo spoke of his "divine madness," encountered as they filmed *Grand Hotel;* he combined the Shakespearean values of a vintage theatrical family with the conduct of a dedicated rake, making plausible the title role in 1926's *Don Juan* and the part of the director Oscar Jaffee in *Twentieth Century. The Sea Beast* was a good try at *Moby-Dick.* In *Dr. Jekyll and Mr. Hyde,* the "Great Profile" brought off the metamorphosis without makeup; after the liver shriveled he played Hyde all too often.

PHOTOGRAPHED IN 1925
BY **JAMES ABBE**

DREW BARRYMORE And it goes on: in 1984 *Vanity Fair* asked George Hurrell, who had photographed on the set of *Grand Hotel*, to shoot John Barrymore's granddaughter, Drew, who was nine at the time. By then she had already knocked 'em dead as Gertie in *E.T.* From cherub to nymph—or brat to tart, if you count *Firestarter*—she fast-forwarded too soon (Steven Spielberg is her godfather; Kurt Cobain's kid is *her* goddaughter), but rebounded in a string of films, including the improbably named *Never Been Kissed*.

PHOTOGRAPHED IN 1984
BY **GEORGE HURRELL**

THE *AMERICAN GRAFFITI* GANG *Before Happy Days, Grease, Laverne and Shirley, Diner, and all the other greasy-kid-stuff evocations of the late 50s and early 60s, American Graffiti vroomed into theaters in 1973, the second feature by a beardy young phenom and car nut named George Lucas. The last Lucas film to be made without the armor and armadas of the Star Wars juggernaut, the picture took just 28 days and $775,000 to shoot and did an astonishing $115 million worth of business. Lucas's nostalgic and gearhead tendencies would get further airings, but never again in such pure, intimate form.*

PHOTOGRAPHED IN 2000
BY **ANNIE LEIBOVITZ**

From left: Paul Le Mat, George Lucas, MacKenzie Phillips, Bo Hopkins, Kathleen Quinlan, Charles Martin Smith, Candy Clark, Richard Dreyfuss, Suzanne Somers, Ron Howard, Cindy Williams, Harrison Ford.

WILLIAM POWELL Long before Mr. Bond, there was an etiquette of the cigarette case, the martini, and the riposte, and its perfectionist exponent was Nick Charles. The superb dandyism of William Powell, concealing the usual steely resolve, made him seem leaner than he really was (and obliterated the trivial fact that the Thin Man was a victim in the movie so titled, not the sleuth in its sequels). Of such mistakes is immortality composed.

PHOTOGRAPHED IN 1930
BY **VICTOR BARNABA**

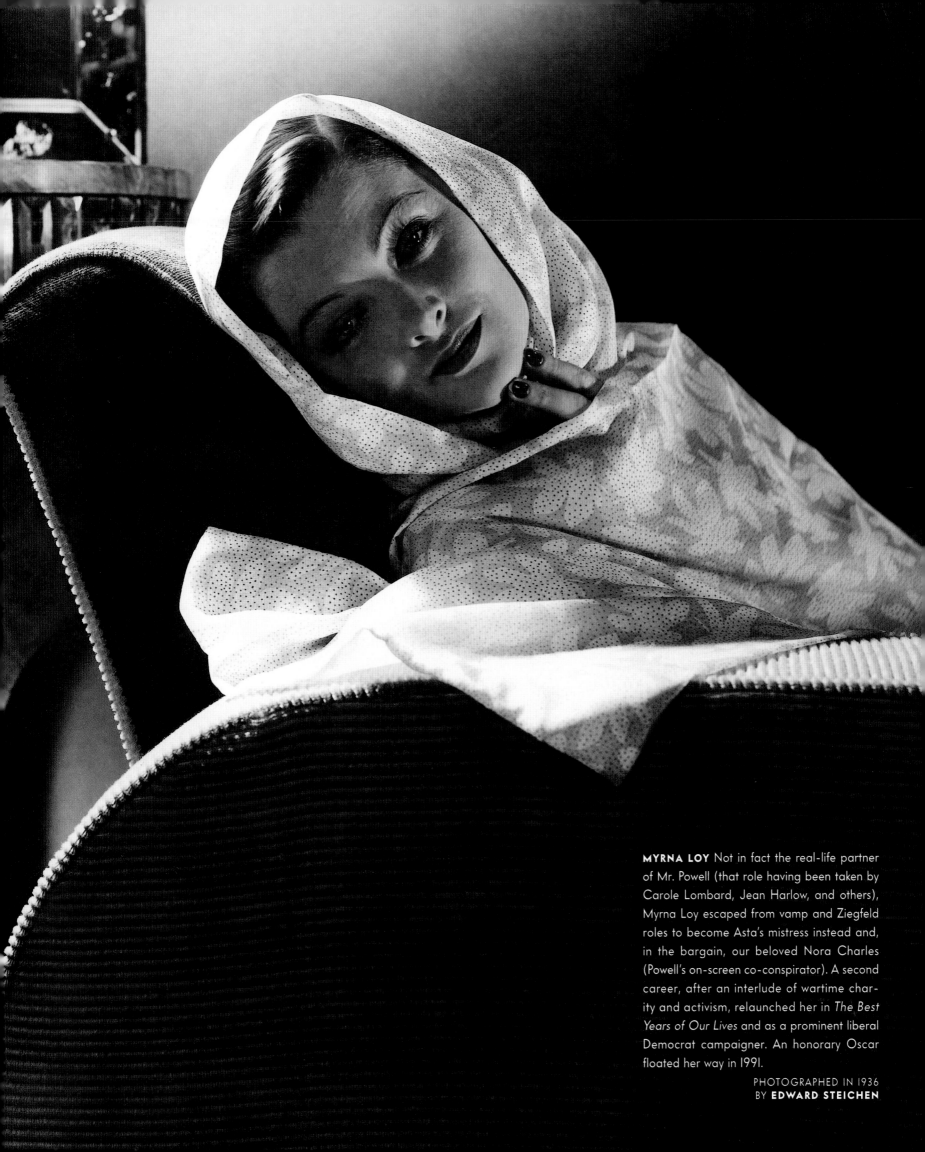

MYRNA LOY Not in fact the real-life partner of Mr. Powell (that role having been taken by Carole Lombard, Jean Harlow, and others), Myrna Loy escaped from vamp and Ziegfeld roles to become Asta's mistress instead and, in the bargain, our beloved Nora Charles (Powell's on-screen co-conspirator). A second career, after an interlude of wartime charity and activism, relaunched her in *The Best Years of Our Lives* and as a prominent liberal Democrat campaigner. An honorary Oscar floated her way in 1991.

PHOTOGRAPHED IN 1936
BY **EDWARD STEICHEN**

LEW WASSERMAN When invited by L.B.J. to be his secretary of commerce, Lew Wasserman turned down the job in order to stay at the Music Corporation of America. He knew where the real power lay. (Not surprising for a guy who was actor Ronald Reagan's agent.) For decades, mentor to an entire industry; also godfather to Jamie Lee Curtis. Sold the Japanese MCA and Universal—for more than 30 years the site of his power lunches, like the one pictured here with longtime colleague Sidney Sheinberg (second from right) and other MCA execs in the studio commissary—before having famous second thoughts in a town where these usually come too late.

PHOTOGRAPHED IN 1995
BY **ANNIE LEIBOVITZ**

By David Kamp

RIVOLI THEATER, NEW YORK CITY,
JUNE 12, 1963

ack in the studio, Johnny Carson was in stitches. *The Tonight Show* had taken the unusual step of hooking up by live remote to the world premiere of *Cleopatra,* and the man he'd deputized to stand outside the Rivoli Theater in Times Square, Bert Parks, couldn't elicit a single upbeat comment from the film's director, Joseph L. Mankiewicz. "Congratulations, Mr. Mankiewicz!" said Parks, agleam with Brylcreem and headwaiter unction. "A wonderful, wonderful achievement!"

Mankiewicz, a stocky, impassive-looking man, had the mien of a Wall Street executive strong-armed into addressing his wife's garden club. "Well," he said warily, "you must know something I don't."

The studio audience roared with laughter. Carson's chuckling bled over the audio track. Parks persevered. "I want to ask you," he said conspiratorially, "whether you are *personally* going to control the sound on the showing of *Cleopatra* tonight? That's the rumor!"

"No," said Mankiewicz, "I think everything connected with *Cleopatra* is beyond my control at the moment."

The studio audience roared again. "Is some of the tension gone?" said Parks, changing tack. "Do you feel a little more at ease now?"

"No, I, uh . . . " Mankiewicz smiled thinly. "I feel as though the guillotine were about to drop."

With that ringing directorial endorsement, the four-hour epic *Cleopatra* unspooled before the public for the first time. It was a crack-up to Carson and company because poor Parks was evidently the only man in town willing to keep up appearances, to pretend that the world had trained its cameras on the *Cleopatra* premiere because it heralded the arrival of a spectacular new filmed entertainment in Todd-AO with color by DeLuxe. The truth was that everyone had come to see the train wreck. Everyone knew that *Cleopatra* was an extraordinarily botched production that had cost $44 million—an unheard-of sum for 1963 which was all the more astounding considering that Hollywood's previous all-time budget record setter, *Ben-Hur,* had only four years earlier cost a mere $15 million, chariot race and all. Everyone knew that *Cleopatra* had nearly gutted the studio that made it, Twentieth Century Fox. Everyone knew that it had taken two directors, two separate casts, two Fox regimes, and two and a half years of stop-start filmmaking in England, Italy, Egypt, and Spain to get the damned thing done.

Above all, everyone knew that *Cleopatra* had given the world "Liz and Dick," the adulterous pairing of Elizabeth Taylor and Richard Burton, irresistibly cast as Cleopatra and Mark Antony. Never before had celebrity scandal pushed so far into global consciousness, with Taylor-Burton pre-empting John Glenn's orbiting of the Earth on tabloid front pages, denunciations being sounded on the Senate floor, and even the Vatican newspaper publishing an "open letter" that excoriated Taylor for "erotic vagrancy." When she signed on for the role, Taylor had already been four times a bride, once a widow, and once a purported home wrecker, but it was during the making of *Cleopatra* that she truly transcended the label of mere "movie star" and became, once and for all, *Elizabeth Taylor,* the protagonist in a still-running extravocational melodrama of star-crossed romance, exquisite jewelry, and periodic emergency hospitalizations.

"It was probably the most chaotic time of my life. That hasn't changed," says Taylor, who has seldom discussed the *Cleopatra* experience publicly.

"What with *le scandale,* the Vatican banning me, people making threats on my life, falling madly in love . . . It was fun and it was dark—oceans of tears, but some good times too."

For old Hollywood, *Cleopatra* represented the moment when the jig was up. No longer would anyone buy the studio system's sanitized, prepackaged lives of the stars, nor would the stars and their agents bow in obeisance to the aging moguls who'd founded the place. It was the moment when every schnook on the street became an industry insider, fluent in *Variety*ese, up to speed on Liz's "deal" ($1 million against 10 percent of the gross), aware that a given film was *x* million dollars overbudget and needed to earn back *y* million dollars just to break even. *Heaven's Gate, Ishtar, Waterworld*—the modern narrative of the "troubled production" began here, though none of these films would come close to matching *Cleopatra* for sheer anarchy, overreach, and bad Karma. Here, too, originated the mixed-blessing concept of "the most expensive movie ever made": in strict economic terms, *Cleopatra* still holds the title. *Variety* estimated *Cleopatra's* cost in 1997 dollars to be $300 million, a full $100 million more than *Titanic's.* Even if you perform a straightforward consumer-price-index conversion of the $44 million figure, *Cleopatra's* adjusted-for-inflation budget comes out at $231 million.

Mankiewicz called *Cleopatra* "the toughest three pictures I ever made," and his epitaph for the film—that it was "conceived in a state of emergency, shot in confusion, and wound up in a blind panic"—is one of filmdom's most famous quotes. Even now the movie's survivors talk of its making almost as if they're discussing a paranormal experience. "There was a certain . . . madness to it all," says Hume Cronyn, who played Sosigenes, *Cleopatra's* scholarly adviser. "It wasn't anything as clear as 'Richard Burton is moving out on his wife, Elizabeth is leaving Eddie Fisher.' It was much more complicated, more levels than that.... Paparazzi in the trees.... We were weeks behind.... Hanky-panky going on in this corner and that.... There were wheels within wheels within wheels. *God,* it was a messy situation."

Although it ended up turning a small profit and winning modest critical acclaim, *Cleopatra* had grim aftereffects on many of its principals. Mankiewicz would never again attain the brilliance and prolificacy of his late-40s-to-late-50s peak, during which he pulled off the still-unmatched feat of winning four Oscars in two years: for writing and directing *A Letter to Three Wives* (1949) and *All About Eve* (1950). "*Cleopatra* affected him the rest of his life," says his widow, Rosemary, who worked as his assistant on the film. "It made him more sensitive to the other blows that would come along." Mankiewicz would make only three more features, concluding with the minor gem *Sleuth* in 1972, and then spend his final 21 years disillusioned and idle, "finding reasons not to work," in the words of his son Tom.

Taylor and Burton, in *Cleopatra's* aftermath, would marry each other twice, make one good movie together, Mike Nichols's *Who's Afraid of Virginia Woolf?,* and otherwise fritter away their acting careers on a series of blowsy, drink-sodden exhibitions of international jet-set filmmaking: *The V.I.P.s, The Sandpiper, The Taming of the Shrew, Dr. Faustus, The Comedians, Boom!, Divorce His, Divorce Hers.*

As for the film's producer, the 68-year-old legend Walter Wanger, he would never make another movie. He had meant for *Cleopatra* to be a happy culmination of a distinguished career that had begun in 1921, when he persuaded Paramount to put Rudolph Valentino in *The Sheik.* Instead, he was forced on premiere night to sit queasily through a movie he hadn't seen, having been aced out of *Cleopatra*'s postproduction phase by Twentieth Century Fox president Darryl F. Zanuck, who targeted him as a prime suspect in the whole mess. And though the concept had been his in the first place, Wanger stood outside the ropes with the hoi polloi, watching as Mankiewicz, Zanuck, Rex Harrison (who played Julius Caesar), and Roddy McDowall (who played Octavian) made their entrances.

And where on this magical night at the Rivoli were the two people everyone wanted to see, Taylor and Burton? In England, where Burton was filming *Becket.* "We'd just had it with *Cleopatra* by then," says Taylor. "The whole thing. It was years of my life." A few weeks later, however, Taylor reluctantly hosted a London screening of the film. She dutifully sat through the picture, mortified by the memories it evoked and the butchery, as she perceived it, of Mankiewicz's vision. Immediately afterward, she hurried back to the Dorchester Hotel, where she was staying—and threw up.

AN INAUSPICIOUS BEGINNING: NEW YORK, LOS ANGELES, 1958–59
"He would never have pulled the plug on Cleopatra. *That would have been like giving up a child."*
—Stephanie Guest, daughter of Walter Wanger

Everyone in the movie business loved Walter Wanger—he spoke well, was Dartmouth-educated, wore Savile Row suits, and was reliably couth and hail-fellow-well-met, the antithesis of the shouters who ran things.

Wanger had wanted to do a Cleopatra picture for years. There had been others—a 1917 silent version with Theda Bara; the opulent Cecil B. DeMille version of 1934, featuring Claudette Colbert; and, in 1946, a soporific British adaptation of George Bernard Shaw's play *Caesar and Cleopatra,* starring Claude Rains and Vivien Leigh. But Wanger hoped to surpass them all with an intelligent treatment and a star in the lead who was, in his words, "the quintessence of youthful femininity, of womanliness and strength." He found his ideal Queen of the Nile in 1951, when he saw Elizabeth Taylor in George Stevens's *A Place in the Sun.*

But that year Wanger was not in the best position to do a deal. After a couple of decades as one of Hollywood's more successful independent producers, responsible for such films as *Queen Christina,* with Greta Garbo, and John Ford's *Stagecoach,* he'd fallen upon a hitless period, the ignominy of which was compounded by the discovery that his wife, the actress Joan Bennett, was having an affair with her agent, Jennings Lang of MCA. On December 13, 1951, in an act that froze Hollywood in disbelief, Wanger staked out Bennett and Lang in the MCA parking lot, pulled out a pistol, and shot Lang in the groin. That Wanger got off as lightly as he did—serving only a four-month sentence at a Southern California "honor farm" in

Cleopatra, with a $44 million budget, was arguably the costliest movie ever made. It also spawned the most frenzied media circus in cinema history. The film's stars, Taylor and Burton, confronted an L.A. throng in 1962.

mid-1952—was in large part a testament to how well liked he was: Samuel Goldwyn, Harry and Jack Warner, Walt Disney, and Darryl Zanuck contributed to his legal fund.

By 1958, Wanger's comeback was in full swing (he had recently produced Don Siegel's thriller *Invasion of the Body Snatchers* and Robert Wise's *I Want to Live!,* for which Susan Hayward would win the 1959 Academy Award for best actress), and his thoughts returned to his dream project. On September 30 he took his first meeting about *Cleopatra* with Spyros Skouras, then the president of Twentieth Century Fox. Skouras, a snow-haired contemporary of Wanger's, was amenable, but he envisioned something more modest than what Wanger had in mind. During their meeting, Skouras had a secretary excavate the ancient script for the soundless 1917 *Cleopatra*—produced by the Fox Film Corporation, Twentieth Century Fox's progenitor—and said, "All this needs is a little rewriting. Just give me this over again and we'll make a lot of money."

Fox was not a well-run operation in the late 50s. All the studios were suffering from the rise of television and the court-ordered dissolution of the studio system, but Skouras and company were having a particularly rough time of it—an internal report published in 1962 reported a four-year loss of about $61 million. "We were the only people who could put John Wayne, Elvis Presley, and Marilyn Monroe in movies and *not* have them do any business," says Jack Brodsky, a Fox publicist during the *Cleopatra* years.

One reason for Fox's weak programming was the departure in 1956 of its founder and resident genius-dynamo, chief of production Darryl Zanuck, who, burned out after 23 years on the job, quit to become an independent producer. Zanuck's replacement was Buddy Adler, who had produced *From Here to Eternity* and *Love Is a Many Splendored Thing* but proved to be an ineffectual executive. As long as Zanuck had been in place, the New York–based Skouras, a Greek immigrant who'd worked his way up from owning a single movie theater in St. Louis, had kept his distance from Los Angeles and the filmmaking process. With Adler, however, Skouras felt no such inhibitions, and began to meddle heavily.

Skouras was no creative genius, but he had made one important strategic move that temporarily "saved" the industry from television—namely, he kicked off the wide-screen era by making *The Robe,* a 1953 biblical epic starring Richard Burton, with the studio's new CinemaScope technology. That film's success ($17 million gross on a budget of $5 million) made Skouras a hero in Hollywood, and soon every studio was rushing out mastodonic sand-swept period epics in rival wide-screen processes such as WarnerScope, TechniScope, and VistaVision.

But by the time Wanger was trying to get *Cleopatra* off the ground, the bloom of CinemaScope had withered. The budget-minded Adler envisioned a modest back-lot picture, costing perhaps a million dollars or two, starring a Fox contract player such as Joan Collins, Joanne Woodward, or Suzy Parker. Wanger continued to argue his case for Taylor, whom Skouras didn't want, because "she'll be too much trouble."

On June 19, 1959, Wanger received his first preliminary operating budget for *Cleopatra:* 64 days' shooting at a cost of $2,955,700, exclusive of cast and director salaries—expensive by melodrama standards, but a piddling amount for an epic. The decade had seen one record-setting mega-production after another, starting with Mervyn LeRoy's *Quo Vadis* (1951, $7 million) and continuing on with Richard Fleischer's Jules Verne fantasy, *20,000 Leagues Under the Sea* (1954, $9 million), Cecil B. DeMille's *The Ten Commandments* (1956, $13 million), and William Wyler's *Ben-Hur* (1959, $15 million).

By late summer, a reputable British writer named Nigel Balchin had been hired to put together a script, a $5 million budget was deemed acceptable, and the names of Taylor, Audrey Hepburn, Sophia Loren, Gina Lollobrigida, and Susan Hayward were being discussed for the title role. On September 1, Wanger made his first formal overture to Taylor, who was in London filming *Suddenly Last Summer* with Joseph Mankiewicz. Over the telephone, she demanded—half-jokingly, she would later say—a million dollars, something no actress had ever been paid for one movie.

Finally, on October 15 Fox staged a photo opportunity at which Taylor pretended to sign her million-dollar contract. The wire services sent out the photo to newspapers across the country, and now Wanger's idea was the world's: Elizabeth Taylor as Cleopatra.

GETTING NOWHERE: NEW YORK, LOS ANGELES, LONDON, 1959–60

"Gentlemen: You are wasting money on Liz Taylor. Nobody wants to see her after the way she treated that sweet little Debbie Reynolds. Everyone loves Debbie. She is what the teenagers call a doll. Ginger Rogers is still popular, but Liz is not liked anymore. I heard a group of teenagers talking about Liz. They said, 'She is a stinker.' They're right."

—Letter sent to Buddy Adler and Walter Wanger
by a woman in Beaumont, California, October 1959

It is the wisdom of those who consider themselves experts on the subject that Mike Todd, the producer-showman behind *Around the World in 80 Days,* was "the love of Elizabeth Taylor's life." But less than six months after Todd died in a plane crash outside Albuquerque in March 1958—leaving the 26-year-old Taylor alone with an infant daughter, Liza, and the two sons she'd had with her second husband, Michael Wilding—she was seen stepping out with her late husband's friend and protégé, Eddie Fisher. Fisher, a pompadoured, haimish 30-year-old pop idol, was famous for his shrewdly publicized union with Debbie Reynolds; together they had two children and were known as "America's sweethearts." But by the time Taylor and Fisher married in Las Vegas in May of 1959, the public goodwill both had built up had evaporated, and they were the target of constant moral dudgeon and tabloid surveillance.

Skouras's intuition that Taylor would be "trouble" wasn't entirely unfounded, in that she had a predisposition toward illness, and alarmed moralists. Then again, she had soldiered on through *Cat on a Hot Tin Roof,* the film she was in the midst of making when Todd died, fulfilled her obligation to *Butterfield 8,* the last film she owed to MGM under her contract there, and delivered a first-rate performance in *Suddenly Last Summer.*

Reaching over Wanger's head, Skouras tapped an old friend, Rouben Mamoulian, to be *Cleopatra*'s director. The 61-year-old Mamoulian was a gifted visualist, was accustomed to policing large groups of people, and had directed the original Broadway productions of *Porgy and Bess, Oklahoma!,* and *Carousel,* as well as the films *Dr. Jekyll and Mr. Hyde, Becky Sharp,* and *Silk Stockings.* But he had a reputation for being temperamental, and his filmmaking skills were rusty—apart from *Silk Stockings,* from 1957, he had made only one movie in the last 17 years. The screenwriter Nunnally Johnson (*The Grapes of Wrath*), whom Fox had hired to write additional dialogue for Balchin's screenplay, was skeptical. "I bet Walter Wanger that [Mamoulian] would never go to bat," Johnson wrote to his friend Groucho Marx. "All he wants to do is 'prepare.' A hell of a preparer. Tests, wardrobe, hair, toenails.... [But] if you make him start this picture, he will never forgive you to his dying day. This chap is a natural born martyr."

Late in 1959, the Fox hierarchy committed its first howler of a mistake: deciding, despite obvious meteorological evidence to the contrary, that England was an ideal place to shoot a sunbaked Egyptian-Roman epic. The decision was money-driven—the British government offered generous subsidies to foreign productions that employed a certain percentage of British crew.

Adler died of cancer the following July. His death created even more of a power vacuum at the studio, but the movie's chief detractor at Fox was out of the way. On July 28, 1960, Taylor finally signed a real contract. The film was to be shot not in CinemaScope but in Todd-AO, a rival widescreen process developed by Mike Todd, which meant that Taylor, as Todd's beneficiary, would receive additional royalties. It was announced that Peter Finch would play Caesar and that Stephen Boyd, Charlton Heston's co-star in *Ben-Hur,* would play Antony. At the Pinewood Studios, located just outside London, John DeCuir, one of the best art directors in the business, began construction on a gorgeous, $600,000 Alexandria set covering 20 acres, featuring palm trees flown in from Los Angeles and four 52-foot-high sphinxes.

Right from the start, Mamoulian's *Cleopatra* was a farce. The first day of shooting, September 28, saw two work stoppages by the movie's British hairdressers, who took issue with the presence of Taylor's specially imported American stylist, Sidney Guilaroff. Only after several weeks of negotiation by Wanger was a fragile truce arranged—Guilaroff would style Taylor at her double penthouse suite in the Dorchester, but would not set foot in Pinewood.

Not that Taylor's presence at Pinewood ever became much of an issue. She called in sick on the third day of shooting, saying she had a cold. The cold grew into a lingering fever, and for the next few weeks she remained ensconced in her suite—attended by her husband and several doctors, including Lord Evans, Queen Elizabeth's physician.

Physically and spiritually, the Eddie Fishers were not a healthy couple at the time. Fisher missed the singing career he'd largely forsaken for Taylor, and knew the $150,000 he was being paid by Fox for vague junior-producer duties was really for being Taylor's professional minder. Furthermore, he was strung out on methamphetamine, having gotten hooked in his grueling touring days on "pep" shots administered by Max Jacobson, the notorious "Dr. Feelgood" who provided similar services to John F. Kennedy.

Taylor was in a continual funk because of her ill health, residual grief over the death of Mike Todd, the grim English weather, and the correct intuition that she'd lent her star power to a doomed, disorganized production. In response, she took to drinking and taking painkillers and sedatives. "She could take an enormous amount of drugs," Fisher told Brad Geagley, a senior producer at Walt Disney, in an unpublished 1991 interview for a never-completed book concerning *Cleopatra.* "She's written up in medical journals somewhere—that's what she's always told me, and I believe her." (Fisher declined to be interviewed for this story, on the grounds that he wants to save his "explosive, blockbuster stuff" for his memoir.)

While Taylor spent the autumn shuttling between the Dorchester and the London Clinic, where she was variously diagnosed with a virus, an abscessed tooth, and a bacterial infection known as Malta fever, Mamoulian was having his own troubles. Balchin's script remained unsatisfactory to him, and in the rare moments when the sky was clear, the illusion of Egypt was nevertheless shattered by the steam visibly emanating from the actors' and horses' mouths.

Production ground to a halt on November 18, when there was simply no more Mamoulian could do without Taylor and an improved script. The plan was for shooting to resume in January, by which time Taylor would presumably be well and Nunnally Johnson would have finished another script polish.

Back in New York, Skouras sent a copy of the current shooting script to Joseph Mankiewicz, who had made his two Oscar-winning pictures for Fox, and asked the director for a frank critique. Mankiewicz was merciless: "Cleopatra, as written, is a strange, frustrating mixture of an American soap-opera virgin and an hysterical Slavic vamp of the type Nazimova used to play ... "

On January 18, 1961, with production resumed but still moving at a glacial pace, Mamoulian, bitter and frustrated, cabled his resignation to Skouras. He left behind about 10 minutes of footage, none of it featuring Taylor, and a loss of $7 million.

"I began to look at my life, and I saw a tough situation. In the hospital all the time—I mean, I became a nurse. I was giving her injections of Demerol. I didn't want the doctors to come. I felt sorry for the doctors. I did it for two nights, and whooo-ee. . . . After two nights I said, 'This is crazy.' I actually faked appendicitis to get away."

—Eddie Fisher,
recalling the winter of 1960–61

A couple days after Skouras accepted Mamoulian's resignation, a desperate voice broke through the static on Hume Cronyn's telephone in the Bahamas, where he owned a remote island with his wife, Jessica Tandy. "Hume?" said the voice. "Where the hell is Joe?"

It was Charles Feldman, Joe Mankiewicz's Hollywood agent. Mankiewicz was staying with the Cronyns, preparing the screenplay for *Justine,* his planned follow-up to *Suddenly Last Summer.* Feldman told Mankiewicz that Skouras was offering the moon for him to rescue *Cleopatra.* The director was skeptical, but that didn't stop him from flying immediately to New York to meet Skouras for lunch at the Colony.

"Spyros," he said, "why would I want to make *Cleopatra?* I wouldn't even go see *Cleopatra.*"

Indeed, gifted as he was, Mankiewicz seemed the last person qualified (or inclined) to helm a big-budget spectacle. "His movies were dialogue-based and staged like plays, like *All About Eve,* where most of the action, where there *is* action, is people coming down stairs or going in and out of doors," says Chris Mankiewicz, the director's older son, who took time off from college to work on *Cleopatra.* Skouras recognized, however, that the elder Mankiewicz was a great writer and skilled diva-wrangler, having finessed the egos of Taylor and Katharine Hepburn on *Suddenly Last Summer,* and Bette Davis on *All About Eve.*

Mankiewicz consented to take over the project when Skouras made an offer he couldn't refuse: Fox would not only place him on salary, but also pay $3 million for Figaro, the production company he co-owned with NBC. For a 51-year-old man whose glorious career had never quite made him rich, the prospect of overnight millionairedom was irresistible. "He was seduced by the opportunity," says Chris Mankiewicz. "He never saw a penny from *All About Eve.* Now, for once in his life, they were all coming to him. All of a sudden you've got the 'Fuck you' money."

Cleopatra seemed, for a flicker of a moment, to be in good, sane hands. Mankiewicz, citing as his inspirations Shaw, Shakespeare, and Plutarch, set about creating a totally new script for the movie. He enlisted two writers to help him, the novelist Lawrence Durrell (whose *Alexandria Quartet* was the basis for Mankiewicz's *Justine* script) and the screenwriter Sidney Buchman (*Mr. Smith Goes to Washington*). Wanger, elated by Mankiewicz's "modern, psychiatrically rooted concept of the film," thought he was at last getting the upscale *Cleopatra* he'd dreamed of.

Alas, this period of promise was when Taylor suffered what probably still qualifies as her nearest near-death experience. Late in February she returned to London from a vacation on the Continent with what her doctors described as "Asian flu," caught while rushing back to attend to her suddenly "appendicitis"-stricken husband. By March, the Asian flu, or whatever it was, had complicated itself into double pneumonia, and Taylor was sedated and prone in an oxygen tent in the Dorches-

ter. On the night of March 4, 1961, she fell comatose. She was rushed once again to the London Clinic, Fisher at her side screaming, "Let her alone! Let her alone!," as paparazzi leaned in to get photographs of her unconscious. The diligence of the Fleet Street press ensured that within hours an international deathwatch was in place, some papers already reporting that Taylor was dead.

"I was pronounced dead four times," says Taylor. "Once I didn't breathe for five minutes, which must be a record." Doctors performed an emergency tracheotomy to alleviate congestion in her bronchial passages. The operation saved her life, and by the end of the month she was back home with Fisher in Los Angeles, convalescing. Several months later she underwent plastic surgery to conceal the incision mark at the base of her throat, but it wasn't successful; the scar is visible in the finished film.

Calamitous as the whole episode was, it produced two seemingly serendipitous effects. First, it bought Mankiewicz six months to get his *Cleopatra* together while Taylor recovered. Second, Taylor's public image was overnight transformed from home-wrecking pariah to heartstring-pulling survivor; the London Clinic received truckloads of flowers and sympathetic fan mail, even a get-well telegram from Debbie Reynolds. "I had the chance to read my own obituaries," says Taylor. "They were the best reviews I'd ever gotten." During her convalescence, she collected a sympathy best-actress Oscar for *Butterfield 8,* a movie she hated.

Mankiewicz decided to junk Mamoulian's footage and reconstruct the movie from scratch —only Taylor, Wanger, and John DeCuir, the art director, would carry over to the new incarnation of *Cleopatra.* To replace Finch and Boyd, Mankiewicz pursued Trevor Howard and Marlon Brando, the latter of whom had played Mark Antony in the director's 1953 adaptation of Shakespeare's *Julius Caesar.* But neither actor was available, so Mankiewicz set his sights on Rex Harrison, whom he had directed in *The Ghost and Mrs. Muir,* and Richard Burton, then starring on Broadway in *Camelot.*

Skouras hated both choices. Harrison, he said, had never made a profitable movie for Fox, and Burton "doesn't mean a thing at the box office." Indeed, Burton, the 36-year-old product of a dirt-poor Welsh mining family, was perceived in Hollywood to be a great stage actor whose film career had never really taken off. But grudgingly, after strenuous lobbying from Mankiewicz, Skouras gave in. Fox bought out the remainder of Burton's *Camelot* contract for $50,000, signed the actor for $250,000, and got Harrison for $200,000.

If you had to peg one of *Cleopatra's* two male stars as a potential troublemaker on the set, it would be Harrison; Wanger later expressed surprise that he had turned out to be "the good boy." Described by several of his surviving castmates as "the Cunt," Harrison was known for being tetchy, difficult, and condescending. Burton, by contrast, was a charmer, adored by his peers for his erudition, basso speaking voice, Welsh-barroom raconteurship, and sexual magnetism. Though notorious for his philandering—he had romanced such co-stars as Claire Bloom, Jean Simmons, and Susan Strasberg, and had shown up at his first meeting with Wanger, at New York's '21' Club, with a Copacabana dancer on his arm—he invariably returned to his wife, the dignified, mumsie-looking Sybil Burton.

One of the few people who remained oblivious to Burton's charms, in fact, was Elizabeth Taylor. She had met him years before *Cleopatra* at a party at Stewart Granger's house, back when she was a contract player at MGM. "He flirted like mad with me, with everyone, with any girl who was even remotely pretty," she says. "I just thought, 'Ohhh, boy—I'm not gonna become a notch on *his* belt.'"

On the back lot of Rome's Cinecittà Studios in 1962, Burton and Taylor were photographed at sunset, as Antony and Cleopatra.

PHOTOGRAPHED IN 1962
BY **BERT STERN**

ENGLAND ALL OVER AGAIN: ROME, 1961

"It appears that the responsibility for increased costs in connection with the production falls into four categories, namely

(1) Elizabeth Taylor
(2) Lack of Planning
(3) Corruption on part of employees
(4) Friction between American and Italian Heads

No effort was made at this time to review the first category, due to the danger involved."

—Excerpt from a report prepared
by Nathan Frankel, C.P.A., who was
retained by Twentieth Century Fox
in 1962 to determine how the studio's
money was being spent on *Cleopatra*

The second go-round of *Cleopatra,* in Italy, was a folly of proportions nearly as epic as the finished film. Once again, the production rushed ahead without a completed script or adequate preparation, an indication of how desperately Skouras wanted to present Twentieth Century Fox's board of directors with a ready-to-release film that would bring in cash and save his regime. Wanger later estimated that if he and Mankiewicz had been given more time to regroup and plan, *Cleopatra* would have cost about $15 million. But Skouras was not exactly at his managerial best in 1961. Taylor, Fisher, and Mankiewicz got a sense of his addled state of mind one night when he joined them for drinks in New York. The others in the group couldn't help but notice that Skouras was addressing Taylor only as "Cleopatra."

"You don't know my name, do you?" Taylor said suspiciously. "You can't remember my name!"

"You are Cleopatra!" Skouras responded.

"You're paying me a million dollars," Taylor said, "and you can't remember my name. Spyros, tell me my name! I'll give you half the money back!"

"Ehh ... ehh ... ," Skouras sputtered, "you are Cleopatra!"

By the summer of 1961, *Cleopatra* was practically all Fox had left; short of funds, the studio had canceled most of its other features and had pinned much of its hope on television. The latest in Fox's series of regent studio chiefs was Peter Levathes, a Skouras protégé who had won good notices as the head of the company's television division.

"We decided to move the production to Rome because we thought Elizabeth Taylor would show up more," says Levathes. "The climate would be more to her liking, and she wouldn't call in sick all the time." At Levathes's urging, Skouras granted Fisher's request to fly in Taylor's personal physician, Rex Kennamer of Beverly Hills, for a fee of $25,000.

Interiors and Roman exteriors were now to be shot at Cinecittà, the massive studio complex six miles outside of central Rome. Ancient Alexandria was being reconstructed at Torre Astura, a hunting estate on the Tyrrhenian Sea owned by Prince Stefano Borghese. Some additional work, mostly battle sequences, would be filmed in the Egyptian desert.

Trawling through the voluminous files and correspondence left in *Cleopatra's* wake, what one takes away is the abject terror Taylor inspired in powerful men. (As Fisher would later say, "One thing I learned from Elizabeth—if you ever need anything, yell and scream for it.") Privately, Wanger, Mankiewicz, Skouras, and Levathes complained about her fragility and erratic work habits, and talked about how she deserved a good telling-off. But in her presence they lost their resolve and genuflected. Skouras and Levathes tried (unsuccessfully) in 1961 to sign her to a four-picture deal with Fox. Wanger set her up in a 14-room mansion in Rome called the Villa Papa, and flew in chili from Chasen's for her. Mankiewicz reportedly shuffled shooting schedules to accommodate her menstrual cycle. "We could only shoot Roman scenes in the Senate [which did not involve Taylor] when Elizabeth was having her period," says Kenneth Haigh, who played Brutus. "She said, 'Look, if I'm playing the most beautiful woman in the world, I want to look my best.' "

But by the time the production had moved to Rome, these men had an even better reason to coddle Taylor than the usual keep-the-talent-happy ethos. Taylor, in the wake of her near-death episode, was now uninsurable. If she walked off or fell ill, the movie—which was Elizabeth Taylor—would represent nothing but red ink.

Mankiewicz, between scouting locations, assembling a cast, and consulting with department heads, wasn't close to having a finished screenplay when shooting began on September 25: a mere 132 pages out of an eventual 327, or most of the film's first half ("Caesar and Cleopatra") and none of its second half ("Antony and Cleopatra"). This meant that the film would be shot in continuity, a costly process that would eventually result in 96 hours of raw Todd-AO negative.

Skouras insisted on moving ahead anyway, arguing that "the girl is on salary"—an allusion to Taylor's renegotiated contract, which called for her to work for 16 weeks beginning August 1, with a guarantee of $50,000 for every week *Cleopatra* ran over. Consequently, Mankiewicz would spend the remainder of the production directing by day and writing by night, an impossibly taxing task that, says his widow, "damn near killed him." (Yet another screenwriter, Ranald MacDougall [*Mildred Pierce*], was drafted in, but Mankiewicz still insisted on writing the actual shooting script.)

Casting was done on the fly: a mid-September flurry of telephone calls brought aboard such actors as Hume Cronyn, Martin Landau, and Carroll O'Connor from America and Kenneth Haigh, Robert Stephens, and Michael Hordern from England. But when the actors arrived in Rome, they discovered half-finished sets, incomplete wardrobes, and an exhausted writer-director who hadn't yet written their parts. Says Cronyn, "I arrived the same day as Burton, September 19, 1961. Neither one of us worked until after Christmas."

"I had a 15-week contract, which was long for those days, but it wound up being almost 10 months," says O'Connor, who played Casca, a Roman senator who puts the first knife into Caesar's back. "In all that time, I worked 17 days."

The chop-chop pace demanded by Skouras resulted in all manner of jaw-dropping blunders that might have been circumvented had there been adequate time to prepare. The beach at Torre Astura, where DeCuir's massive replica of Alexandria was under construction, turned out to be laced with live mines left over from World War II; a $22,000 "mine-dredging" expenditure was added to *Cleopatra's* ledger. On top of that, the set was adjacent to a NATO firing range. Wrote Wanger in his diary, "We will have to arrange our schedule so we are not working when the big guns are blasting." And because Italy had no facilities for processing Todd-AO film, the day's rushes had to be sent all the way to Hollywood and then back to Rome before the director could view them.

DeCuir's sets were grandiose and beautiful, but because no one had kept close tabs on his work, Mankiewicz and his crew discovered too late that they were almost unmanageably big. The fake Roman Forum (which cost $1.5 million to build) dwarfed the real one up the road; so much steel tubing was required to hold it up that *Cleopatra* exacerbated a countrywide shortage, palpably affecting the Italian construction business.

As DeCuir's Rome grew, Twentieth Century Fox began to shrink. Earlier in the year, Skouras, desperate to stanch the hemorrhaging of the company's resources, had engineered the sale of the studio's 260-acre Los Angeles lot to the Aluminum Company of America for $43 million, a transaction that would come to resemble Peter Minuit's $24 deal for Manhattan. Though the studio continued to lease 75 acres for its own use (eventually reacquired), the remaining acreage was now being developed into Century City, the gigantic office-building-and-shopping-center complex that stands south of Beverly Hills today. "You could see the village from *The Song of Bernadette,* New York, castles, a real railroad station," recalled Cesare Danova, a Fox contract player who portrayed Apollodorus, Cleopatra's majordomo. "And the first thing that I saw [upon returning to the lot in 1962] was a truck from the Acme Wrecking Company. Everything was coming down. This was a potent sign for me—that the end had come to an entire world."

The sheer size and obvious disorganization of *Cleopatra* made it an easy mark for anyone practiced in the art of graft—a circumstance not lost on many of the Italians hired to work on the picture. "The Italians are wonderful at designing things, but they have this natural proclivity for larceny," says Tom Mankiewicz, the director's younger son, who, like his brother, Chris, took time off from college to work on the film. "Once you start saying, 'All right,

I need 500 Praetorian-guard outfits, I need 600 Nubian-slave outfits, I need 10,000 soldier outfits'—this is like an *invitation.* And there was no one to stay on top of it all. If you wanted to buy some new dinnerware or a set of glasses for your house, it was the easiest thing to put it on the budget of *Cleopatra.*"

"Later I got to see the studio's breakdown on the money waste," says Taylor. "They had $3 million for 'miscellaneous,' and $100,000 for paper cups. They said I ate 12 chickens and 40 pounds of bacon every day for breakfast. What?"

Skouras, though the man with ultimate authority, placed a lot of the blame for the film's rampant disorganization on Wanger. "You have to know Walter Wanger well," Skouras later told an interviewer. "He is a fine man, but he likes to have lots of people to help him. Off the record, he does not want to work so hard." Levathes felt that Mankiewicz was a prima donna whose extravagant requests were being indulged by Skouras regardless of financial consequence. Wanger complained with some justification that Skouras and Levathes were undermining his authority by circumventing him in favor of Mankiewicz and the department heads, but too often he merely complained. The surviving actors and crew remember the producer eventually devolving into a sweet but powerless "greeter" whose most visible duty was to escort visiting European royals to the set.

As a bout of torrential, London-like weather precluded outdoor shooting for much of the fall of '61 (at a cost of $40,000 to $75,000 for every day rained out), many of the film's principal actors realized that they were going to be in Rome at least through the spring of '62. So they moved out of the luxurious Grand Hotel and into their own apartments, becoming idle, semi-permanent residents of the city. Given that Fox had to keep the actors on salary the whole time—Hume Cronyn at $5,000 a week, Roddy McDowall at $2,500 a week, Martin Landau at $850 a week, etc.—the cost pileups were tremendous.

At one point in autumn, Skouras and Levathes approached Burton to see if he'd mind terribly if the movie ended with Caesar's assassination, thereby cutting out half of the plot and roughly 95 percent of Antony's part. Burton was succinct. "I'll sue you until you're puce," he told them.

Given the messy state of affairs, morale remained remarkably high on the set. "Everyone was in a very gay way," says O'Connor. "We knew the picture was going to be O.K., even if it wasn't going to be one of the greats." The rushes were impressive enough to prompt hope in some quarters that the film was en route to greatness. On Christmas Eve, Fox publicist Jack Brodsky wrote the following to Nathan Weiss, his colleague in New York: "The first 50 pages of the second act have just come from Mank's pen and they're fabulous. Burton and Taylor will set off sparks, and already Fisher is jealous of the lines Burton has."

HELL BREAKS LOOSE: ROME, WINTER 1962

"For the past several days uncontrolled rumors have been growing about Elizabeth and myself. Statements attributed to me have been distorted out of proportion, and a series of coincidences has lent plausibility to a situation which has become damaging to Elizabeth ... "

—Statement issued by
Richard Burton, then disavowed
by him, on February 19, 1962

L*e scandale,* as Taylor and Burton later termed their affair, didn't begin until their work together did, in December or January, after Mankiewicz had written enough material for them to start rehearsing the film's second half. "For the first scene, there was no dialogue—we had to just look at each other," says Taylor. "And that was it—I was another notch." Burton

As Cleopatra entered Rome, 6,000 extras filled out the scene, shot in May 1962. Taylor, in the sphinx's lap, was tugged along by "Nubian slaves."

further endeared himself to Taylor by showing up hung over. She had feared that he would lord his talent over her and make fun of her lack of theatrical training; instead, she found herself steadying his trembling hands as he lifted a coffee cup to his lips. "He was probably putting it on," Taylor says. "He knew it would get me."

As for Eddie Fisher, he had not been having the best of times in Rome. Though he was on the *Cleopatra* payroll and was trying to learn how to become a movie producer, his presence wasn't expected or needed at Cinecittà. "I remember Eddie one day walking onto the set, trying to be funny, and shouting to Mankiewicz, 'O.K., Joe, let's make this one!' " says Brodsky. "No one reacted. It cast a pall."

"Eddie and I had drifted way apart," says Taylor. "It was only a matter of time for us. The clock was ticking."

But right through the end of January, the only suspicion that Fisher held was that Burton was encouraging his wife to drink too much. In his self-described capacity as a nurse, Fisher took exception to the influence the Welshman's prodigious boozing and peaty *joie de vivre* were having on Taylor, who had grown tired of her husband's predilection for dining in. "Remember," says someone who worked on the production, "Elizabeth was a very self-indulgent person at that time, a sensualist who'd just been confronted with possible death, and was probably rebounding from it by tasting as much life as possible."

Several people associated with *Cleopatra* point out that sensualism and high living were the order of the day in Rome, particularly with so little work for the actors to do. "There was a tremendous sense of being in the right place at the right time," says Jean Marsh, who played Antony's Roman wife, Octavia, well before her PBS fame as the creator and star of *Upstairs, Downstairs.* "Fellini was there, and Italy was the capital of film. And the film was so extravagant, so louche, it affected everyone's lives. It was a hotbed of romance—Richard and Elizabeth weren't the only people who had an affair."

Taylor and Burton filmed their first scene together on January 22. Wanger happily noted in his diary, "There comes a time during the making of a movie when the actors become the characters they play.... That happened today.... It was quiet, and you could almost feel the electricity between Liz and Burton."

Some people on the set, including Mankiewicz, knew already that there was more going on than just electricity. At one point Burton had stridden triumphantly into the men's makeup trailer and announced to those present, "Gentlemen, I've just fucked Elizabeth Taylor in the back of my Cadillac!" Whether or not this boast was for real, it *was* true that he and Taylor were using the apartment of her secretary, Dick Hanley, for trysts.

On January 26, Mankiewicz summoned Wanger to his room at the Grand Hotel. "I have been sitting on a volcano all alone for too long, and I want to give you some facts you ought to know," he said. "Liz and Burton are not just *playing* Antony and Cleopatra."

"Confidentially," Wanger later told Joe Hyams, his collaborator on *My Life with Cleopatra,* a rush-job account of the film's travails published in 1963, "we all figured it might just be a once-over-lightly. That is what Mr. Burton figured, too. I know it. He told me."

S everal firsthand accounts support the idea that Burton began his dalliance with Taylor with only short-term pleasure in mind. Brodsky recalls the actor's genuine surprise, as the weeks advanced, to find himself in the midst of both an intense affair and an international incident: "He said to me, 'It's like fucking Khrushchev! I've had affairs before—how did I know the woman was so fucking famous!' "

Mankiewicz and Wanger harbored hopes in the early going that the situation would simply blow over. But Taylor's notoriety since her grieving-widow days had made her the most-hunted tabloid prey in the world. Well before the affair had begun, the Roman gutter press had planted informants in Cinecittà and arranged paparazzi stakeouts of the Villa Papa. Word got out fast, even before Fisher knew anything was going on.

As February dawned, rumors were swirling so madly around Rome—"the whispering gallery of Europe," as Wanger called it—that Fisher could no longer ignore or brush off the gossip. One night early that month, as he lay in bed beside Taylor, he received a heads-up telephone call from Bob Abrams, his old army buddy and Jilly Rizzo–like amanuensis.

Fisher hung up the phone and turned to his wife. "Is it true that something is going on between you and Burton?" he asked her.

"Yes," she said softly.

Quietly, defeatedly, Fisher packed and spent the night at Abrams's place. The following day, he returned to the Villa Papa, and for about two weeks slept by Taylor's side, hoping that the situation would somehow resolve itself. There was never any kind of knock-down-drag-out confrontation. "She just wasn't 'there' anymore," Fisher said in 1991. "She was with *him.* And I wasn't 'there.' She talked to him once at the studio, in my office, with all kinds of people around. And she was talking love to him on the telephone. 'Oh, dahling, are you all right?' With this new British accent."

By mid-February the rumors had gone worldwide, and Taylor-Burton innuendo was everywhere. *The Perry Como Show* ran a comic "Cleopatra" sketch in which a slave named Eddie kept getting in Mark Antony's way. Taylor was visibly upset, and the entire production was in a bad way. Mankiewicz, run-down from his Sisyphean work schedule, had become feverishly ill. So had Martin Landau, who had a large part (as Rufio), and whose illness necessitated the cancellation of a day's worth of shooting. Leon Shamroy, the cinematographer, a cigar-chomping sexagenarian known for his seen-it-all stoicism (he had shot the Fox epics *The Robe, The Egyptian,* and *The King and I,* as well as the Gene Tierney classic *Leave Her to Heaven*), collapsed from exhaustion. Forrest "Johnny" Johnston, the film's production manager, fell gravely ill and died in Los Angeles in May.

Morale back home was also low. Pro- and anti-Skouras factions were taking shape on the Fox board, and rumors swirled of a coming putsch. "This was where my hair went gray," says Levathes, who is now 86. "I used to look younger."

Burton, contrite, met with Wanger and volunteered to quit the production if that was what was best. Wanger counseled against this option, arguing that "what would solve the problem [is] putting an end to any basis for the rumors."

In the meantime, Burton's older brother Ifor, a powerfully built man who functioned as the actor's bodyguard-factotum, used his fists to get the message across. "Ifor beat the living shit out of Burton," says a *Cleopatra* crew member. "For what he was doing to Sybil. Beat him up so that Richard couldn't work the next day. He had a black eye and a cut cheek."

Both Fisher and Sybil Burton decided it best to flee the situation. He headed by car for Gstaad, where he and Taylor owned a chalet; she left for New York. But before either had gone, Fisher paid a visit to the Burtons' villa for a heart-to-heart talk with Sybil. "I said, 'You know, they're continuing their affair,'" Fisher recalled. "And she said, 'He's had these affairs, and he always comes home to me.' And I said, 'But they're still having their affair.' And she went to the studio, and they closed [production] down. And that cost them $100,000. And the day I left Rome, it cost them another $100,000. Elizabeth screamed and carried on. Work stopped that day. They had that in honor of me."

When Fisher, having driven as far as Florence, called Rome to determine his wife's whereabouts, he discovered that Taylor was in Hanley's apartment, accompanied by Burton, who was enraged that the singer had meddled in his marriage to Sybil. Burton took the telephone. "You nothing, you spleen," he said to Fisher. "I'm going to come up there and kill you."

Instead, Burton summoned the courage to tell Taylor their affair was over, and left for a short trip to Paris, where he was playing a small part in Darryl

In June 1962, Burton and Taylor, with their affair out in the open, relaxed on their boat off the coast of Ischia. "It's like fucking Khrushchev!" Burton said. "How did I know the woman was so fucking famous!"

PHOTOGRAPHED IN 1962
BY **BERT STERN**

Zanuck's Normandy epic, *The Longest Day*. That night, Hanley called Wanger to say that Taylor would be unable to work the next day. "She's hysterical," Wanger wrote in his diary. "Total rejection came sooner than expected."

The following day, February 17, Taylor was rushed to the Salvator Mundi Hospital. The official explanation was food poisoning. Wanger, who cooked up a story about some bad beef she had eaten, had, in fact, discovered Taylor splayed on her bed in the Villa Papa, groggy from an overdose of Seconal, a prescription sedative. "It wasn't a suicide attempt," says Taylor. "I'm not that kind of person, and Richard despised weakness. It was more hysteria. I needed the rest, I was hysterical, and I needed to get away."

Taylor recovered quickly, but news of her hospitalization compelled both Fisher and Burton to fly back to Rome, which only fanned the flames of rumor. On February 19, Burton, eager to extinguish these flames, issued a statement addressing the "uncontrolled rumors . . . about Elizabeth and myself." The statement took pains to provide reasons why Sybil and Eddie had left town (she was visiting Burton's sick foster father; he had business matters to attend to), but never outright denied that an affair was going on. It was a crucially unsavvy nondenial denial, and the Fox publicity team was apoplectic. The studio got Burton to disavow the statement and pin the blame for its release on his press agent, but it was too late: now the papers had a peg upon which they could hang their "affair" stories. Taylor-Burton was an out-in-the-open phenomenon.

"It was not a help to the production," says a crew member. "You know how she got time off for her period? Now she was having three or four periods a month."

THE WHIRLWIND: ROME, SPRING 1962

"It's true—Elizabeth Taylor has fallen madly in love with Richard Burton. It's the end of the road for Liz and Eddie Fisher."

—Louella Parsons's syndicated column, March 10, 1962

"The report is ridiculous."

—Eddie Fisher's response

In the aftermath of Taylor's hospitalization, all the aggrieved parties tried to re-arrange themselves as they had been before. Fisher threw his wife a 30th-birthday party on February 27 and presented her with a $10,000 diamond ring and an emerald-studded Bulgari mirror. Burton told the press he had no intention of divorcing Sybil. But it was to no avail—the Taylor-Burton affair continued, as did the reporters' pursuit.

Privately, there were cruel scenes between Burton and Fisher, with the former visiting Villa Papa and boasting to the latter, "You don't know how to use her!," or turning to Taylor and saying, with Fisher present, "Who do you love? Who do you love?" Fisher never fought back. Where others saw wimpiness and retreat, Wanger, in recorded conversations with Joe Hyams, his book collaborator, ascribed a kind of nobility to the singer's pacifism. "Eddie always took the position that this is an evil man, and he had to stand and protect her when she was misled by this terrible guy," he said. "He wanted to hold his family together." Fisher left Rome for good on March 21, 1962.

Cleopatra was now about halfway finished, but it still lacked its biggest, most challenging scenes: Cleopatra's procession into Rome, the arrival of her barge at Tarsus, the battles of Pharsalia, Philippi, Moongate, and Actium. Moreover, there remained several weeks' worth of "Antony and Cleopatra" scenes to be filmed. The fictive and the personal dovetailed to the point where even the actors got confused. "I feel as if I'm intruding," Mankiewicz said one day as his shouts of "Cut!" went unabided by Taylor and Burton during a love scene. In a less pleasant coincidence, the very day that Burton announced to the press he would never leave Sybil was the day Taylor had to film the scene in which Cleopatra discovers that Antony has returned to Rome and taken another wife, Octavia. The screenplay called for Cleopatra to enter Antony's deserted chambers in Alexandria, pick up his dagger, and stab his bed and belongings in a rage. Taylor went at it with such gusto that she banged her hand and needed to go to the hospital for X-rays. She was unable to work the next day.

The day-to-day developments of Taylor-Burton were now a full-time news beat. Martin Landau remembers a night shoot on the island of Ischia involving Taylor and Burton where the crew's spotlights, once turned on, revealed

paparazzi bunched up like moths. "Behind us was this cliff, with shrubbery and growth coming out of it," he says, "and there were 20 photographers hanging off these things, with long lenses. A couple of them fell—30 feet!"

In actuality, the affair was, as Taylor would note a few years after the fact, "more off than on." "We did try and resist," she says today. "My marriage with Eddie was over, but we didn't want to do anything to hurt Sybil. She was—is—such a lovely lady." Taylor still won't discuss the scenes and machinations that went on between the Fishers and the Burtons, calling the subject matter "too personal," but other observers on the set remember moments when the lovers' similarly combustible personalities caused near explosions. In the midst of *le scandale,* Burton was also carrying on with the Copacabana dancer he'd been seeing in his *Camelot* days; one day Taylor took exception to her presence on the set, prompting Burton to shove Taylor slightly and snarl, "Don't get my Welsh temper up." In another instance, Burton showed up for work wrecked, again with the "Copa cutie," as she was known on the set, in tow. When he finally rallied himself into performing condition, Taylor admonished him, "You kept us all waiting." To which Burton responded, "It's about time somebody kept you waiting. It's a real switch."

Far more so than Taylor, Burton was flummoxed, unable to choose between his wife and lover, desperate to have it both ways. Speaking to Kenneth Tynan in *Playboy* after *Cleopatra* had wrapped, he futilely tried to defend the Liz-Sybil arrangement with a choice bit of baroque doggerel. "What I have done," he said, "is to move outside the accepted idea of monogamy without investing the other person with anything that makes me feel guilty. So that I remain inviolate, untouched."

For all its unpleasant side effects, Burton was elated by his new worldwide fame. Kenneth Haigh remembers him "calling me into his room and saying, 'Look at this! There are about 300 scripts! The offers are piling up everywhere!'" Hugh French, Burton's Hollywood agent, began boasting that his client now commanded $500,000 per picture. "Maybe I should give Elizabeth Taylor 10 percent," said Burton.

Alas, the seesaw nature of the affair was not conducive to the efficient completion of what was now routinely described in the papers as a "$20 million picture." Between his euphoric highs, Burton was drinking heavily on the set. Taylor, too, became erratic, alternately showing up unprecedentedly early to work on scenes with Burton and failing to show up at all. A production document titled "Elizabeth Taylor Diary" indicates that on March 21, the day Fisher departed, Taylor was dismissed from Cinecittà at 12:25 P.M. after "having great difficulty delivering dialogue."

The unexpected work stoppages didn't always bother Mankiewicz, who welcomed the opportunity to catch up on his writing and his sleep. He was by now a physical ruin, sometimes writing scenes the night before they were to be shot. A stress-related dermatological disorder caused the skin on his hands to crack open, forcing him to wear thin white film cutter's gloves as he wrote the script longhand. Somehow, he retained his equanimity and sense of humor. When an Italian newspaper alleged that Burton was a "shuffle-footed idiot" deployed by the director to cover up the real scandal—that it was Mankiewicz who was having an affair with Taylor—Mankiewicz released a statement declaring, "The real story is that I'm in love with Richard Burton, and Elizabeth Taylor is the cover-up for us." (The same day, Burton shuffled up to Mankiewicz on the set and said, "Duh, Mister Mankeawitz, sir, do I have to sleep with her again tonight?")

Astonishingly, there had been a time, early on in Rome, when the Fox brass had chastised their publicity department for not getting *Cleopatra* enough attention. By April and May of 1962, as *le scandale* superseded news coverage of the Mercury-Atlas space missions and the U.S.-Soviet tensions that were leading up to the Cuban missile crisis, it was almost impossible to keep up with the whirlwind. Fisher was briefly hospitalized in New York with exhaustion, and after his release took to opening his nightclub act with the song "Arrivederci, Roma." A congresswoman from Georgia named Iris Blitch called on the attorney general to block Taylor and Burton from re-entering the country, "on grounds of undesirability." And in April, the Vatican City weekly, *L'Osservatore della Domenica,* printed a 500-word "open letter," signed only "X.Y.," that began "Dear Madam" and went on to say, "Even considering the [husband] that was finished by a natural solution, there remain three husbands buried with no other motive than a greater love that killed the one before. But if we start using these standards and this sort of competition between the first, second, third, and the hundredth love, where are we all going to end up? Right where you will finish—in an erotic vagrancy ... without end or without a safe port."

The complicity of the Catholic Church in the sport of Liz-bashing undid Taylor's nerves at the worst possible moment for the production. She was due at last to film Cleopatra's entrance into Rome, the centerpiece of the entire picture. The premise of the sequence, commonly known as the procession, is that Cleopatra, having borne a son to Caesar in Egypt, must now go to her lover's home turf to present herself to the Roman public. If they accept her, then her dream of a globe-straddling Egyptian-Roman empire is realized; if they boo and hiss, she is finished. Mankiewicz, hewing to Plutarch, addressed the situation precisely as Cleopatra did: by devising the most lavish, eyeball-popping spectacle he could think of, a NASA-budgeted halftime show.

As Caesar and the senators watched, agog, from the Forum's reviewing stand, a seemingly endless parade of exotica would stream through the Arch of Titus: fanfaring trumpeters, charioteers, scantily clad dancing girls with streamers, an old hag who changes magically into a young girl, dwarfs tossing sweets from atop painted donkeys, comely young women tossing gold coins from atop painted elephants, painted Watusi warriors, dancers shooting plumes of colored smoke into the air, a pyramid that bursts open to release thousands of doves, Arabian horses, and, for the finale, a two-ton, three-story-high, black sphinx drawn by 300 Nubian slaves, upon which would sit Cleopatra and her boy, Caesarion, both resplendent in gold raiment.

Originally the procession was to have been one of the first things shot, in October, but bad weather and inadequate preparation made a hash of that plan, forcing Fox to pay out money to various dancers, acrobats, and circus-animal trainers to ensure their availability through the spring. (Furthermore, the original elephants that had been hired proved to be unruly and destructive, one of them running amok on the Cinecittà soundstages and pulling up stakes; the elephants' owner, Ennio Togni, later attempted to sue Fox for slander when word got out that his pachyderms had been "fired." Said a disbelieving Skouras, "How do you slander an elephant?")

Six thousand extras had been hired to cheer the queen's entrance and ad-lib reactions of "Cleopatra! Cleopatra!," but Taylor, mindful of their Roman Catholicism and the Vatican's recent condemnation, feared an impromptu stoning. Comforted by Burton and Mankiewicz, she summoned the courage to be hoisted atop the sphinx. When the cameras started rolling, she assumed a facial expression of blank hauteur and felt the sphinx rolling through the arch. "Oh my God," she thought, "here it comes."

But the Roman extras neither booed nor (for the most part) shouted "Cleopatra! Cleopatra!" Instead, they cheered and yelled, "Leez! Leez! *Baci! Baci!,*" while blowing kisses her way.

OPERATION HOMESTRETCH: ROME, ISCHIA, EGYPT, SPRING-SUMMER 1962
"Mr. Skouras faces the future with courage, determination ... and terror."
—Groucho Marx, speaking at a testimonial dinner held in honor of Spyros Skouras at the Waldorf-Astoria in New York, April 12, 1962

Taylor had bought a Rolls for husband Eddie Fisher, which he drove in Rome. After Taylor dumped him for Burton, Fisher dumped the car at the airport.

In the spring of '62, Skouras saw the writing on the wall. He knew that his reign as Fox president wasn't going to last much longer. By May he was stricken with prostate trouble, and when he arrived in Rome on May 8 to screen a five-hour rough cut of *Cleopatra*-to-date, he had been fitted with a temporary catheter and was heavily sedated—and fell asleep several times during the screening. Satisfied nevertheless with what he saw, he began a push to finish the film as quickly as possible.

The month had begun with Taylor indisposed on account of what Wanger described as "the most serious situation to date." On April 21, Taylor and Burton, without forewarning any members of the production, left Rome to spend the Easter weekend at Porto Santo Stefano, a coastal resort town a hundred miles to the north. Unprotected by handlers and publicists, they were surveilled the entire time by a swarm of reporters and paparazzi, and the following day newspapers around the world ran pictorial stories of their "tryst at seaside."

"It was like hell," says Taylor. "There was no place to hide, not in this tiny cottage we had rented. When we were driving somewhere, they ran us into a ditch by jumping in front of the car. It was either Richard hits them or he swerves over, so we swerved over."

One of the Porto Santo Stefano "tryst" stories appeared in the London *Times,* which infuriated Sybil Burton, who was at home in England with the Burtons' two small daughters, Kate and Jessica. Sybil had studiously ignored the London tabloids, but to have the Taylor-Burton affair splashed across the *Times* was the last straw. She went to Rome on April 23 to await her husband's return. Wanger, fearing a public scene, detained her at the Grand Hotel for as long as he could.

In the meantime, Taylor returned abruptly and solo from Porto Santo Stefano, and was rushed, for the second time in four months, to the Salvator Mundi Hospital. The following day's papers carried news of a "violent quarrel" that had prompted Taylor to walk out on Burton as he stood, smoldering, on the porch of the stucco bungalow they were staying in. "Burton told her to go and get rid of herself, and she tried to," Wanger later said confidentially. "This was the one time that she really took an overdose and she was really in danger." Taylor again denies that suicide was her intent, saying that, as had been the case in February, she needed some respite.

The hospitalization could be explained away with the old standbys "exhaustion" and "food poisoning," but the reason she didn't work again until May 7—that she had a black eye and facial bruises—could not be so tidily addressed. Skouras, in a letter to Darryl Zanuck several months later, matter-of-factly referred to "the beating Burton gave her in Santo Stefano. She got two black eyes, her nose was out of shape, and it took 22 days for her to recover enough in order to resume filming." But Taylor maintains that the truth was what the press was told—that her bruises were incurred during the ride back from Porto Santo Stefano. "I was sleeping in the backseat of the car," she says, "and the driver went around a curve, and I bumped my nose on an ashtray."

Once Taylor's bruises healed, she went back to work. But more bad luck followed. The winds came up on some of the days the extras and dancers had been convened to continue work on the procession, canceling shooting at a cost of $250,000. A successfully completed scene that required Antony to slap Cleopatra to the ground—a loaded proposition made more so by the fact that Taylor had a bad back—was erased when the film was damaged in transit back to the United States; June retakes would be necessary. Then, on May 28, word slipped out to Levathes that Taylor had filmed Cleopatra's death scene, in which she commits suicide by letting an asp bite her hand. The death scene was, in the eyes of Fox's impatient executives, the one sequence the film could absolutely not do without. Knowing it existed, Levathes headed for Rome to shut down the picture.

On June 1, Wanger met with Levathes and learned that, effective the following day, he was being taken off salary and expenses. This was in every sense a quasi-firing, in that no one discouraged him from continuing to work on the film. So continue he did, contesting, with Mankiewicz, the New York office's demands that Taylor's last day be June 9, that the battle of Pharsalia sequence be canceled, and that all photography be completed by June 30. (A week later, back in the States, Levathes fired Marilyn Monroe from her abortive final film, *Something's Got to Give.* A Fox spokesman said, "No company can afford Monroe and Taylor.")

In haste, the *Cleopatra* production moved to the Italian island of Ischia, which was standing in for both Actium, the ancient Greek town near whose shores Octavian defeated Antony, and Tarsus, the Turkish port of the Roman Empire where Cleopatra made her second great entrance, aboard a barge. (The barge, complete with gilded stern and Dacron purple sails flown in from California, cost $277,000.)

It was off Ischia that a paparazzo named Marcello Geppetti took the photograph that most enduringly represents the Taylor-Burton affair: a shot of Burton planting a kiss on a smiling Taylor as both sun themselves in bathing suits on the deck of an anchored boat.

Taylor completed a successful take of Cleopatra's arrival aboard her barge on June 23. By studio decree, it was her last day on the picture—272 days after Mankiewicz had begun at Cinecittà, 632 days after Mamoulian had commenced shooting at Pinewood.

Battle-sequence work in Egypt would keep Mankiewicz busy through July, and battles with Fox occupied him in the weeks prior. While still on Ischia, the director learned that Fox was killing yet another crucial sequence, the battle of Philippi. Mankiewicz was enraged, having planned for the Philippi conflict to open the film's second half. On June 29, he sent a strongly worded telegram to Skouras and the Fox brass:

WITHOUT PHARSALIA IN MY OPINION OPENING OF FILM AND FOLLOWING SEQUENCES SEVERELY DAMAGED STOP BUT WITHOUT PHILIPPI THERE IS LITERALLY NO OPENING FOR SECOND HALF SINCE INTERIOR TENT SCENES ALREADY SHOT SIMPLY CANNOT BE INTELLIGIBLY PUT TOGETHER STOP . . . WITH MUTUAL APPRECIATION OF RESPONSIBILITIES AND SUGGESTING THAT MINE TOWARD THE STOCKHOLDERS IS NO LESS THAN YOURS I SUGGEST THAT YOU REPLACE ME SOONEST POSSIBLE BY SOMEONE LESS CRITICAL OF YOUR DIRECTIVES AND LESS DEDICATED TO THE EVENTUAL SUCCESS OF CLEOPATRA.

Fox placated Mankiewicz by allowing Pharsalia to be partially reconstituted via two days' worth of hasty shooting in some craggy Italian hills—and then *Cleopatra* moved on to Egypt for additional battle work.

The Egypt trip, from July 15 to July 24, was the by-now-customary fiasco, marred by delays, poor sanitary conditions, a threatened strike by the locally hired extras, and government wiretaps on the telephones of Jewish cast and crew members; adding injury to insult, there was the further deterioration of Mankiewicz's physical condition—he required daily B_{12} shots to keep going, and one shot hit his sciatic nerve, rendering him barely able to walk.

Principal photography was now complete. But Mankiewicz would have more to contend with in the film's lengthy postproduction phase: a new Fox regime. Back on June 26, under pressure, Skouras had announced his resignation as president, effective September 20.

ENTER THE MUSTACHE:
NEW YORK, LOS ANGELES, PARIS, LONDON, SPAIN, 1962–63
IT LOOKS LIKE MUSTACHE WITH ZEUS AS PLANKHEAD.
—Cable sent from Jack Brodsky
(in Fox's New York office) to Nathan Weiss
(in Fox's temporary Rome office), July 6, 1962

"Mustache" was Darryl Zanuck. "Zeus" was Skouras. Upon Skouras's resignation, Zanuck, whose family was still the single largest shareholder of Fox stock, made a play to take control of the faltering company he had co-founded in 1933. By outmaneuvering the various board factions and their designees for president, he engineered a coup that by

summertime had installed him as president and relegated Skouras to a largely ceremonial chairman-of-the-board position (ergo, "Zeus as plankhead").

Zanuck surveyed the state of affairs at Fox like a police chief arriving at a morbid crime scene—*move away, pal, show's over.* He shut down virtually all Fox productions save *Cleopatra,* dismissed most of the studio's employees and executives, lowered the thermostats, shuttered most of the buildings on the shrunken back lot, and replaced Levathes with his own son, producer Richard Zanuck.

Mankiewicz and Darryl Zanuck had a complex love-hate relationship that more often tipped toward the latter. But the director was relieved to know there was now a decisive man at the top, and someone who knew the ins and outs of picture-making to boot. "When I finished a screenplay, the first person I wanted to read it was Darryl," Mankiewicz said in 1982, recalling the days when Zanuck was Fox's chief of production. It was Zanuck who resolved one of Mankiewicz's biggest writerly dilemmas—how to pare down an overlong screenplay entitled *A Letter to Four Wives*—by suggesting that Mankiewicz eliminate one of the wives.

Back in Los Angeles, Mankiewicz and his editor, Dorothy Spencer, prepared a rough cut of *Cleopatra* that ran five hours and twenty minutes and reflected his desire to present *Cleopatra* in two concurrently released parts, with separate tickets required for each: *Caesar and Cleopatra,* followed by *Antony and Cleopatra.* Fox had long been against the idea, because of the exhibition logistics involved and because no one was interested in seeing Taylor make love to Rex Harrison.

Mankiewicz made a date with Zanuck to screen the film on October 13 in Paris, where the new Fox president lived (and continued to work, even though he was running an American studio). As this date approached, Wanger sent Zanuck a series of obsequious letters and telegrams, begging to be fully reinstated as producer: I BESEECH YOU, DARRYL . . . NOT TO AGGRAVATE THIS SITUATION AND FURTHER DAMAGE MY STATUS AS PRODUCER OF CLEOPATRA BY NOT BRINGING ME TO PARIS . . . I APPEAL TO YOU AS A MAN NOT TO DO THIS TO ME. Zanuck's cold-shoulder reply was that Wanger was welcome to come along provided he paid his own way.

The October 13 screening did not go particularly well. Zanuck said little to Mankiewicz as the lights went up except "If any woman behaved toward me the way Cleopatra treated Antony, I would cut her balls off."

Mankiewicz grew nervous when a week passed without him hearing anything further. On October 20, he sent a letter to Zanuck requesting an "honest and unequivocal statement of where I stand in relation to *Cleopatra.*"

On October 21, he got his statement. "On completion of the dubbing, your official services will be terminated," Zanuck wrote. "If you are available and willing, I will call upon you to screen the re-edited version of the film." Elsewhere in the letter, which ran to nine single-spaced pages, Zanuck described the existing battle sequences as "awkward, amateurish . . . second-rate film making" with a "B-picture" look; said that the film "over-emphasized in some places the *Esquire*-type of sex"; described Wanger as "impotent"; contrasted Mankiewicz's handling of *Cleopatra* unfavorably with his own handling of *The Longest Day;* and alleged, "You were not the official producer, yet in the history of motion pictures no one man has ever been given such authority. The records show that you made every single decision and that your word was law."

A few days later, Zanuck released the following statement to the press: "In exchange for top compensation and a considerable expense account, Mr. Joseph Mankiewicz has for two years spent his time, talent, and $35,000,000 of 20th Century–Fox's shareholders' money to direct and complete the first cut of the film *Cleopatra.* He has earned a well-deserved rest."

In response, the director told the press, "I made the first cut, but after that, it's the studio's property. They could cut it up into banjo picks if they want."

Privately, Mankiewicz sent Zanuck yet another letter that painstakingly refuted every charge made against him in the October 21 correspondence: "I am, I suppose, an old whore on this beat, Darryl, and it takes quite a bit to shock me . . . but never could I imagine the phantasmagoria of frantic lies and frenzied phony buck-passing that you report [in] your letter!"

By December, however, the two men's temperatures had cooled, and they recognized that their cooperation was necessary to get *Cleopatra* into releasable form. Zanuck conceded to Mankiewicz that the previous regime's cutbacks on Pharsalia and Philippi had been a mistake, and so, in February

1963—at a cost of $2 million—*Cleopatra's* company of soldiers was reconvened in Almería, Spain, to do battle. Further bits and pieces were shot in—irony of ironies—Pinewood Studios in England, where the whole mess had begun with Mamoulian 29 months earlier.

When the reshoots were done, Mankiewicz, with Zanuck looking over his shoulder, edited *Cleopatra* down to its 243-minute premiere length. Though they were publicly allies again, the director was unhappy with this version and still thought Zanuck had done him a disservice by not allowing *Cleopatra* to be shown in two parts. When Mankiewicz was asked to participate in a fluffy NBC tribute program called *The World of Darryl Zanuck,* he said he'd do it only if they retitled it *Stop the World of Darryl Zanuck.*

Nevertheless, *Cleopatra,* at last, was done.

CODA: NEW YORK, ETC., 1963–

"She is an entirely physical creature, no depth of emotion apparent in her kohl-laden eyes, no modulation in her voice that too often rises to fishwife levels. Out of royal regalia, en negligee or au naturel, she gives the impression that she is really carrying on in one of Miami Beach's more exotic resorts than inhabiting a palace in ancient Alexandria."

—Judith Crist, evaluating Taylor's
performance in her review of *Cleopatra*
for the *New York Herald Tribune,*
June 13, 1963

Cleopatra opened at the Rivoli Theater to mixed reviews, Crist's being the most damning, Bosley Crowther's, in *The New York Times,* being the most enthusiastic ("a surpassing entertainment, one of the great epic films of our day"). A viewing unprejudiced by temporal context reveals the movie to be mediocre-to-good, a tribute to Mankiewicz's salvaging abilities and the fact that, for all the waste, you do see a lot of the money up on the screen—the movie looks handsome and expensive in an old-fashioned, 2,000-artisans-at-work way, as opposed to the contemporary, postproduced-in-the-computer-lab way. The procession sequence is as mind-boggling as it's supposed to be.

Taylor's Cleopatra comes off as an imperious harridan, a seething Imelda, but she's actually effective—you believe her dream of empire. Still, you can't help but notice the inconsistency of her physical appearance throughout the film, a consequence of the events and upheavals she was enduring. At times, she's skinny and youthful; other times, she's fleshy but ravishing; still other times, damned if she isn't Mrs. John Warner foretold. The male leads' fortunes are more contingent upon the circumstances under which Mankiewicz wrote their parts. Whereas Harrison gets all the good lines, Burton looks ludicrous and spends most of his screen time shouting, flaring his nostrils, and huffing around Alexandria in a strangely tiny mini-toga (he shows more leg than Cyd Charisse). Not that poor writing was entirely to blame—Mankiewicz's completed screenplay contains nuanced, character-building Antony scenes that never should have ended up on the cutting-room floor.

Business at the Rivoli was good, and the movie sold out for the next four months; Skouras, his exhibitor's skills coming to the fore, had shrewdly arranged a deal whereby Fox collected $1.25 million in advance guarantees from the theater before a single ticket had been sold. Applying this strategy worldwide, he collected $20 million in pre-release grosses.

The movie was never the runaway hit Wanger had dreamed of, but a year after its release it was one of the top-10 grossers of all time, and in 1966,

Paparazzi hounded the couple as they left a Rome nightclub in April 1962. Burton was drunk; Taylor still had on her Cleopatra eyeliner from that day's shoot.

when Fox sold the television broadcast rights to ABC for $5 million, *Cleopatra* passed the break-even mark. The studio had by then rehabilitated itself—*The Sound of Music,* which had come out a year earlier and cost $8 million to make, was an unexpected megahit, grossing more than $100 million.

But the travails of *Cleopatra* did not end at the Rivoli. Subsequent to the New York premiere, Fox chopped the film down further. For the Washington, D.C., and London premieres, a three-hour forty-seven-minute version was shown. When the film went into wide release, it was even shorter, running at three hours and twelve minutes. If big-city moviegoers were gypped out of seeing Mankiewicz's vision realized, most Americans were gypped out of seeing a comprehensible film.

Recently, with the support of the Mankiewicz family and Fox's current studio chief, Bill Mechanic, archivists have been laboring to reconstruct a six-hour "director's cut" of the film that would do better justice to Burton's part, and the film as a whole, than the 243-minute "opening night" version currently available on video. Their efforts have revealed that Mankiewicz's cynical divination of *Cleopatra's* ultimate fate—that it would end up as the world's most expensive banjo picks—wasn't that far off. The *Cleopatra* he envisioned has scattered to the winds. Some missing footage has turned up in the hands of private collectors. Other bits and pieces have been discovered, uncatalogued and a mile deep in the earth, in an underground storage facility in Kansas. Further bits have turned up in even stranger places: Richard Green and Geoffrey Sharpe, two eagle-eyed *Cleopatra* enthusiasts in London who are assisting Fox in the restoration efforts, noticed that Charlton Heston used chunks of excised Mankiewicz footage to flesh out his 1972 low-budget vanity production of Shakespeare's *Antony and Cleopatra.*

Appropriately, the saga of *Cleopatra* dragged unhappily on for several more years after its release, a dénouement of bad blood, threats, and lawsuits. Taylor, Burton, and Fisher sued Fox for their proper shares of the grosses. Fox sued Taylor and Burton for breach of contract, specifically citing the former for, among other things, "suffering herself to be held up to scorn, ridicule, and unfavorable publicity as a result of her conduct and deportment." Wanger sued Skouras, Zanuck, and Fox for breach of contract. Fox sued Wanger right back on the same grounds. Skouras contemplated a libel suit against Wanger for the way he was portrayed in the 1963 book *My Life with Cleopatra,* and another suit against the publicists Brodsky and Weiss for the way he came across in their book from 1963, *The Cleopatra Papers.* By the late 60s, after several GATT-like rounds of depositions and negotiations, all of these various actions were eventually resolved.

The matter of the Fishers and the Burtons also stretched well beyond *Cleopatra's* production life span. When principal filming was completed, Burton returned once more to his wife, and Taylor, for the first time in years, had no man in her life. By early 1963, however, the two had reunited to do another movie, *The V.I.P.s,* a London-based production that gave them an excuse to take adjacent suites in the Dorchester. Sybil Burton filed for divorce that December; Fisher, after months of ugly public exchanges with Taylor over the division of their property, finally gave up the ghost on March 5, 1964, when he failed to contest her petition for a Mexican divorce.

Burton was playing *Hamlet* in Toronto when Taylor's divorce was finalized; she was with him. They married in Montreal on March 15. The following night, Burton was back in Toronto playing the Dane. After taking his curtain call, he presented his wife to the audience and declaimed, to the audience's delight, "I would just like to quote from the play—Act III, Scene I: 'We will have no more marriages.'" □

STANLEY KUBRICK Reclusive, obsessive, brutally devoted to his craft, Stanley Kubrick registered the anxieties of the 20th century and made the first film convincingly set in the 21st. In *Dr. Strangelove* he satirized the greatest external threat of all; in *A Clockwork Orange* he anatomized the enemy within. Capable of miniature, as in *Lolita*, and epic, with *Spartacus* and *Barry Lyndon*, he traced the outlines of our time from the trenches of the First World War (*Paths of Glory*) to Vietnam's desolation row (*Full Metal Jacket*).

PHOTOGRAPHED IN 1963

JACKIE COOPER AND **MICKEY ROONEY**
Dirty faces, but no angels. Jackie Cooper was the screen's archetypal newsboy and urchin of the Depression years, who grew up to play editor Perry White in all four Christopher Reeve *Superman* spectaculars. Mickey Rooney graduated from his success as Puck in *A Midsummer Night's Dream* (1935) and as the puckish Andy Hardy—his alter ego in 16 pictures—by way of marrying eight Mirandas (including Ava Gardner) and turning into Caliban in *Baby Face Nelson* in 1957. See why contenders are often called kids?

PHOTOGRAPHED IN 1996
BY **HERB RITTS**

EDDIE BRACKEN AND **DONALD O'CONNOR**
From the days of the vaudeville circuit, and still up for a song and a dance: Donald O'Connor (right) portrayed Huck Finn and Buster Keaton in his day, tap-danced with Gene Kelly (*Singin' in the Rain*), and in 1992 became a dad by playing Robin Williams's father in *Toys*. Eddie Bracken was a veteran of the "Our Gang" comedies (and also a vet in Preston Sturges's *Hail the Conquering Hero*). More recently seen in *Rookie of the Year*—back to boyhood.
PHOTOGRAPHED IN 1997
BY **PEGGY SIROTA**

HOLLYWOOD ISSUE COVER, 2000 From left: Penélope Cruz, Wes Bentley, Mena Suvari, Marley Shelton, Chris Klein, Selma Blair, Paul Walker, Jordana Brewster, Sarah Wynter.

PHOTOGRAPHED IN 1999
BY **ANNIE LEIBOVITZ**

BLYTHE DANNER AND **GWYNETH PALTROW**

Blythe spirit. Ms. Danner appeared in *Man, Woman and Child* in 1983; her man is director and producer Bruce Paltrow, and her child—her daughter—was ever perched for kindred pursuits. From the start, which was as young Wendy in *Hook*, Gwyneth showed good breeding. After classics such as *Emma*, she caught even the bard's eye in *Shakespeare in Love*—and got an Oscar in return. Very talented in *The Talented Mr. Ripley* (1999).

PHOTOGRAPHED IN 1995
BY **DAVID SEIDNER**

LILLIAN AND **DOROTHY GISH** In D. W. Griffith's *Orphans of the Storm*, they played abandoned waifs. (To re-create the grim mood of the set, misty portraitist James Abbe posed them under an umbrella, forsaken and bathed in a halo of gloom.) Waifs they weren't. Adopted by filmgoers everywhere, the Gishes became the grandest sisters in silent film. Dorothy, younger by five years, was dubbed the "female Chaplin"; Lillian gained renown in Griffith features such as *The Birth of a Nation, Intolerance,* and *Broken Blossoms.* If nothing else, Miss Lillian had staying power: she made 84 films in 75 years (1912 through 1987).

PHOTOGRAPHED IN 1921
BY **JAMES ABBE**

CARNAL KNOWLEDGE 30TH COLLEGE REUNION Candice Bergen, Art Garfunkel, Jack Nicholson, Ann-Margret, Mike Nichols

Hands down, *Carnal Knowledge* is the screen's wittiest, smartest, and most acutely entertaining depiction of masculine self-loathing. Maybe it's a little too rough on the boys (Garfunkel and roommate Nicholson, King of the Amherst Make-Out Artists), but unlike other relics of the Battle of the Sexes, early-70s division, this film still lacerates. Credit is due Nichols's mordantly precise direction, Jules Feiffer's stiletto-funny script, and a quartet of withering, revelatory performances. For Bergen, Garfunkel, and Ann-Margret, the movie was a breakthrough; for Nicholson, in the wake of *Easy Rider* and *Five Easy Pieces*, another notch on the bedpost.

PHOTOGRAPHED IN 2001
BY **ANNIE LEIBOVITZ**

MIRIAM HOPKINS The first-ever full-length Technicolor movie took author William Makepeace Thackeray's scheming protagonist and awarded *her* the title. Otherwise, *Becky Sharp* (1935) would have been properly baptized *Vanity Fair*, after Thackeray's 1847 satirical novel—one of several sources from which the magazine derives its name. Miriam Hopkins was the centerpiece, as she had been in *Trouble in Paradise* and would be again in *The Children's Hour*. This Georgia peach tried to outbitch Bette Davis and nearly won, but wasn't Becky always deceptively sweet?

PHOTOGRAPHED IN 1935
BY **ANTON BRUEHL**
AND **FERNAND BOURGES**

CAROLE LOMBARD Ms. Lombard (here on a Hollywood soundstage) might well have been astonished at the telegram F.D.R. sent to her man, Clark Gable, when she died in a plane crash on a War Bonds tour in 1942. "A great artist ... she is and always will be a star," wrote the president. "Well whaddaya know!" one imagines the star of *Twentieth Century* and *My Man Godfrey* exclaiming. "Wait till my old Mack Sennett partners get a load of this." Killed just as she'd done her best, in Lubitsch's *To Be or Not to Be.* PHOTOGRAPHED IN 1931 BY **CECIL BEATON**

PULP FICTION If "violence is as American as cherry pie," as H. Rap Brown put it, then here is that pie's upper crust. With their 1994 film, *Pulp Fiction*, Bruce Willis, director Quentin Tarantino, Uma Thurman, Samuel L. Jackson, and John Travolta gave a fresh, affectless patina to the cruel and amoral, rendering casual gunplay as American as a Quarter Pounder with Cheese and changing the look of independent films forever. Tarantino, who'd color-coded *Reservoir Dogs*, became our unchallenged Mr. Noir.

PHOTOGRAPHED IN 1994
BY **ANNIE LEIBOVITZ**

By Christopher Hitchens

Nobody knows how it came by its name. Most probably, some city booster or real-estate hopeful of the 1890s wanted a beckoning title for some borderline property. And the whole cosmology of America tends toward the West, the Occident, the quenching of the sun in the sea. But the other quasi-magical street names of the United States are, when you unpack them, even more trite.

They say the neon lights are bright on Broadway . . . so let them.

The avenue I'm taking you to—*Forty-Second Street?* Park is banal, Madison was a politician, Fifth is a digit, Pennsylvania is a state, Bourbon is a drink. Only the alchemy of layered association invests these addresses with any patina. But Sunset, no matter how vulgar and obvious its origin, is quite something. I'll meet you on Sunset . . . It started on Sunset . . . Make a left on Sunset. You can't say that doesn't sound exotic.

Sunset runs from the newest hardscrabble immigrants at one end to the oldest and richest immigrants at the other. It traverses 25 miles of megalopolis, and where it ends, the United States of America comes to a stop. As it curves like a graph, you can read off much handy information about the condition of the national libido, the national economy, the national cuisine, the national composition, and the national dreams, to say nothing of some local cultural gossip that has become the costly thread from which international legend is made. If you can fake it here, you can fake it anywhere.

All things considered, I'm glad that I took my cruise along the strip—in the company of the great Billy Wilder—in torrential rain. One can forget that Wilder's imperishable *Sunset Boulevard,* which opens with a stencil of the title on the edge of a dingy pavement, is shot partly in a downpour: "a great big package of rain," as the deceased narrator puts it, "oversized—like everything else in California." Mr. Wilder consented to give me the tour on day one of what became the great Los Angeles flood of 1995. The few heroic sluts on this great working-girl turf looked as if they might offer to wash our windshield instead, and through the deluge I swear I glimpsed a sodden hustler clutching a soggy sign reading: WILL DIRECT FOR FOOD.

The torrents were a reminder that you never step into the same stream twice, and no observant person has ever seen identical Sunsets. Its nature is protean. Mr. Wilder is one of its archaeologists and historians. He sees it clearly, but he can see it as it once was. "When I came here in 1934—stayed at the Chateau Marmont for 70 bucks a month—half of this wasn't even paved. There was a bridle path from Hollywood to Holmby Hills. Douglas Fairbanks and Mary Pickford bought their place in Beverly Hills as a hunting lodge."

Everything that Wilder sees reminds him of something else. "That was Ciro's," he says, pointing at what is now the Comedy Store. "There was a big scandal there when it was reported that Paulette Goddard was doing it on the table and on the dance floor with Anatole Litvak. I never asked her—she was married to Charlie Chaplin and Erich Maria Remarque—but I asked him on his oath and he swore that her shoulder strap just slipped and all he did was kiss her on the breast."

We approach the Virgin Megastore, former site of Schwab's drugstore (known in *Sunset Boulevard* as "headquarters"). "Mervyn LeRoy told me that he didn't discover Lana Turner there, no matter what you read. He found her in another drugstore, just across from Hollywood High School."

Here are, and were, the clubs that defined what was hot for those who liked it that way. "There was a lot of illegal gambling and drinking at the Clover Club in the 1930s," says Wilder semi-fondly. "I saw David Selznick boozing it up in there before he made *Gone with the Wind.*"

At Le Dôme, the power-lunch parlor where Barry Diller created panic in 1992 by snacking with David Geffen right after he left Fox, Wilder talks about pictures. "Expensive as they are now, studios try and keep 'em popular. They're either very broad or very cautious—they like it best if it's a picture they've already seen. That was always true, but we made *hundreds* of pictures. Even then, they liked to do test-marketing, only they did it with preview cards. One card for *The Lost Weekend* told me it was a great movie but I should take out all the stuff about drinking and alcoholism. Another time I went to Long Beach with Ernst Lubitsch for a preview of *Ninotchka,* and he was reading the cards in the car on the way home. Started laughing and wouldn't tell me why, but finally passed me the card that said, 'Great movie. I laughed so hard I peed in my girlfriend's hand.'"

Wilder was a part of "the emigration of genius," the exodus of gifted anti-Nazi Germans and Austrians that brought Thomas Mann and Theodor Adorno and Bertolt Brecht to the California coast. Had he met these heroes? "I was introduced to Mann at a Kaffeeklatsch for exiles run by Salka Viertel, who was married to the director. I was so impressed—he'd won the Nobel Prize in the 20s—that I don't remember what he said or if I said anything."

He reminisces briefly about Will Rogers, who made the transition from vaudeville and silent pictures to talkies, and about Howard Hughes, who shared the Rogers passion for the new fad of aviation and once crashed a plane within earshot of Sunset. And then it's time for him to go back out into the rain.

Returning to the bar to relish the memory of lunch for a few moments, I am hailed from a good table by a very handsome black man who looks familiar. "I love your work, man," he says, leaving me quite undone. I ask a waiter discreetly. "That's Billy Dee *Williams,*" he whispers hoarsely. "He was in *Lady Sings the Blues* and . . . " The whole screen career and credits follow. Sunset—where every waiter is a producer/director. And you should see the signed star pix by the till at Gil Turner's liquor store on the corner of Doheny.

I reflect, after the great Wilder has left me, that at least in his day there must have been less talk about how great it all *used* to be. You couldn't hold forth about how everybody should have been here 30 or 40 years earlier, because nobody really had been. Yet, on further reflection, all of *Sunset Boulevard* is about glory days departed. "I *am* big," responds Norma Desmond when Joseph Gillis tells her she used to be big. "It's the pictures that got small." Sunset may have been a great developer's idea for a name, but it does have the infallible connotation of the blazing hours just before darkness falls. Between the blaze and the *noir* falls the lengthening shadow. You can catch it in conversation: What if the Japanese wise up? What if the Japanese go *broke?* Hurry it up, buster. The strip is changing faster than you are.

Lost Angeles. That's it in a phrase. Some of the sites are easy to spot. Down the road is that health-nut hangout the Source, where Woody Allen was so hilariously discomfited in *Annie Hall,* vindicating his suspicion that L.A.'s only cultural advantage was the permission to make a right on red. There's the Chateau Marmont, where John Belushi OD'd, just after Michael Eisner's wife had seen him watching one of his reruns and found herself thinking . . . *Sunset Boulevard.*

There's the St. James's Club, so English and Anglophile that it's even on the corner of Kings Road, where Tim Robbins went to keep his fateful non-

appointment in *The Player* (with a stalker who used the name Joe Gillis, as it happens) and ended up hearing one of the funniest pitches ever delivered. But even the St. James's has opened under new management and become the Argyle, having already been the Sunset Towers apartment building and the home of Marilyn Monroe, Jean Harlow, and Clark Gable. It used to be said that the St. James's had been a skyscraper before it got "fucked flat."

Other corners and sites can be unearthed or recovered with just a few strokes of the archaeologist's brush. In *The White Album,* Joan Didion recounts being told, "You turn left at the old Mocambo," as she sought directions to Sammy Davis's place in the hills above Sunset. She didn't know where "the old Mocambo" was, but didn't have much trouble finding out. Yet listen to the old-timers talk about the fabled Garden of Allah, which used in Wilder's day to be just opposite the Marmont, and you need a trowel or a shovel, not a brush.

"The Garden of Allah was created by a fizzling silent-movie star called Alla Nazimova," says Marc Wanamaker, nephew of Sam and a meticulous local historian and archivist. "She was just like Gloria Swanson in *Sunset Boulevard,* only more savvy. She had a Spanish Mediterranean–style house and she added an *h* and turned it into an apartment complex which saw her through her slump. Scott Fitzgerald stayed there. Charles Laughton and Elsa Lanchester were there. The Errol Flynn and John Barrymore rat pack partied there."

Now there's a bank and a McDonald's enclosed in mini-mall architecture on the site. (When you've seen one cluster of generic stores grouped under one management or one roof, you've seen a mall.) The only tenuous connection remaining from the industry is Jay Ward's animation studio, home of

Director Billy Wilder, then 90, in the backseat of a 1965 Mercury Montclair convertible, giving directions at the corner of Sunset and Horn.

Dudley Do-Right and Rocky and Bullwinkle. A tacky and tattered statue of the goofy moose and the stupid squirrel still bestrides the sidewalk, one of those glimpses that one gets from the car as Sunset unspools itself.

The most frequent and sonorous commonplace about the City of Angels, and about its inhabitants, is that no sense of history adheres. Wrong. Hang out with Marc Wanamaker, or with Mike Davis, author of the amazing *City of Quartz: Excavating the Future in Los Angeles,* and you elicit an intense feeling for the ways in which the immediate past has fired the mold of the present. Sunset did not uncurl itself toward the ocean like some blind tendril seeking the light. It fought its way as part of a process of ambition and acquistion that still shows at every bend. One consequence is the way in which Sunset crosses the borders of three municipalities: Los Angeles, West Hollywood, and Beverly Hills.

Until 1984, West Hollywood was an autonomous, unincorporated district. As a result, the area between Doheny and Marmont known as "the strip"—the area lovingly photographed building by building by Ed Ruscha in 1966—was a law unto itself, a border town with frontier values. In the 1930s and 1940s it was a magnet for gambling, bootlegging, clublandism, and the informal or commercial carnal-knowledge industry, and some of this ethos still hangs about it like tattered finery.

"It was known as the Las Vegas of L.A.," says Wanamaker, "with its own sheriffs on one side of the line and the L.A.P.D. on the other."

The irony, of course, was that *Las Vegas* soon became the Las Vegas of L.A. "The big billboard in front of the Marmont was taken over by the Sahara Hotel in Vegas," Wanamaker says. "Putting that on the strip was a sign that the strip was on the way out. Behind the sign, incidentally, is the site of Preston Sturges's original Players Club, now called Roxbury."

The big Marmont billboard (Joan Didion says that she used to sit at Spago and tell what was new by the Sunset billboards) has been occupied for some years by the Marlboro cowboy. He looks even more rugged now that you can't light up anywhere on the strip. Asking diffidently at Dan Aykroyd's House of Blues if I could smoke, I was told by a stunning African-American hostess, "Honey, didn't we *have* this very conversation last year? You promised you'd stay healthy so I could bear your child." Just like that. Behind her, a large notice read, THIS JOINT IS DEDICATED TO THE MEMORY OF OUR DEAR BROTHER RIVER. Did Mr. Phoenix die in here? "No, honey, but he was an *investor*." Oh, O.K. I'll go and smoke outside, then.

Despite this attempt to impose a herbivorous style on all of California, there are still points of resistance along the strip. And the strip, after all, is where Humphrey Bogart was filmed outside the Trocadero in *Stand-In* (1937), and Robert Cummings exited the same club in *Hollywood Boulevard* (1936). *Hollywood Story* (1951) was shot at LaRue. There is a tradition of louche life to live up to. And so Bret Easton Ellis's affectless bastards cluster in Carneys railcar diner on the strip, and his narrator in *Less than Zero* is knocked back by a Sunset billboard that reads, cryptically, DISAPPEAR HERE. If you have some time and money on a Saturday night, you can still get into trouble at the Viper Room or, if you want to feel more traditional about it, at the Whisky or the Roxy.

But if you want unauthorized excitement these days, it's eastward you should turn your horse's head. As Sunset dips downtown toward its terminus at Union Station, which is now the hub of a metro system that, in somebody's dreams, Angelenos will one day use, the street names mark the transition. The old Brooklyn Avenue, once home to the immigrant Jewish community, has been renamed after a struggle. It is now called Cesar Chavez.

In this district, new Chinese expansion meets the Hispanic underclass, and if you get up early enough you can see the day laborers waiting on the sidewalk for drive-by employers. Good-luck stores, some of them selling the mystique of Santería, cater to the needs of those who most need a break. It's in this rather incongruous setting, by the crumbling walls of the old Mother Cabrini orphanage, that you can see the almost unvisited Fort Moore monument, just off Sunset at Hill Street. Cracked and faded, its waterfall no longer tumbling, it celebrates the conquest of California by the United States and the founding of Los Angeles by Anglos.

You would not guess, from these white stone reliefs of heroic Mormons and Yankees, how John Charles Frémont, "the Pathfinder" in California history, described his 1843 expedition as it moved south: "Our cavalcade made a strange and grotesque appearance . . . guided by a civilized Indian, attended by two wild ones from the Sierra; a Chinook from the Columbia; and our own mixture of American, French, German—all armed; four or five languages heard at once; above a hundred horses and mules, half-wild; American, Spanish and Indian dresses and equipments intermingled."

As you move west along Sunset to Echo Park, it's worth a slight detour to see the Neutra and Schindler architecture up the hill (in an area now noted chiefly for clubs and dives consecrated to the polymorphous perverse). Hereabouts, too, is the Short Stop bar, watering hole of street cops, where you used to be able to see Joseph Wambaugh. As he phrases it so delicately in *The Choirboys*, "Spermwhale had persuaded Baxter to take him to the Sunset Strip once after work to meet Foxy and the two policemen were taken backstage by a burly assistant manager. Foxy was standing nude in her dressing room combing her pubic hair and pushing the vaginal lips back inside before the second show." Wambaugh was a Cal State English student when Christopher Isherwood was a professor, and admires his *Goodbye to Berlin*. Nice to feel the air of divine Berlin decadence seeping onto Sunset.

At Sunset and Hillhurst, as you work your way back toward the strip from downtown, there once stood the colossal set of D. W. Griffith's *Intolerance*, which for two years was the most striking edifice in the city. (Griffith's *In Old California* was the first movie ever shot in Hollywood.)

The first comedy club, showing up on the right, brings one back onto the strip from the eastern approach. My guide this time, George Schlatter, used to be a nightclub booker for MCA until his lovely wife, Jolene, made an honest man of him, and set him on the stony upward path that led him to conceive *Rowan & Martin's Laugh-In*.

"There was a real café society in those days," says George, referring to the period in the early 50s when Sophie Tucker, Mae West, Nat Cole, and Sammy Davis were the aristos. "People did dress and dine a little." Listening to George, you can hear Bobby Troup doing "Route 66" (another magical American road name), and picture Sammy Davis tap-dancing at Ciro's before grabbing—and *playing*—every instrument in the band. "After Sammy came back from his eye injury, the whole town came out to see his first gig. Cooper was there. Gable and Bogart were there. Frank and Dean were playing cards at the stageside."

In contrast to Wilder, George was in Ciro's on the night of the Paulette Goddard—Anatole Litvak *scandale*. "If you believe the thousands of people who say they saw it, she sank beneath the table and he stayed upright and grinning." In 1954, Darryl Zanuck gave a huge party with a circus theme at Ciro's, and climaxed the bash by doing a trapeze act himself. "Can you imagine a studio head doing that today?"

On this world and its doings, Hedda Hopper and Louella Parsons were able to feed nightly and create the whole business of celebrity and showbiz journalism. Army Archerd, who was columnar legman for the gossip writer Harrison Carroll, still writes for *Variety*, but otherwise we're talking about a lost world. And some of it, as I listen to George, turns out not to have been so romantic. "When I got the account for the Crescendo club, Billy Eckstine was rumored to be a silent partner because blacks couldn't get a license on the strip. A couple of us had to get together and buy Judy Garland's old house for Sammy Davis, putting it in my name because of the 'no blacks' rule."

Schlatter and others were able to bust the color bar using showbiz success as a lever. "The time came when we could say to people, here or in Vegas, 'You want to book Sammy, you have to let him and his guests stay in your hotel.' And they had no choice." He talks fondly of the night Marlene Dietrich walked down the street to Bugsy Siegel's place with Lena Horne and Pearl Bailey for company and the doors fell open and the Jim Crow era was over.

And here's the Bullwinkle statue again. It used to face a twirling cowgirl statue, and in the opening scene of *Myra Breckinridge* Myra/Myron looks out at it from the penthouse terrace of the Chateau Marmont, which had once had a view of the splendors of the Garden of Allah. "Ah yes, the Garden of Allah," says Gore Vidal today. "I used to stay there because of Sam Zimbalist, my MGM producer, who was Alla Nazimova's pet even though she was absolutely queen of the dykes. We worked on *Ben-Hur* there. But my cabin was next to Errol Flynn's, and his day began at midnight, so that I had to move out because of all the shrieks and splashes from the pool."

It's touching to summon the ghost of the young Vidal wishing that Flynn would pipe down and let him get on with re-creating Roman decadence for the silver screen. There are all sorts of glamorous ghosts and phantoms in this *quartier*. Marc Wanamaker, for one, remembers how Ciro's outlived café society and metamorphosed into a rock club in the 1960s. Here the blissed-out young came to gaze upon the Doors, whose blissed-out name was borrowed from *The Doors of Perception*, one of Aldous Huxley's California meditations from the days when he was scheming pre-Leary voyages of the imagination from a bit further along the boulevard in West Hollywood.

By now we have left the wok and the burrito behind, and the joys of nouvelle are about to unfold themselves. Sunset Plaza, a ritzy stretch of restaurants, luxury stores, and hairdressers, begins to presage the more gorgeous and formal tones of Beverly Hills. Since this area is still privately held, by the old, established Montgomery family, it has been able to avoid the sorts of tawdry development that elsewhere make the boulevard feel, in Ed Ruscha's useful phrase, "all malled out."

Joan Didion describes the intersection of Sunset and La Brea as "the dead center of nothing," but along the strip the heart still lifts a bit, and it becomes possible to believe that the odd dream might actually come true. Dyan Cannon really was pedaling along it on her bike when she was hailed from a smart car and asked if she was in the movies. On replying in the negative, she was told that she ought to be, and would be.

You can only guess at the change by looking at Ruscha's Warholian set of 1966 foldout photographs, and it may become clearer when he presents his three-dimensional, three-decade work in progress of the entire boulevard, but the difference is made by the fact that for these blocks you get a north-south perspective as well as an east-west one. As if on a generous step cut out of some exotic hillside, you can look down and look over in one direction, and look up yearningly in the other (toward the plush European-style homes and mansions known to some as "the Swish Alps").

The very word "strip" has something snappy, urbane, and Runyon-esque about it: a stretch of big shoulders, big wads, and wised-up, street-smart elements—an air of optimism, or at least of euphoria. Perhaps this is why, even as Sunset begins to shade into the manicured gentility of Beverly Hills, people like to stress its gamy and risky side. Arguments occur about the precise location of "Dead Man's Curve," a fated corner just by the Beverly Hills city limits, where Jan of Jan & Dean survived a triple-fatality smashup in April 1966, only two years after pushing the road-accident hit "Dead Man's Curve" to No. 8 on the charts. Jon Wiener, biographer of John Lennon, who teaches at U.C. Irvine, directed me to the entry in *The Penguin Encyclopedia of Popular Music* which said that "it was years before [Jan] could remember an entire song lyric."

I think that the likeliest spot for Dead Man's Curve is on the corner of Sunset and Carolwood (Barbra Streisand's street), where there appears to be a sort of wayside shrine. But that could be to Barbra. We are entering the neighborhood where casual laborers run roadside stands with big signs saying, STAR MAPS HERE. Within bull's roar of the shrine, you can pinpoint the homes of Engelbert Humperdinck and Jayne Mansfield (the mapmakers provide a tasteful asterisk for the deceased). Marilyn Monroe and Walt Disney lived on Carolwood, I was intrigued to learn, and Tony Curtis and Burt Reynolds also.

Even in the drenching rain of the worst floods in memory, it is possible to visualize the lushness and grace of the area, the amazing combination of seclusion and ostentation that gives character to the equally seductive combination of wealth and fame. "Around here," says George Schlatter, who is from around here, "you don't ask if people have a tennis court. You ask do they have a north-south tennis court, to keep the sun out of their eyes. You don't ask if they have a pool; you ask what heating system their pool has."

Voyage up Rodeo to Sunset and imagine you are giving a tour to a starstruck newcomer. Swing by Jackie Collins's new place on Beverly Drive, go over four blocks to Lucille Ball's house on Roxbury, with Gene Kelly just down the street and the Kirk Douglas home on Rexford. Then, just above Sunset, you might get a glimpse of the Knoll, where Marvin and Barbara Davis find it amusing to entertain.

Mrs. Davis is the force behind the Carousel of Hope, a charity for children with diabetes, and at her last fund-raising gala managed to get Hillary and Barbra and the Duchess of York and Steven Spielberg and Tom Hanks and Governor Pete Wilson all at one table. In case they got bored with one another, they were entertained by Placido, by Kenny G., by Jay Leno and Neil Diamond and Phil Collins (whose home, now his wife's, was then at Sunset and Hillcrest). Not too shabby and, at 10 grand a couple, not too bad from the diabetes-research point of view.

It's true that there's the odd mud slide and earthquake. (Local gag: "I've bought a place on Mulholland. My agent says it'll be beachfront one day.") But nowhere else in the world puts you so neatly in reach of skiing in one direction and surfing in another, positioned beautifully for the yachts of Catalina and the dune buggies of the pristine desert, with night-blooming jasmine thrown in. After working on *Lolita* with Stanley Kubrick, Nabokov went butterfly hunting in Mandeville Canyon.

But I'm straying from the free association with lawlessness, chance, and life in the raw. Down the road from the Beverly Hills Hotel—still closed while it is redone to the taste of the new owner, the Sultan of Brunei—is a vast empty lot. It marks the spot of the neighborhood's most famous arson. A Saudi princeling, tiring of austere desert morality, decreed himself a pleasure dome

here and placed a row of pornographic caryatids with their pudenda fronting the street. The resultant fire-setting shows that there is a final arbiter of taste in this neck of the woods, and that its judgment is swift and sure.

Through Bel Air we bowl, tipping our hats to the Ron and Nancy Reagan home on St. Cloud Road, which not long ago changed its street number. This was not to throw star-map rubberneckers off the trail, but resulted from the fact that the Reagan address was 666. On learning that this number was the mark of the beast in the Book of Revelation, they did what anybody would have done and altered it to 668. You can't be too careful.

These gentle hills and undulant canyons conceal a lot more coiled superstition, diabolism, and violence than they disclose at first review. The Sharon Tate house on Cielo Drive; the old Houdini house of tricks; some whispered-about houses that cater to rather specialized tastes. And don't forget that, as Mike Davis reminded me, the whole effort of sculpting these hospitable slopes was undertaken first with high-pressure water-blasting and, when that failed, by the discharge of many tons of TNT.

But it was in escaping violence and disorder that Thomas Mann came to stay at the Beverly Hills Hotel for a few days in April 1939. "We are charmed once more by this landscape," he wrote. "Its slight absurdity is outweighed by the manifold charms of nature and life. Perhaps we shall someday build a hut here." And build quite a decent hut he did. Having stayed for a time in Brentwood on North Rockingham, and then on Amalfi Drive, he settled just off Sunset on San Remo Drive: "Where the house is to be built, numerous lemon trees have been felled, and the foundation of the little house appears in the form of a trellis on the ground. Thus at my visit yesterday, I saw the space for my future study, in which my books and my desk from Munich will stand."

Here he wrote *Doctor Faustus.* The family that now occupies the house is friendly and gracious about receiving pilgrims, as Mann himself was when the 14-year-old Susan Sontag came over shyly to crave a meeting almost half a century ago. From this address he kept in touch with neighbors like Arnold Schoenberg, caught a dangerous flu after making a pro-Roosevelt speech in a foggy garden in Bel Air, and, at the home of the composer Hanns Eisler, met Charlie Chaplin: "I laughed for three hours long at his imitations, scenes, and clownings and was still wiping my eyes as we got into the car." At this period, Mann was composing the foreword to a newspaper for German P.O.W.'s, so the laughs were not numerous. Hollywood ought to be more boastful than it is about this period of generosity and genius in its past.

Leaving Holmby Hills, the boulevard opens out a bit and becomes almost countrified.

"There are tributaries from every direction," says John Gregory Dunne, "but Sunset is the string that binds it all together." Up this canyon or that road, as he can tell you from his elaborate knowledge, lived Kenneth and Kathleen Tynan, and Christopher Isherwood and Don Bachardy. L.A. mayor Richard Riordan is O. J. Simpson's current neighbor. Sunset serves to connect them to the amorphous idea of "El Ay" and the California dream.

(I did seriously consider leaving Mr. Simpson out of this account, just to be able to say I had done it. But there was no avoiding the police sawhorses that marked off the end of Rockingham, where Michelle Pfeiffer has put her house on the market and where Michael Ovitz and Stanley Sheinbaum—liberal fund-raiser *extraordinaire*—are still clinging on.)

Unlike most good things, Sunset doesn't really come to an end. It just peters out, amid a tacky modernist welter of junk-food stops and unsightly commerce. It almost literally dribbles away into the sand. Perhaps that is as it should be. It can be more satisfying to look back than to look forward. When I asked Billy Wilder what he made of Andrew Lloyd Webber's musical version of *Sunset Boulevard* he paused, not entirely for effect, before saying, "I thought to myself, This thing could make a great movie someday." □

A dapper Wilder, 44, in a publicity photograph taken for the 1950 release of his seminal motion picture *Sunset Boulevard*.

LORETTA YOUNG *Vanity Fair* loved her as the wife of Richard the Lionhearted in DeMille's *The Crusades* in 1935, and loved her again, 64 years later, as her still-crusading self—a queen of Catholic charities. She tried everything once, from *Platinum Blonde*, with Frank Capra (1931), to the bishop's wife in *The Bishop's Wife* (1947), to a stint as TV's tasteful grande dame in the respectable 1950s. She elected *not to talk about* whether her daughter was the child of Clark Gable, with whom she made *The Call of the Wild* in 1935. For this restraint, much honor.

PHOTOGRAPHED IN 1999
BY **FIROOZ ZAHEDI**

THE THREE AMIGOS Frank Sinatra, Shirley MacLaine, Dean Martin Sometimes called the Clan (but perhaps "Rat Pack" sounded better to Sammy Davis Jr.), Sinatra and company by no means excluded girls from their tree house. They positively adopted Shirley MacLaine during the filming of *Some Came Running* in 1958; she remained one of the gang through *Ocean's Eleven* and six other pictures. For their sake, she suffered a cruel arm-twisting from Frank's Mob pal Sam Giancana, as well as the pangs of a major pash for crooner Dino. Through it all, Sinatra was the straw that stirred the cocktail. No singer turned actor—not even Elvis—loomed larger in American culture for a longer spell: 1939 through those whirlwind Reagan years. PHOTOGRAPHED IN 1966

DAVID GEFFEN Rodin rendered his *Thinker* with brow knit, chin on curled hand: the history of Thought coiled into one mortal hunch. For our pages, our Rodin—Ms. Leibovitz—has depicted this Brooklyn-born oracle of Malibu as the Deal-Maker (confidant of a galaxy of A-list stars and insiders, DreamWorks co-founder, billionaire record-*Macher*), perpetually cradling a receiver, whether in bed or on his Gulfstream IV or at the roaring shore. In the sun-splashed principality of The Phone Call, a surfside Geffen is often that anchor on the other end of the line.

PHOTOGRAPHED IN 1989
BY **ANNIE LEIBOVITZ**

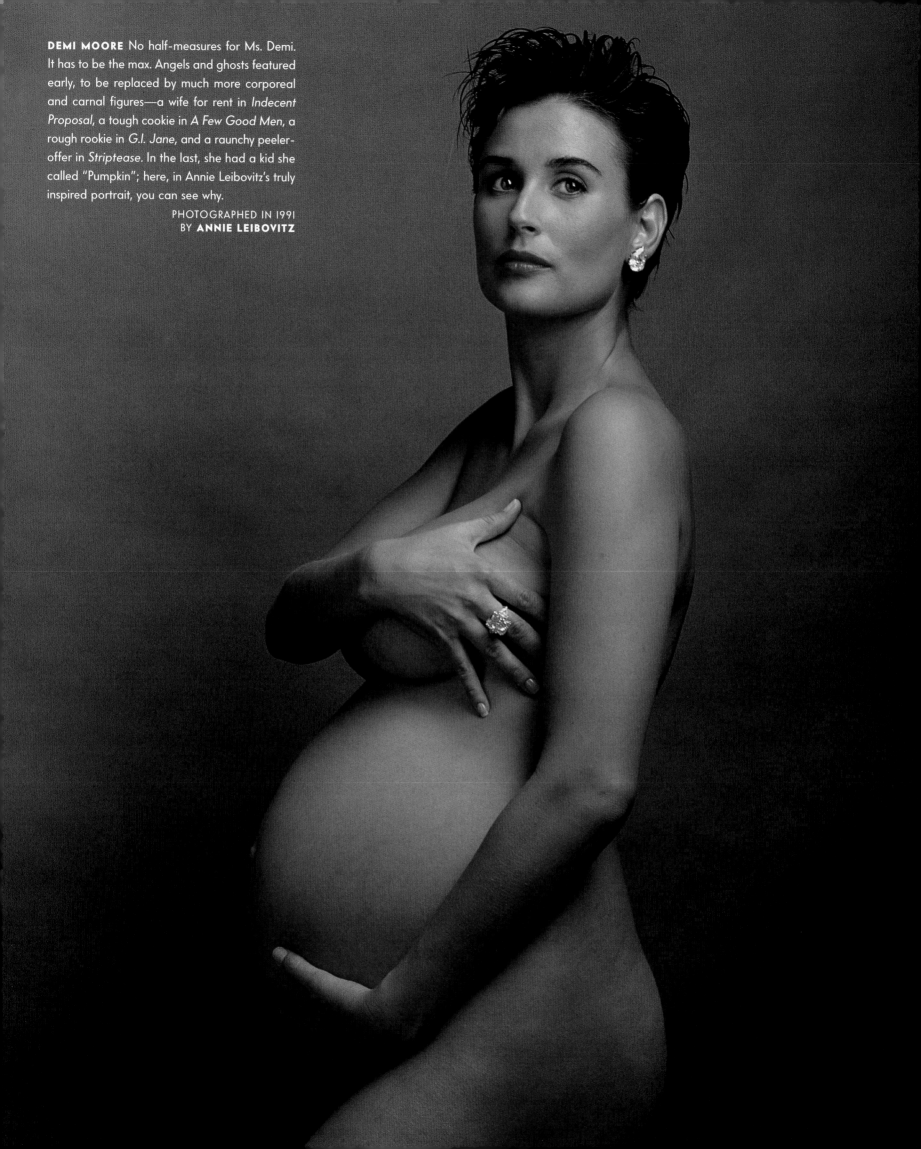

DEMI MOORE No half-measures for Ms. Demi. It has to be the max. Angels and ghosts featured early, to be replaced by much more corporeal and carnal figures—a wife for rent in *Indecent Proposal*, a tough cookie in *A Few Good Men*, a rough rookie in *G.I. Jane*, and a raunchy peeler-offer in *Striptease*. In the last, she had a kid she called "Pumpkin"; here, in Annie Leibovitz's truly inspired portrait, you can see why.

PHOTOGRAPHED IN 1991
BY **ANNIE LEIBOVITZ**

BETTE DAVIS Posing for Horst—for *Vanity Fair's* November 1932 number—she was being written up as a Bright Young Thing. (The title of this study: *A Boston Ingénue*.) Within two years she would play the embittered waitress in *Of Human Bondage*, and a bitch-goddess would be born. Clawing the studios all the way, and able to convey suffering and sacrifice with the bat of a sightless lash (*Dark Victory*), she was the quintessential woman at bay in *Jezebel* and *All About Eve*. In later years she made the macabre and melodramatic her own, as Fierce Old Thing, battling co-star Joan Crawford in *What Ever Happened to Baby Jane?*

PHOTOGRAPHED IN 1932
BY **HORST P. HORST**

TOM CRUISE *Vanity Fair* used this boy as a fashion model in 1984. He was still just one of the crowd when Francis Ford Coppola made *The Outsiders.* Uncredited in *Young Guns;* much credited for *Top Gun.* Soon he proved his Oscar mettle in *Rain Man* and *Born on the Fourth of July.* Post-bratuate career with *The Firm;* shaping up gloriously in *Jerry Maguire* and *Magnolia;* future missions quite possible.

PHOTOGRAPHED IN 1996
BY **ANNIE LEIBOVITZ**

MATT DAMON Yet another of Coppola's many, many adopted screen children, he appeared in *The Rainmaker*, leaving schoolboy roles behind and graduating to parts (in *Good Will Hunting, Saving Private Ryan, The Talented Mr. Ripley*) that let him be the Harvard dropout that he really is. And the boy can write—at times with buddy (and *Good Will Hunting* Oscar partner) Ben Affleck. Damon's Bostonian in the non–Henry James, George V. Higgins kind of way.

PHOTOGRAPHED IN 1997
BY **BRUCE WEBER**

KATHARINE HEPBURN A lioness in spring, netted by Cecil Beaton. If David O. Selznick ever made a blunder, it was to deny her the part of Scarlett O'Hara because, he believed, she couldn't convey the sex. But it was exactly this combination of sex with mind, and with independence, and with love, that bewitched directors George Cukor (*Holiday*) and Howard Hawks (*Bringing Up Baby*)—and the rest of us. Just look at the "spinster" she played in *The African Queen*. Of her four Oscars, three (for *Guess Who's Coming to Dinner*, *The Lion in Winter*, and *On Golden Pond*) were awarded when she was over 60, and that doesn't say a tithe of it.

PHOTOGRAPHED IN 1935
BY **CECIL BEATON**

ISABELLA ROSSELLINI AND **DAVID LYNCH** *Vanity Fair* once described David Lynch as "the most assured and inventive movie stylist this country has produced since Martin Scorsese" (who, like Lynch, it so happens, once kept house with Ms. Rossellini). Perhaps if it's your day job to spin out *Eraserhead*, *Dune*, and *The Elephant Man* (replete with mutants and grotesques), and to hatch television's creepy *Twin Peaks*, it is restorative to contemplate the faultless beauty of Ingrid Bergman's daughter, born in the aftermath of filmdom's most celebrated *scandale*, who became a figure of hypnotic presence in Lynch's *Blue Velvet* (1986). Maintaining the mood, Leibovitz evokes Magritte in this remarkable photograph.

PHOTOGRAPHED IN 1986
BY **ANNIE LEIBOVITZ**

ALFRED HITCHCOCK Unmistakably English, "Hitch" nonetheless earned his designation as *auteur* by creating movies that bore his distinctive inscription far beyond his requisite cameo, which he played, on occasion, in bulbous silhouette. His British period—*The Lady Vanishes, The 39 Steps*—drew the attention of Hollywood, where the titles *Rebecca, Rear Window, The Man Who Knew Too Much, North by Northwest,* and *The Birds* now need no signature. Nor, in suggesting something repressed and sinister in this least jolly of the fat men, do the titles *Suspicion, Notorious, Vertigo, Psycho,* or *Frenzy.* Painted, here, by another master who played with our perceptions.

ILLUSTRATED IN 1973
BY **ANDY WARHOL**

HOLLYWOOD ISSUE COVER, 2001 From left: Nicole Kidman, Catherine Deneuve, Meryl Streep, Gwyneth Paltrow, Cate Blanchett, Kate Winslet, Vanessa Redgrave, Chloë Sevigny, Sophia Loren, Penélope Cruz.

PHOTOGRAPHED IN 2001
BY **ANNIE LEIBOVITZ**

OLIVIA DE HAVILLAND Staying power: that's what it took to be Errol Flynn's girl in five Warner Bros. blood-and-thunder jobs, including *The Charge of the Light Brigade.* It's also what it took to sue her studio for unfair treatment (and win), to quarrel massively with her sister, Joan Fontaine (and live), to lobby for the part of Melanie in *Gone with the Wind* (and get it). Her two Oscars, for *The Heiress* and *To Each His Own,* were postwar. Removing herself to Paris, she became ever more regal and played Wallis Simpson's TV aunt as late as 1988.

PHOTOGRAPHED IN 1999
BY **ANNIE LEIBOVITZ**

GARY COOPER The Montana outdoorsman became Mr. America and played many of its emblematic roles—John Doe (in *Meet John Doe*), *Sergeant York*, Longfellow Deeds (in *Mr. Deeds Goes to Town*), Lou Gehrig (in *The Pride of the Yankees*). Ernest Hemingway himself picked Cooper for the part of Robert Jordan in *For Whom the Bell Tolls*. Reserved to the point of being monosyllabic as Marshal Will Kane in *High Noon*, he personified the connection (in talkies) between the strong and the silent.

PHOTOGRAPHED IN 1930
BY **EDWARD STEICHEN**

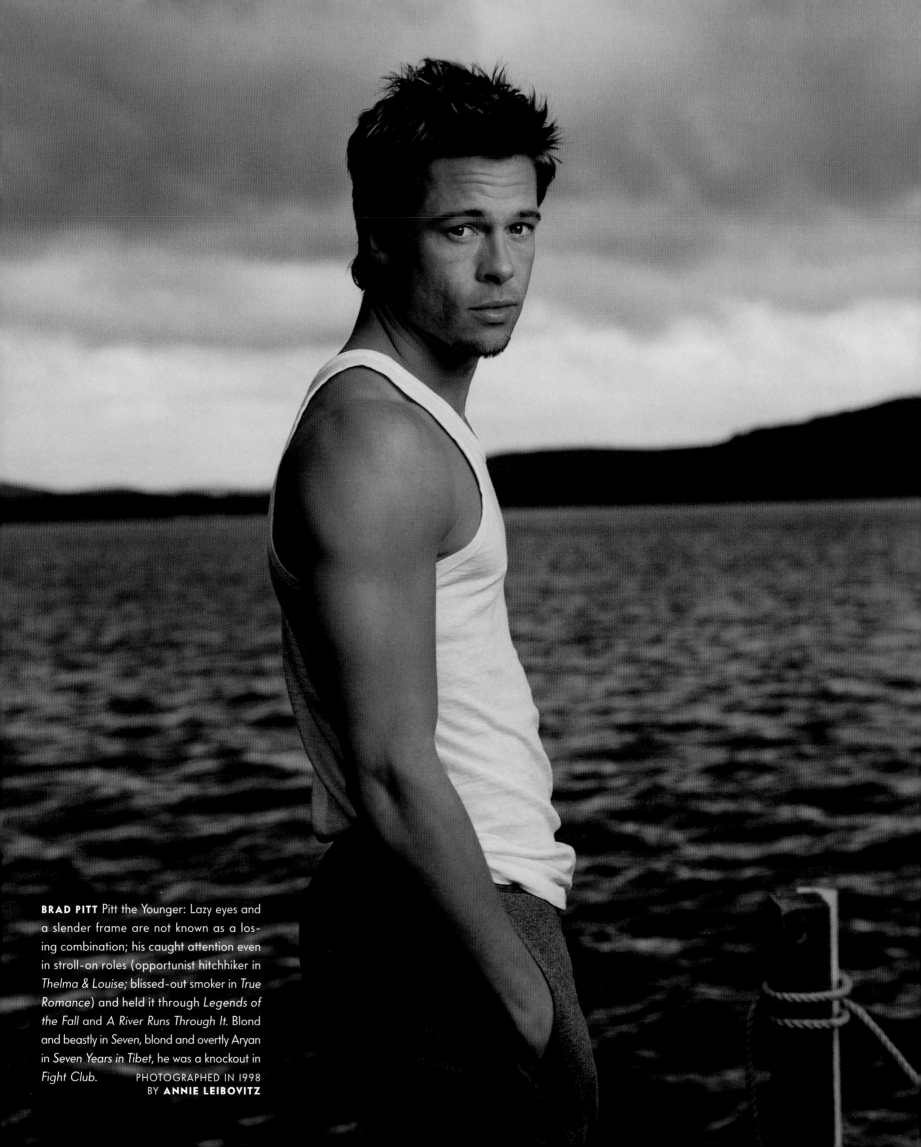

BRAD PITT Pitt the Younger: Lazy eyes and a slender frame are not known as a losing combination; his caught attention even in stroll-on roles (opportunist hitchhiker in *Thelma & Louise;* blissed-out smoker in *True Romance*) and held it through *Legends of the Fall* and *A River Runs Through It.* Blond and beastly in *Seven,* blond and overtly Aryan in *Seven Years in Tibet,* he was a knockout in *Fight Club.* **PHOTOGRAPHED IN 1998 BY ANNIE LEIBOVITZ**

THE THREE GRACES Michelle Pfeiffer, Jodie Foster, Meg Ryan
Blondes of a feather ... but perhaps it's wrong to say good things
come in threes, when they come so very individually. Think of life
without *Married to the Mob, Taxi Driver,* or *Sleepless in Seattle.*
Or, to put it another way, without that lounge act in *The Fabulous
Baker Boys,* without that cage confrontation in *The Silence of
the Lambs,* or without the deli-orgasm scene in *When Harry Met
Sally ...* Protean to a degree—one has played a convincing
feline, one a persuasive candidate for angelhood, and one is an
accomplished director in her own right—together they share an
achievement: having purged dumbness from blondeness for
good and all.   PHOTOGRAPHED IN 1999
                                            BY **HERB RITTS**

LEONARDO DiCAPRIO Wherefore art thou, Leonardo? Having taken the unromantic parts of bullied adolescent (*This Boy's Life*) and challenged younger brother (*What's Eating Gilbert Grape?*), he became the most butch and modern screen Romeo of them all in Baz Luhrmann's racy *William Shakespeare's Romeo and Juliet*. For this generation of young womanhood, his portrayal of the doomed and fragile Jack Dawson, in *Titanic*, has probably deposed Romeo as the reference point in any case.

PHOTOGRAPHED IN 1997
BY **ANNIE LEIBOVITZ**

F

By Dominick Dunne

ortuitous" is the word I often use to describe my arrival at *Vanity Fair* 17 years ago. It was a perfect match. From childhood on, I had been mesmerized by Hollywood and read everything I could find about it. I knew what Fatty Arbuckle had allegedly done to that starlet in the St. Francis Hotel in San Francisco, and what Paulette Goddard had done to Anatole Litvak under the table at Ciro's. As an adult I had moved from New York to Los Angeles and worked in the television-and-film industry. For a year or so, I lived in Harold Lloyd's beach house in Santa Monica, a few houses down from Marion Davies's huge showplace, which William Randolph Hearst had built for her to use when they weren't at San Simeon. Mae West was another neighbor. My late wife and I soon became part of Hollywood high life and went to dinner at the houses of many of the people who appear in this book. I saw up close how stars and moguls lived. I watched Warren Beatty and Kim Novak dance the sexiest dance I ever saw at a party at the Holmby Hills mansion of the Ray Starks, which had previously been the home of Humphrey Bogart and Lauren Bacall. I saw Loretta Young at swell parties ask for money for a home for unwed mothers every time anyone said a four-letter word. When I left that world and became a writer, I felt as if somehow I had been guided to this magazine, which is so good at getting Hollywood and its influence on American life right.

As a bit of a social chronicler, I love the pictures in this book that capture the private lives of very public people: Sophia Loren ogling the exposed bosom of Jayne Mansfield at a post-premiere dinner; Clifton Webb entertaining Laurence Olivier and Vivien Leigh at a Sunday lunch; Judy Garland belting out a tune at a party at the home of Jean Howard, the photographer who took the picture, and her husband, the agent Charles Feldman; a marital moment caught by Edward Steichen of Irving Thalberg, the MGM wonder boy, and Norma Shearer, who for years was the queen of MGM, at their beach house in Santa Monica; the haunting face of Marilyn Monroe; and the familiar Slim Aarons picture of Clark Gable, Van Heflin, Gary Cooper, and James Stewart in white-tie and tails, roaring with laughter at a New Year's Eve party in the private room at Romanoff's in 1957. I have always been fascinated by the secrets and scandals of Hollywood—the love affairs, the divorces, the suicides, the murders, the forgeries, the firings, the double crosses, the perversions, the failures. That kind of stuff can get tacky in the wrong hands, but *Vanity Fair* writers invariably find the heart of the matter in a classy way, with the sort of details available only to the cognoscenti. A good example is Patricia Bosworth's article about the 1958 stabbing murder of Johnny Stompanato, the gangster lover of Lana Turner, by the star's teenage daughter, Cheryl Crane. I lived right around the corner in Beverly Hills, and I remember standing outside Lana's big white rented house

and watching Jerry Giesler, the lawyer to the stars, arrive at the scene. I thought I knew all there was to know about that dark Hollywood tale, but Bosworth brings new dimensions to it. The photographs that accompany the story show Turner as still beautiful but just slightly over the hill, just emerging as a camp icon in the films of Ross Hunter. I am in awe of the photo department at *Vanity Fair*, which always comes up with pictures that not only illustrate a story but also enhance it.

In my days in the picture business, I produced one of Elizabeth Taylor's films. She told me then that she couldn't remember when she wasn't famous. In 1985, I interviewed her for *Vanity Fair*. She was recently out of the Betty Ford Center, where she would later meet her seventh husband, Larry Fortensky. Her great friend Rock Hudson was terminally ill, and she was starting her work for AIDS. We were at her house in Bel Air. It was a movie star's house, and—movie star that she has always been—she was late coming downstairs. She said that she didn't want to talk about Richard Burton, whose first marriage to her had come undone on the film we had made together. She told me she had gone to an A.A. meeting and almost caused a riot—people stood on chairs to look at her. She's funny, and the story made us laugh. The photographs for the story were shot later, in London by Helmut Newton. It was pouring rain, and Elizabeth was late as usual. The stylist, who was coming from Paris with the dress by Yves Saint Laurent that Elizabeth was to wear, got held up by customs, so we couldn't start the shoot until late in the afternoon, with a substitute dress from the Emanuels, who had designed the wedding dress for Princess Diana. It was red velvet, and Elizabeth, adorned with dazzling diamonds, looked simply beautiful. She was used to creating chaos around her while remaining calm herself. She began to tease Helmut, and he enjoyed it, and suddenly everything clicked, for she was playing the role she plays better than anyone else: Movie Star.

Recently I went back to Hollywood for Academy Awards week. When I lived there, stars used to dress up and go to parties and live in big white houses. They all lived near one another, they all went out to dinner at Chasen's and Romanoff's, and Louella Parsons and Hedda Hopper wrote about them in their gossip columns every day. In the way that royals really feel comfortable only with other royals, the stars of that period sought one another out when they wanted to socialize. But that all stopped, and for a couple of decades Hollywood put on a different face. What I feel these days is that the style I saw out there years ago is back, and I think *Vanity Fair* has a lot to do with it. Our party on Oscar night brings the old-time glamour to the surface again. For proof of that, you have only to look at the party pictures in this book. □

MARLENE DIETRICH This—from *Vanity Fair* of January 1936—is the only known color image that remains from the voluminous archive of photographer Anton Bruehl and his collaborator, Fernand Bourges. But Mar-laay-na was as colorful in black and white; could make strong men laugh or cry; could do tragedy or cabaret; could be an angel in blue or suggest that the Devil was a woman.

PHOTOGRAPHED IN 1936
BY **ANTON BRUEHL**
AND **FERNAND BOURGES**

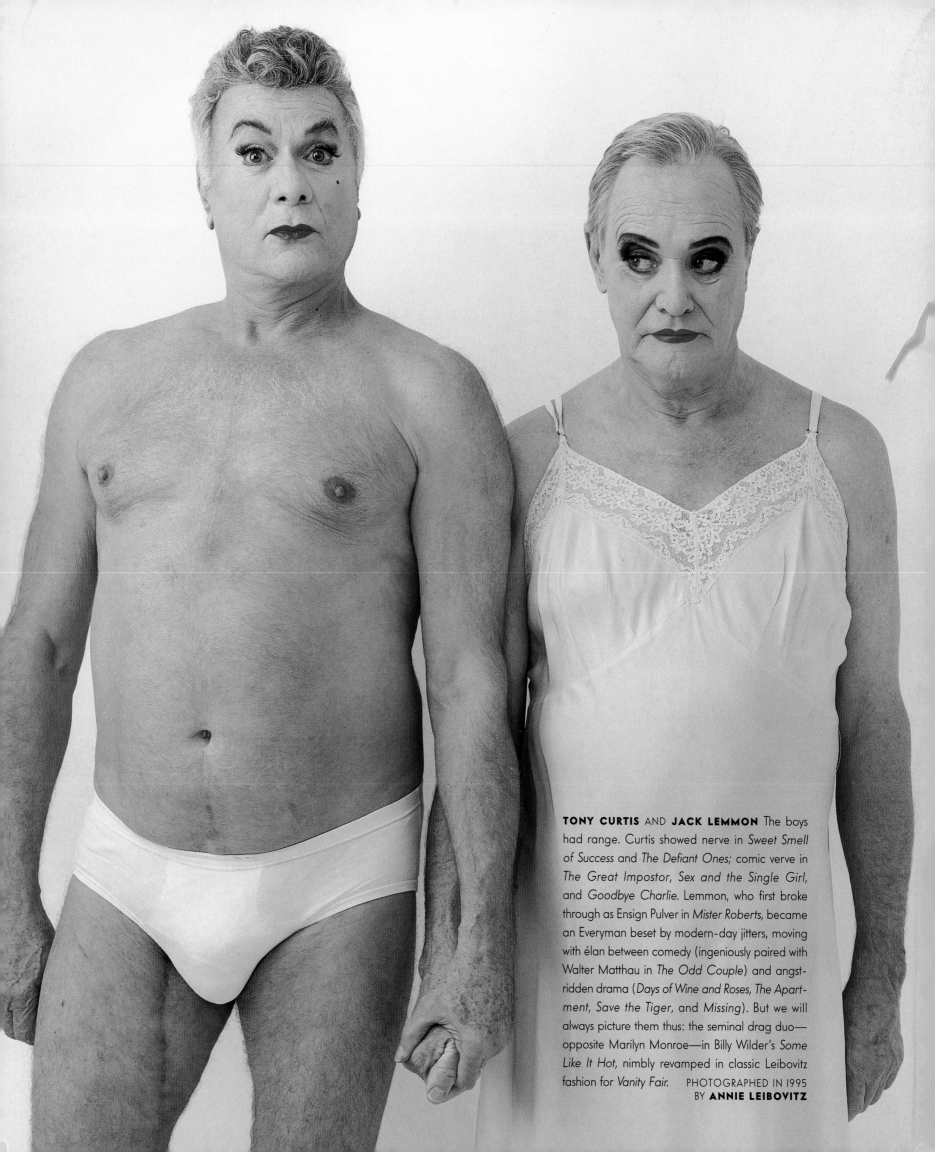

TONY CURTIS AND **JACK LEMMON** The boys had range. Curtis showed nerve in *Sweet Smell of Success* and *The Defiant Ones;* comic verve in *The Great Impostor, Sex and the Single Girl,* and *Goodbye Charlie.* Lemmon, who first broke through as Ensign Pulver in *Mister Roberts,* became an Everyman beset by modern-day jitters, moving with élan between comedy (ingeniously paired with Walter Matthau in *The Odd Couple*) and angst-ridden drama (*Days of Wine and Roses, The Apartment, Save the Tiger,* and *Missing*). But we will always picture them thus: the seminal drag duo—opposite Marilyn Monroe—in Billy Wilder's *Some Like It Hot,* nimbly revamped in classic Leibovitz fashion for *Vanity Fair.* PHOTOGRAPHED IN 1995 BY **ANNIE LEIBOVITZ**